ALTERED
LOVES

ALTERED LOVES

*Mothers and Daughters
During Adolescence*

TERRI APTER

FAWCETT COLUMBINE   NEW YORK

A Fawcett Columbine Book
Published by Ballantine Books
Copyright © 1990 by Terri Apter

All rights reserved under International and Pan-American Copyright Conventions. Published in the United States by Ballantine Books, a division of Random House, Inc., New York, and distributed in Canada by Random House of Canada Limited, Toronto.

http://www.randomhouse.com

This edition published by arrangement with St. Martin's Press.

Library of Congress Catalog Card Number: 91-70648
ISBN: 0-449-90631-0

Text design by Holly Johnson

Manufactured in the United States of America

First Ballantine Books Edition: September 1991
10 9 8 7 6 5 4

CONTENTS

ACKNOWLEDGMENTS

I need to thank all the mothers and daughters who let me into their homes, talked about themselves and allowed themselves to love one another and fight one another while I watched them. Without them the book could not have been written, and without them and people like them, the book would have no meaning.

The bulk of this book was written during the academic year 1987–8 which I spent in Berkeley, California. I want to thank Nancy Chodorow for introducing me to the wealth of psychological studies and data at the University of California in Berkeley. I benefited from the Family Dynamics Seminar in the Human Development Institute, from the Psychoanalytic Grand Rounds at Herrick Hospital, and from Dr. Martin Schreier's efforts to make the work at Children's Hospital Oakland so accessible.

In memory of Ann Duncan

INTRODUCTION

The mother/daughter relationship, remarked Adrienne Rich, "is the great unwritten story." What remains unwritten, however, is not a story about the problems mothers and daughters have with one another, or the way in which the relationship can harm, limit, and even cripple—all that has taken up much printer's ink in the last fifteen years. What is unwritten is the positive side to these problems, the way in which mothers and daughters fight in order to grow, the way in which their arguments aim, and often succeed, at self-confirmation and self-validation. What remains unwritten is the story about how connection between mother and daughter, and indeed between child and parent, remains a strength, not an immaturity.

Adolescence, too, is a developmental phase which has received very poor press. As in many other aspects of our lives, psychoanalytic theories have influenced how we see our psychological and emotional aims. Many parents and most mental health professionals accept the assumption that during adolescence a child is trying to separate from her parents. It is through separation, it is thought, that adult identity is achieved. The adolescent's typical behaviour is seen in light of this assumption. Teenagers express anger and even hatred towards parents, it is thought, because they are trying to break the childhood bonds of love and dependence. Teenagers hold different opinions and views, it is said, because they want to rebel against their parents. Adolescence has been seen as a parent/child version of divorce, whereby the child gives up her early love and admiration for the parent, and turns instead to friends, to lovers, to idols who have the glamour, the infallibility, the perfection which she once saw in her parents. The depressive moods common to adolescence have been seen as a symptom of mourning, for the parent is as though dead to the child, just as

1

the child the parent once knew seems usurped by a sexually mature, but infantile and irrational stranger bent on making life hell.

One simple drawback of this accepted theory of adolescent development is that it takes no account of what we know about a girl's development into womanhood. For a girl never separates herself from others, and marks the boundary between herself and others in quite the same way a boy has been thought to do. What in fact I discovered when I looked at female adolescent development, was that neither girls nor boys developed into adulthood along such clear cut lines of individuation and separation, that they continued to develop through their parents, just as they continued to care deeply about their parents. Adolescents tried not to separate from parents, but to negotiate a new relationship with their parents that would work in their new maturity.

In adolescence a crucial shift occurs from childhood dependence to a complex engagement with a parent. The shift is a matter of emphasis. Even a very young child cares how her parent sees her, and will fight for recognition of an individuated self. By 8 or 9, the child usually has some grasp of what responses and expectations are appropriate to her character. Thus she can experience both outrage and gratification: she measures her worth and her skills. The parent (especially the mother) will have contributed greatly to the child's individuality: the normal parent will have responded to new skills, rejected excessive dependence, and given her child a little push and shove towards autonomy. The anger and resistance of a very young child is always limited by the terrible fear her dependence harbours, but the adolescent characteristically and even predictably engages in fighting which has been misconceived as a struggle to break free of the parents. Rather, the adolescent shakes the parent into a new recognition and appreciation of her new and emerging self. The parent often resists this claim upon her attention, for the adolescent demands recognition long before she, objectively, deserves it. She asks for recognition of a self that is barely recognisable. She continues to need her parents' irrational admiration, whereas her parents now tend to view her more objectively, and to fear the consequences of irrational expectations. Preoccupied with her self, the adolescent sees enormous changes, whereas the parent sees the child she knew all along. For the parent, new developments are superficial and evanescent. For the adolescent, they are thrilling and profound. But whether or not the parent is impressed, she will be called upon to give a response. The maturing child's self-concept, self-esteem, goals and ideals are never formed in isolation from the parent.

We need a new model of adolescent development, one which makes sense of the continued love between child and parent, and one which makes sense of the continued support an adolescent seeks from her parent. We need to understand, also, why parents and adolescents do tend to have troubled times, and to follow the strange and sometimes distorted aims of their quarrels. While adolescents do work very hard to change the relationship, only in severe circumstances—when severed by political or social turmoil, or by the cutting edges of excessive pride, vanity, greed (a modicum of such vices does no substantial harm), or by a deep threat to one's development, to one's sense of integrity and direction—are these bonds unbound. Even then, there linger loose ends which irritate us throughout our lives, and which we find ourselves tinkering with, tying up in odd ways to disguise or repair the loss.

Human development is relational. We are born into relationships of dependence and love. We grow within such relationships, which change as we grow, and which most of us continue to live in and through throughout our lives, however much we, and our mothers, and our relationships with them have changed. The conclusion many of us have come to, because we continue to feel very strong bonds with our parents, is that we are failed adolescents, that we are slow to achieve the task of adolescence. Instead, I believe that the traditional tasks of adolescence have been misconceived, and that the traditional theories of adolescence have outlived their rightful span as a half-truth.

The traditional theory of adolescent development has further glaring inadequacies when it addresses female development. For if, as Anna Freud said, adolescence was the "stepchild" of psychoanalysis, the forgotten subject, the subject most easily neglected, and glossed over as a re-emergence of earlier issues, or a recapitulation of a previous drama, then female adolescence was at a double disadvantage; not even a stepchild, but the abandoned child, the child repeatedly put out for adoption, when the adoption refused to "take." For both the earlier phase of female development and the subsequent "recapitulation" or re-enactment were hidden behind the weight of the masculine blueprint. When one psychoanalytic scholar was asked to write a chapter on female adolescence for a textbook, she concluded there was not enough good recent material to supply a separate chapter.[1]

The traditional, or classical view of adolescence, the view that has been so important in its popular impact, has reached us not so much through Freud's theories of the sexual dynamics of childhood—though it is supposed that Oedipal tensions recur with the sexual awakening of adolescence—but rather through Margaret Mahler's analyses of separation and individuation. Mahler believed that the infant is born into a symbiotic phase, wherein he does not understand that he is separate from the mother. He experiences himself and the mother as an indivisible unit. Eventually, at about five months, there is a "hatching" phase wherein the infant catches on to the boundaries of something which begins to have an identity and a powerful, invigorating meaning—a self. Gradually the child is able to mark the boundary between himself and his mother, to extend and test it. As he develops there remains a tension between this separateness and the union he once felt with his mother. He continues to be wary of the power of that initial symbiosis which was enormously comforting and reassuring, but which also submerged and stifled the self.[2]

Anyone familiar with feminist psychology writings or recent writings about women's psychology will recognise key terms here, terms which signal supposed differences between male and female development. Recent attempts to understand the special ways a woman views her self and her obligations have emphasised the continuing strength of this very early phase when she sees herself as linked to others, when she makes no firm distinctions between her self and her mother.[3] Unlike a boy who emerges from the symbiosis of his first attachment to realise his distinction from the mother with whom he felt blended in infancy, a girl continues to see herself as joined, not only by love but by sex, gender and feeling, to her mother. In establishing and protecting his gender identity a boy works to define self-boundaries, to mark a distinction between himself and others. A girl, however, is likely to define her self in relation to others, and to assess personal meaning and success largely in terms of her ability to remain connected to others and to fulfil the demands others make upon her.

This account of different gender developments and different quality of self-boundaries, though still compelling, has been discredited. All children are in fact born with a sense of themselves as separate from their mother. Though they do not immediately have an adult sense of self, we can see through their persistent and structured attempts to engage the mother, to form a relationship with her, that they respond to her as to another person. They seek responses from her. They watch and depend upon her responses. They fix attention on someone outside themselves and work very hard to establish a rapport with her.[4] The assumption that a child first experiences her self and her mother as one is countered by observations of how the child actually behaves towards her mother. Nevertheless, it does seem that the girl is less good at individuating herself from her mother, grows up with less rigid boundaries between her own needs and others' wishes, identifies herself not as a separate being, but as a being in relation to others, and therefore defines herself as "warm" or "loving" or "helpful" rather than "competent," or "ambitious" or "successful." She defines herself in terms of how she is with others, not in "objective" or autonomous terms.[5]

Whether one sees this continued closeness—indeed this fluid boundary between mother and daughter—as a strength, as a capacity for comfort and a willingness to care, or as a weakness, a limitation (as did Freud, along with many of the feminists writing on women's psychology in the 1970s), a failure to de-

fine the self and to give it firmness, direction and expansive-
ness, it shows the different point from which girls and boys
approach adolescence, and marks their very different passage
through adolescence.

So what, I wondered, happens during adolescence, during
this so-called second individuation stage, wherein the child,
though having a sense of herself as a separate physical being,
and knowing her way around the grammar of her self and others, tries to effect a "final" separation from a mother from
whom she has never quite effected an infantile separation?
Whereas her brother comes to his gender identity—that is, becomes aware of himself, and of himself as a boy—by noting
that he is different from his mother, the girl never learns to see
herself as fully separate from her mother; she never so keenly
challenged the identity of a self in opposition to that early overwhelming attachment, and so grows up to see herself as part
of another, as a being whose identity is confirmed in relation
to another. Whereas the adolescent boy already possesses the
full confidence in his difference from the person who had once
encompassed him and through whom he had the first stirring
of a self, whereas he has already fought for identity by marking
self-boundaries and protecting himself from that early emotional suffusion, the girl approaches adolescence with a sense
of self still formed by that early fluidity. Perhaps, then, she does
not come to adolescence with good potential, or readiness for
separation, for the independence, the autonomy that has been
thought to be the stuff of male adolescence.

When feminists began to write about female psychology,
and began to attack the influences of their strong relational self,
of their unwillingness to put themselves first or to assert themselves, they saw as the crucible of these differences the unique,
lonely and isolated attachment between mother and child. The
social reinforcement of this relationship then came under fire,
for it was the mother's sole possession of the infant that crip-
pled gender identity, that turned sons into people who, in order
to have a male identity, must deny (or at any rate tightly control and guard) the dependency, connection and love-suffusion
they, as infants, experienced through the mother.[6] And this first

passionate love between mother and child turned girls into people who were somehow ill-defined, incomplete, willing to sabotage themselves because they feared the all powerful mother they had both loved enormously and, because of the terrifying power that love had given her, hated. Men and women, it was thought, conspired together to keep woman in check, because they both wished to destroy the monstrous female power they witnessed as infants. Thus the institution of motherhood, the way in which a woman's bond to the home made her the tyrant of her child, became the target for complaint. But the emphasis was always on the mother's power, and the influence of this power, during infancy. The gender intensification that so clearly takes place during adolescence was seen as minor, a simple reinforcement of the type of reactions that occurred earlier.

Alongside these criticisms of the social structure of motherhood came a series of attacks upon the mother herself. Not only was the initial power of the mother at fault, but so too was the mother's bondage to her role. If her infant was in her power alone, then she was in the infant's power. Solely responsible for the domestic care of this demanding creature, she demanded from her child all the reinforcement, all the gratification her domestic slavery prohibited her from seeking elsewhere. The spate of "awful mother" literature actually began by stressing mothers' effects upon sons. It began with Freud's portrayal of the woman making vicarious use of her son's masculinity. A son, Freud believed, offered a woman her one chance to possess the phallus she so desperately desired. The image of the hungry woman feeding vicariously on her son's love, was enlarged and enlivened in fiction. At the same time critics were hyping their discovery of the jealous mother in D. H. Lawrence's *Sons and Lovers*,[7] "Momism," or the denigration of the mother's loving interference of the son, found its great comic expression in the writings of Philip Roth.[8] The enemy to maturity was the intrusive mother whose love destroyed because she refused her son's right to his distinct self-boundaries. The "Momism" of the 1960s gave way to many feminist versions of maternal evils. The mother grew into the tyrant that victims become, and forced her daughter into the victim's role. Having her own needs for self-definition and self-expansion thwarted, she sought to hold on to her daughter, to tie her alongside her, a companion in her loneliness, a participant in her frustration, and a buffer against the great threat of envy. The mother needed her daughter to prove that fulfilment was not an option, to assure herself that she had not missed out. Even as the mother seemed to wish her daughter well and want the best for her, she also feared a competitor, and she feared proof that her sacrifices, her limitations were not necessary.

Thus it was the mother who denied her daughter the right to pursue sexual fulfilment.[9] It was the mother who denied her daughter the right to self-esteem, and it was the mother's envy that made the daughter afraid to reach her potential and thereby exceed her mother's status.[10] Like Snow White, the daughter accepted the poison apple because she needed to believe that her mother loved her.

Whether it was the limitations of the mother herself, or the limitations of motherhood as an institution which isolated mother and child, making them both victims of domestic tyranny and domestic frustration, the mother/daughter bond emerged as a terrible, ambiguous thing, with bitterness masquerading as love, and bondage masquerading as attachment. Even less radical approaches to mothering presented the attachment to her, and the relational self that emerged from that attachment, as a loss, or dimming of the self, as a failure to pursue self-interests. But gradually feminists began to shift from criticism of characteristic female views and priorities to an appreciative understanding of them.[11] The characteristics now under such scrutiny emerge not in infancy or childhood but in adolescence. During this phase the girl displays a distinctive moral outlook, which emphasises—at least theoretically—concern for others and a refusal to seek her own ends at others' expense. During this phase, too, she exercises new skills in attachment, revelation and reflection. In these developments her mother plays a crucial role.

But what role does the mother play? It is always assumed that the same-sexed parent provides a role model for the child, but what are the mechanisms of this identification? Mothers and daughters are closer certainly than daughters and fathers, and tend to be closer, more often, than mothers and sons, especially during adolescence. There are more outright fights between mother and daughter, but these arguments are strangely sought after, and strangely productive. Not only has the story of the differences between boys and girls in adolescence yet been untold, but also, as I worked on the story, it rapidly became clear that the story of a girl's adolescence has a great bearing on untold aspects of a boy's adolescence. The traditional theory of adolescence not only fails to account for adolescent girls' development through their mother, but also fails to describe a large proportion of a boy's development. Indeed, I came to the conclusion that though there was more uniformity of development among girls, among boys one could see a large number who were, in respects of attachment and relational thinking, more like girls than like other boys.

To help underline the difference between the traditional subjects of psychological studies and my own, as well as to find some use for the current vacillating status of a general pronoun, I use "his" or "him" when referring to the adolescent as traditionally described, and I use "her" or "she" to refer to my mostly female subjects, or to any other specifically female study.

I was able to interview sixty-five mother and daughter pairs, from two different countries—Britain and the United States. Eighteen pairs were English, though four pairs I interviewed when living in England were citizens of other countries: one pair from Argentina, one from Bengal, one from India and one from Ireland. Five pairs were Scottish, and thirty-eight were American. Ten of the pairs from England and Scotland were selected from responses to advertisements I submitted to national magazines in 1986. The rest were selected randomly from a list of employees to which I was given access by a large technical firm with offices in Cambridge. By "random" I mean that I contacted every fourth name on the list and inquired if there were any adolescent daughters in the family and if so whether the mother and the daughter would grant me interview time. By combining the two methods of selection I hoped

to solve the problem arising from the possibility that people
who wrote to me in response to an advertisement which stated
I was writing a book on mothers and adolescent daughters
might have special interests or special problems. The people I
selected from the employees list only had to consent—they did
not have to put themselves forward. The distinction may be
subtle, and indeed there was no perceivable difference between
the two groups, but I could not know that from the outset.
Five people from the employees list who had adolescent daughters refused to be interviewed, either by declining directly or,
more obliquely and confusingly, failing to be home at the
agreed time, or failing to leave enough time for the interview.
The reasons for this ambivalence would undoubtedly be of interest, though I have no means of discovering them.

My selection of pairs in America was roughly parallel to
my selection in the United Kingdom. I advertised in a local
weekly paper and one national magazine, and received a wealth
of replies which I sifted through, but in the end made relatively
less use of than those I received in Britain, partly because the
replies frequently indicated the misinterpretation that I would
help them with mother or adolescent daughter problems. "Discussing a relationship" clearly has therapeutic overtones in the
American idiom. It was touching and, frankly, intriguing to
hear various cries of complaint or despair or anger, but when
I wrote explaining that my role would not be therapist but
observer, many did not reply. In the end I selected ten pairs by
this method, as I had in England, though this represented in
England fifty per cent of the replies and in America ten per
cent. Eighteen other pairs were contacted through state and
private schools—seven came from northern California, four
from Chicago, and seven from Washington DC. The reasons
for this choice were largely ones of convenience since I was
visiting these cities in America: but there was also the attraction
of taking samples from the west coast, the midwest, and the
east coast. To make contact with the students I first approached
the principal of the school, who then referred me to a few
teachers, who then offered to put my case to a class, or who
allowed me to give a brief address to a class, or in one case, to

an assembly of the entire school. I explained my interest to the students who then brought the suit to their mothers—for only if their mothers consented could the interviews and study proceed. I used a similar technique to contact and select seven mother/daughter pairs of late adolescence who were freshmen and sophomores—first and second year students at college or university. Few mothers declined to participate when a daughter put the suggestion to her, though of course it may be that daughters who are keen to talk and to be open and to reveal themselves are raised by similarly inclined mothers. Indeed, there was no perfectly "clean" or "random" method of selection, though I hoped to avoid excessive bias by switching the methods of selection. The remaining three mother/daughter pairs were contacted through informal information from social workers.

I tried to interview families from a variety of social backgrounds, and succeeded to a large extent, though there are certain gaps I could not fill. Though two mother/daughter pairs were very wealthy, none came from what could be called an upper class background with the unusual complications of title or land. Only three pairs came from what could be called a deprived background, and of these three, each was black and each from California. In each of these decidedly poor families there were added problems of alcoholism or delinquency. I cannot therefore believe this was a fair representation. Other pairs of low income (but not poverty stricken) families did not suffer similar problems. My sample of Hispanic families was so small (only one!) not because the adolescent girls were reluctant to come forward, but because their mothers would not participate—and these were the only mothers to decline a daughter's suggestion. The reasons they gave were that their English was not good enough, or that through the interview their name would get on some kind of "list," or that there was no need for discussion, since their daughters were "okay."

The technical firm whose list of employees I used, employed people in a wide range of tasks, from cleaners to computer scientists to business managers. The socioeconomic range was very wide in the state schools I used, and surprisingly wide in the private schools, especially in northern California. What was less varied in the private schools was race, though there was a good mix in the university and colleges from which I took my sample of late adolescents. Among the American group were nine black families, four Chinese pairs, one Hispanic and the remaining twenty-four were white.

I preferred to interview these pairs in person, seeing the mother and daughter separately for some time—between one and three hours each. Then I requested the opportunity to observe them together. The ideal set-up was that I would first spend an evening in each home, and the mother and the daughter would decide "who went first." I usually found myself in the sitting room with the mother and the bedroom with the daughter, which was very much her private place. Initially these interviews were taped, but later I used a portable computer. The bother of using the keyboard when conducting an interview was actually less intrusive than the tape, which made many participants nervous—they wanted the opportunity, if necessary, to "take back what [they] said." There was also much reassuring eye contact and a peaceful filling-in of pauses as I used the computer. I would try to let some time, but not too long a time, elapse before meeting the pair again. I wanted a day or two to peruse or write up the various interviews but I did not want so much time to elapse that new problems or new perspectives would arise. This ideal formula was not always achieved. In fact, I was able to use this formula in only thirty-two pairs—less than fifty per cent of the pairs I interviewed. The deviations from this pattern ranged from the minor to the extreme. In some cases the mother and daughter were so excited and so interested in what one another was saying that they could not keep apart. Eventually the interview became a cross conversation, with each adding to or amending what the other was saying. The energy and amusement level in such cases was high, as each countered or endorsed the other's descriptions. Perhaps a more rigorous or experienced interviewer would have prohibited such shenanigans, but I could see no professional reason to stick strictly to my interview formula. The point was to extract information, and different people respond to different approaches. Only when the revelation of information became a stimulus for anger, as happened in at least two cases, did I feel that the modifications of descriptions were being unduly controlled either by fear or by the heat of the moment.

The need to observe the mother and daughter together was mandatory. There was a tendency in the private conversations to emphasize either the rosy or the drab in their relationship. Discriptions of family behaviour involve more sophistication in spotting the causes of normal domestic aggravation than most of us are readily capable: it involves saying who was at fault, who tried hardest, who had least patience. Moreover, especially during this dynamic stage, descriptions of family members tend to be extreme. All those "I never"s and "she always" while perfectly sincere, are also perfectly ridiculous. The difficulty with observation, however, is that another person is never a fly on the wall. A camera could almost become such a thing if it were left there long enough. People can control the expression of their feelings some of the time, but not all of the time, and by and large, the people who were willing to participate in this book were not highly motivated to control, but rather to express their feelings, and for their feelings to make some contribution. I tried to set up an entire day for observing the mother and daughter together, though sometimes it was only part of a day when the mother and daughter had planned special time to be together. I was observing them when they both wanted to be together, so that I saw them interact, but did not always see them when each wanted to be free of the other. I was observing them together when they chose to be together and I conclude that they had a strong urge to interact and that this interaction plays a crucial part in the daughter's development. I try to overcome this potential bias by balancing the observation work with the interview work.

I consider those interviews and studies which followed, or closely approached, this format, the core of my study; but, as I have said, less than fifty per cent of the pairs I studied followed this format. Fourteen pairs selected from those who replied to my advertisements were interviewed by telephone.

Three people followed this interview up with written after-thoughts or amendments. Three pairs proved impossible to interview separately, since there was far too much noise in the house, too many interruptions, too much interest in what the mother or the daughter was saying to keep away, or the house was simply too small. For the remaining nineteen pairs there were interviews but no follow up observation session—I was travelling, they were busy, one partner fell ill, other appointments cropped up, the weather was preventing their planned activity. Such difficulties made me receive all the information I did get with a delicious sense of greed.

I began the interviews in the winter of 1985, and finished with them in the summer of 1988. During that period the shape and content of the interviews changed, for I was being persuaded to change my view of the central aims and character of this relationship. I started the project with the theoretical question: how does the daughter deal with the problems of separation from her mother during adolescence? Like most people interested in adolescence at that time, I saw the "task" of adolescence as separation from the parent, and I set out to understand how the daughter "succeeds" or "fails" to separate from the person to whom she has been closest. So from the winter of 1985 to the spring of 1987, my aim was to discover the mechanisms, techniques, catalysts and inhibitors to separation and individuation. How did the daughter become "her own person"? How did the mother respond to the daughter's independence? Which of her responses encouraged and which impeded separation? How did the girl protect her emerging self-boundaries? I asked the daughter how she felt about the mother, what annoyed her most, what she resented, when she became most angry, what she thought was unfair, where she thought she and her mother differed most, whether she thought her mother knew her or understood her, whether she cared what her mother thought, whether she tried not to care, or whether she became highly annoyed with what her mother thought about her, or expected of her, or the restrictions put upon her. I asked whether she wanted to be like her mother, whether she thought she was like her mother, whether she admired her mother.

Everyone who collects information through interviews needs some blueprint, some question base to obtain and organise data, but in interviews of this kind it is also essential to let the person interviewed lead the interviewer. If the interviewer sticks to the question base rigorously then she may miss essential points. The aim of my questions was to uncover the character of the relationship, and therefore I had to be led by the people I interviewed without facing the later nightmare, familiar to anyone collecting information, of realising that I had overlooked certain questions. So I followed any lead, and listened to the girls as they described or mused about what their mothers thought of them and what they thought of their mothers, and how their mothers should see them, and what their mothers failed to understand or what they would always understand. Gradually this influenced the kind of questions I asked. Rather than shaping the interview to discover how the daughter was separating from her mother I learned to ask, "How are you retaining your attachment to her?" "How are you trying to persuade her to see you differently?" "Are you succeeding?" "How angry or frustrated do you become when you do not succeed?"

Listening to a number of people on similar subjects and in similar settings, certain patterns emerged. Where I was expecting to hear about the need to be one's own person, or be independent, or have more freedom, I was hearing far more about what their mothers saw or did not see, what they thought. There are checks easily made upon one's "recognition" of a pattern. Were these references striking because they were unexpected or because they were numerous? I counted the number of such references and included words such as "her perceptions," "her view is," "she thinks I'm," "the way she sees things," "her view of me is," and I came up with a minimum of three per interview, an average of twelve. In contrast, references to separation, had an average of one, and to autonomy, an average of four.

This kind of count does not prove anything. The exercise was little more than a game to check my sense of being overwhelmed by these references. This in itself urged me to ask more questions along these lines: "How does your mother see

you?" "How do you see her?" "How do you feel when she
sees this or that in you?" "Can you influence how she sees
you?" The counting game did not give rise to a new model of
adolescent development, but it led to new confidence in my
temptation to turn away from traditional expectations and ex-
plore the relationship from a different angle.

The only other references to approach the "seeing/under-
standing/thinking" category were those of "telling me what to
do," "thinking she knows what's best," "thinking she knows
me better than I know myself," "thinking she knows all about
me," "not letting me figure out things for myself." These complaints did not arise in every interview, as did the issues of how
I see my mother and how she sees me, but the average appearance in all the interviews was eight. These complaints lie between two issues: autonomy and controlling the self-image/
reflection. A daughter can complain that her mother is always
telling her what to do because this curtails her freedom, or she
can complain that her mother is always telling her what to do
because her mother does not "see," "appreciate" or "understand" what she truly is. "Leave me alone!" which is the familiar cry of an adolescent daughter in the face of her mother's
advice, admonishment or direction, might be a bid for separation, or might be a cry of frustration at her mother's slowness
in seeing what the daughter is capable of, or how complex the
daughter's feelings are—or seem—in contrast to the daughter's
new and increasing self-awareness. She wants to be left alone
because her mother's responses are not right, do not seem appropriate. She wants to be left alone because her mother is
failing to help her, yet she continues to seek help in establishing
her self-image, her self-confidence. In the context of the other
information I was getting from adolescent daughters I felt that
the traditional balance—that of seeing the rejection of the
mother's advice, perception, interference as a bid for separation—was inaccurate, weighted by theory. In the context of
their continued efforts to correct and control the mother's views
and responses, it seemed that the aim was not to be left alone
but to change some of the patterns of responses and the expectations. The bid for autonomy was as much a bid for the recognition of autonomy as a bid for freedom from constraints.

The analysis of this type of data is highly intuitive, in that everything heard or observed has to be interpreted and put into a context and measured without any well-tried or widely accepted tool for measurement. Patterns are spotted, but other patterns may be missed, and the favoured patterns may be misconstrued or over emphasised. It is easy to see why some might prefer to deal with questionnaires and analyze the data from the questionnaires, where the replies are well contained. The difficulty with these however is that the questions, once answered, cannot be put into different contexts, and often the interpretation put upon them is inflexible or presumptuous. The answers are constrained by the questions—whereas in an interview, the interviewer can get some sense of whether there is something wrong with the question, or whether the next question, or prod—for the aim may simply be to keep the participant talking—should be modified, and a new track taken. Nevertheless, I certainly made use of material gathered from others' extensive questionnaires; but for the core of this book they would have been sadly inadequate.

The interviews with the mothers also contained hints that a model of adolescent development involving separation and conflict was either inadequate or inappropriate. Most mothers were pleased that the daughter remained close to her, continued to confide in her and seemed "still to like" her. Yet each mother who felt happily close to her daughter believed that she was particularly "lucky." Her personal experience with an adolescent daughter did not persuade her to change her expectation that an adolescent would be difficult, unruly, and surly. It merely persuaded her that she and her daughter were exceptions. Though some pairs at some times suffered from the nightmare of stereotype conflicts, the "exceptions" were the rule.

I asked the mothers whether they found their daughters troublesome or worrisome, what they found most troublesome or difficult with their daughters, what they worried about most, what they hoped for, what they feared, what they enjoyed about their daughters, what they resented, what they admired. I knew there were many questions that I could ask, but whose answers I would have to treat with caution, or scepticism. "Do you feel

envious of your daughter's youth?" "Do you resent her
beauty?" "Do you begrudge her youth or her scope of choice
and opportunity?" "Do you fear that your husband admires
her more than you?" These are common assumptions, or assumptions about common problems and difficulties between
mothers and adolescent daughters which can be addressed in
an interview, but any material about them taken in interview
must be treated with caution. The assumption is that such feelings are unconscious, and the reason for subjecting them to
censorship is obvious: mothers do not like harbouring envious
or mean feelings towards a child. In the end I was persuaded
that these feelings are not common, are not basic to the character of the relationship, that they need not be assumed to characterise the relationship; but I am in no position to deny that
they exist, or that when the relationship is severely problematic
a therapist or analyst has reason to look for them, to suspect
or even expect them. In denying that certain types of problems
are prevalent, I deny that they characterise the central character
of the relationship.

I doubt, however, that in speaking to mothers alone that I
ever would have been persuaded to change the bias. The notion
that the adolescent is trying to separate, and to become autonomous, to break with childhood ties, to tear out the childhood
loves and ideals, is firmly rooted in parents' and professionals'
expectations and interpretations. Social workers dealing with
the adoption of older children spoke of the special difficulty of
adopting teenagers who must become attached to the adoptive
parents, but who are also trying to separate. Parents bemused
by the demands of an adolescent child believe they must "let
go" or permit the child to separate, while they maintain a disciplinary hold upon the child. The mothers I spoke to were
diffident about their attachments and their daughters' needs. It
seemed that they responded in one way and reflected in another. They responded to their daughters' needs for disclosure,
conversation, confidences, and yet they also felt that this was
not quite what the daughters wanted. What was happening
however was that the daughters wanted their confidences and
responses and conversation, but also were trying to correct

them, to change the form or quality of the mother's response. The difference is easily clouded by a biased interpretation: the daughter complains of what she gets, but not because she does not want the mother to respond or interfere, but rather because she wants some control over her mother's responses; she now wants to feed in something and to influence her mother's response and to create a new dimension in the relationship. It is easy to interpret the numerous corrections and criticisms as a rejection of any interference whatsoever. The constant corrections lead the mother to conclude: "Nothing I say is right," "She wants me to keep my mouth shut," whereas the daughter is simply geared to correct and amend and influence, to feel her power of influencing the mother's view of her. She wants her mother's mouth open, and she wants the opportunity to complain about it. Complaint and criticism are forms of influence and correction. I think it would be an enormous help to the mother to look at her daughter's needs in a new light, to take a new pride in their battles, to feel more positive about the contribution she is making to her daughter's development at this time. She takes more than a back seat driver's position, and she has a right to acknowledge this.

The observation sessions underlined these aims. The interchanges were full of "identity reminders"—of the daughter indicating to the mother that she could do something, that her own view was strong, that the way she felt had validity in and of itself. The mother was frequently warned off a certain track, sometimes through the tone of voice. "Mo-o-ther," with the elongated vowel exhaled in a sigh, was very common, and the mother recognised it as such. She showed her recognition either by laughing at the familiar sound, or by smiling with some discomfort and an embarrassed sideways glance, or by getting angry and warning her daughter off with: "Now, none of that," or "I've had enough of that." There was the attempt to re-establish authority or dignity, as the daughter reminded her that she too had authority. The daughter was intent upon changing the mother's habitual responses. Clashes came when expectations were disappointed. The cry of "Mo-o-ther" indicated that the mother was being all too much herself, and not responding to change. Always, in a quarrel, the daughter seemed to be begging something from the mother, to be making some request, to be frustrated by the mother's failure to meet her demand. These were not quarrels of people drawing apart, but of people who were trying to correct one another's behaviour, perceptions, or world view. The daughter was criticising the mother for still being herself, for not changing, for not being sufficiently susceptible or sensitive to change, and she complained if the mother refused to see how she had changed. When they were not quarrelling or bickering, the daughter was prodding her for responses, telling her about herself. The daughter's eyes were often on the mother—she looked at her mother more often than her mother looked at her. She would watch her mother when she nearly finished talking, and then would watch her while she waited for a response. (She would often punish the mother for watching her: a grimace or shudder or a glare from the daughter frequently cut off a mother's querying or curious gaze.) This pattern of watching and waiting was the same whether the mother and daughter were outside the home or inside the home. Sometimes it was clear that the daughter knew the mother would be riled, and she waited with some humour to see what would pop up, while the mother tried to control herself, or tried to digest what was being revealed or requested. Sometimes the daughter watched with more anxiety than amusement. Sometimes she watched with eagerness—and surprisingly, that was when she was most likely to respond to the mother's response with anger—the mother was insufficiently enthusiastic, her response to the daughter did not match the daughter's enthusiasm. The daughter was offering something of herself—as a gift, as a proof in need of a teacher's mark, as a piece of theatre, an entertainment. The mother's task was to receive the gift appropriately. The adolescent daughter's task was to teach her mother, sometimes a very slow pupil, what appropriate meant.

From the information I was gathering I had a clear sense that something was incomplete or unbalanced in the traditional theory of adolescent development, in particular of female adolescent development in relation to the mother. But mine was a relatively small study, and however convinced I was that mothers and daughters were working together, sometimes stressfully but nonetheless purposefully, on the daughter's development, the weight of the traditional theory remained against me. It was an enormous boost to the organization of my material when I learned of work currently being done by a group of psychologists at Harvard Medical School and in the Division of Child Development and Family Relationships at the University of Texas at Austin. Starting with the observation that we continue to care for our parents throughout our lives, that we remain attached to them, they have put together a model of adolescent development which involves "connectedness" and "individuation," as opposed to the more traditional notions of "separation" and "individuation." The adolescent—both girl and boy—is seen to develop in relation to the parents' views. This is not merely a matter of the parents' views being fed into their psychology as a mechanical cause, but the parents' techniques of validation and confirmation influence the way in which the adolescent builds her sense of self. This type of parental input has long been recognised in early stages of development, as the infant self gains character and solidity. What is startling and original about this new work is the presumption, first, that this kind of parental input (this input as reflection) continues during adolescence, and, secondly, that its techniques and meaning change. These psychological studies, still in progress, offer the enlightenment of a new language for thinking about adolescent psycho-dynamics, and I make no apology for leaning so heavily on the succinct, simple perspective that has arisen from their sound and subtle work.[12]

I take adolescence as lasting from 11 or 12 until about 21. This is a long phase, encompassing puberty and taking it into what is sometimes considered as young adulthood. Even with this extension I could not find evidence of separation. The mothers themselves did not see the daughter as "leaving home" until well into her twenties. Going away to university or college, for example, did not mean that she was "all grown-up" or that she had left home—she was only away for a while. Different mothers took different things as indicators of the final home-leaving. Sometimes it was when the daughter, or the daughter and her husband/boyfriend bought their own house, or were setting up home in another city. Some mothers took getting a job and setting up home in another city or getting married as the final blow. The emphasis was on the daughter's belongings being removed from the parents' home to another residence which was the daughter's own.

It is during the third, not the second decade of life that children ease away from emotional and psychological focus upon the parents. Yet often daughters in their thirties return to focus on their mothers. They become intrigued by what life was like for her. Having spent so much time and energy on getting her to see life from their point of view, they are struck, fascinated by some unexpected story as they consider life from their mother's angle, remembering her at their age now. What I found throughout these interviews was that adolescent daughters continued to care deeply about their parents, and in particular retained a strong attachment to their mother which they very much wanted to preserve. The more I studied the relationship between mothers and daughters during adolescence, the more intricate and potentially positive it seemed to me. Daughters worked deliberately upon their mothers to get recognition and acknowledgement of the newly forming adult self. They offered a hundred reminders each day that the habitual ways of viewing them were not quite right. Mothers responded to their daughter's efforts, but themselves offered reminders—with more or less diffidence, often depending upon the daughter's age—of what the daughter should be doing, thinking, feeling, or becoming. Communication itself was a type of argument about self-definition and self-justification. The arguments were sometimes more and sometimes less hostile. They were often filled with love and delight. They were often filled with anger and frustration. But the aim of the argument was never to separate; it was always characterised by the underlying demand, "See me as I am, and love me for what I am."

NOTES

1. Ann Petersen's response to Joseph Adelson's request for a chapter on female adolescence for Adelson (1980).
2. Mahler, 1975.
3. Chodorow, 1978.
4. Stern, 1985.
5. Gilligan, 1982.
6. Dinnerstein, 1976.
7. Lawrence, 1948.
8. Roth, 1969; 1972.
9. Friday, 1979.
10. Cohen, 1986.
11. Sassen, 1980; Friedan, 1981; Gilligan, 1982; Apter, 1985.
12. I refer to the recent work of Harold Grotevant and Catherine Cooper, Stuart Hauser and Sally Powers, David Bell and Linda Bell, James Youniss and Robert Ketterlinus, Susan Silverberg and Laurence Steinberg. Much of the June, 1987, issue of *Journal of Youth and Adolescence* is devoted to their new model.

Chapter 1

THE BEAUTY AND THE
BEASTLINESS

WHAT IS ADOLESCENCE?

She stood before the mirror and she was afraid. It was the summer of fear, for Frankie, and there was one fear that could be figured in arithmetic at the table. This August she was twelve and five-sixth years old. She was five feet and three quarter inches tall, and she wore a number seven shoe. In the past year she had grown four inches, or at least that was what she judged. . . . Therefore, according to mathematics and unless she could somehow stop herself, she would grow to be over nine feet tall. And what would be a lady who is over nine feet high? She would be a Freak.[1]

Sometimes, when I lie in bed at night, I have a terrible desire to feel my breasts and to listen to the quiet rhythmic beat of my heart.

Each time I have a period—and that has only been three times—I have the feeling that in spite of all the pain, the unpleasantness, and nastiness, I have a sweet secret, and that is why, although it is nothing but a nuisance to me in a way, I always long for the time that I shall feel that secret within me again.[2]

I was sitting at a party, just sitting with the girls, and watching the boys goof off, and I could feel that awful trickle from my vagina onto the pad, and I kept staring at the boys, and thinking they were so lucky, because they didn't have to bother with this. And then it got to me, how I was sitting with the girls, and how they all went through it—or were bound to go through it—

24

and I felt real attached to them, like I was bound to
them with chains, but I also felt proud, like we had this
secret—which wasn't just the secret of Jane-itch (what
we call having our period, because the boys talk about
Jock-itch, and if you say it real quick you can sound
like you're saying Jan-ich) but a pull towards another
kind of thing, other than that goofing off they were
into, and even though my stomach was aching, I
wanted to fly up, way above those boys. (Berkeley
High student, aged 13 years)

The developing girl is both a freak and a wonder. She experiences her growth both as a sweet secret, a personal mystery,
and as something which is being imposed upon her from the
outside, something taking her over, turning her familiar self
into something gargantuan, ugly, and above all strange. She
knows that intimate changes are occurring within her, and they
involve the most private and vulnerable parts of her self, yet
many of these changes are also glaringly public. She has to
adapt not only to the emergence of a sexual woman within her,
but also to others' treatment of her as a sexually developed
female. She may feel confused and isolated by the change in
others' behaviour towards her. She may be convinced that these
bodily changes will appear as ungainly to others as they do to
herself. On the other hand, her very vulnerability may be the
wedge with which she fits into another's sensibility, in particular to the sensibility, which is growing into empathy, of other
girls, who need to share confidences, as they share her confusion, her ignorance, her excitement, and her fear.

Many psychologists or sociologists writing today about
adolescence, believe that adolescence is an artificial phase, thrust
upon us by an industrial society. Adolescence is seen as an enforced delay of maturity. In contrast to developmental phases
such as infancy, sexual maturity, or old age, which are "set"
by a natural time clock, adolescence is seen as an artificial bar-
rier necessary to modern youth because their society makes
enormously complex demands upon them. They require extra
time to prepare themselves for adulthood. Margaret Mead's

work on adolescents growing up in pre-industrialised societies seemed to show that it was possible to pass from childhood to adult status easily, mildly, without protest, without rebellion, as long as the children facing adulthood had a very clear idea of what their lives would be, were well prepared for these lives, and in addition, did not face the anxiety and confusion of making choices.[3] Adolescence, with its typical features of "storm and stress," mood swings, rebelliousness, excess energy, it was thought, is not a universal feature of development, but an adaptation enforced upon contemporary children by the complexity of their society. The extensive range of choices for adult roles, the continuous threats of failure, the paucity of support in face of failure, cloud the paths to adulthood, and delay maturity.

Until the industrial revolution, there was a far simpler timescale and curve of development from youth to maturity. Puberty, which marked reproductive maturity, marked entry into adulthood—just as it does now in pre-literate, or some pre-industrialised societies, which often have rituals to mark this change in status, and hence which have ways of making the transition clear, both to the child and to others. Hence there need be no fighting about adult versus child status—the centre of so many fights within families in Western society.

Adolescence may in fact be necessary to industrialised society. This society is so complex that in order to prepare for adult status, the developing child must hold back, learn a variety of skills, take a variety of tests, face multiple choices which involve a kind of "moratorium" on development, an enforced extension of the age of irresponsibility. Adulthood is mastered only very slowly, and the child must be given lots of lessons and lots of chances before he can step up and claim the diploma of adulthood.

ADOLESCENCE AND PUBERTY

There is no doubt that as our society shapes the possibilities and influences the goals of adults, so it invades and structures the life of the adolescent. Yet adolescence has been recognised as a stage of human development since medieval times—long, long before the industrial revolution—and, as it is now, has long been seen as a phase which centres on the fusion of sexual and social maturity. Indeed, adolescence as a concept has as long a history as that of puberty, which is sometimes considered more concrete, and hence much easier to name and to recognise. The root meanings of the two words show the difference between the pedestrian and the abstract: puberty is derived from a word meaning "to grow hairy," referring to the growth of pubic hair as one of the secondary features of sexual maturity, whereas adolescence is derived from the term "adolescere," "to grow up,"—a notion that leaves room for a good deal of controversy. Yet, surprisingly, puberty too lacks an easy, definite marker.

So bound up is our development with the fortunes and the sins of our society, that puberty itself, the allegedly simple, concrete fact of sexual maturity, is a volatile and vague concept. The age of puberty has been falling steadily, probably as a result of improved nutrition and rapid weight gain during childhood, and is now believed to have, in middle-class Western populations, reached its lowest possible level. Puberty is now seen as preceding, and hence separate from adolescence, whereas some generations ago it would have made more sense to see puberty and adolescence as closely linked, because the physical and psychosocial changes would have come together. In pre-industrial society, puberty would more reasonably have been a marker for adult status, because it came several years later than it does now. Moreover, the onset of puberty is not as clear as crystal. Puberty is normally thought to indicate sexual maturity. Could puberty in girls, then, not be marked as the onset of menstruation? But menstruation does not actually mark sexual maturity. Girls are usually infertile for several years after the onset of menstruation. Is puberty the onset of those hormonal changes which trigger the growth spurt and menstruation? In terms of endocrinological changes, the gonadotrophin hormone levels begin to rise in both boys and girls around age 7 or 8. This marks the end of the hormonal suppression which has been in effect since soon after birth. The mechanisms of

these changes are not understood. No one knows why the suppression ends, what triggers it, so it is difficult to mark the
beginning of these changes, and hence to use it as a marker for
the beginning of puberty. And when does puberty end? Normally the end of puberty is thought to be signalled by hormonal cyclicity, when a regular pattern is established. But just
as we know nothing about the onset of hormonal changes,
nothing is known about the mechanisms leading to the stabi-
lisation of the hormonal cycle, so they are difficult to pin-point.
And since hormonal cyclicity may not be established until several years after menstruation begins, the endocrinological or
hormonal boundaries of puberty may range from age 7 to 17.
So, clinically, the boundaries and the definition of puberty are
as vague, and summon as little agreement, as those of adolescence. I think if we can see how open-ended puberty is, we
will lower our standards for some highly objective, or absolute
account of adolescence.

Adolescence is certainly not the same recognisable development at all times and in all societies,[4] but if it is a creation of
our society, it is only so to the extent that we are all its crea-
tions. Even so, we all feel our life's story individually, and as
belonging uniquely to ourselves. More general issues have
meaning for us as they shape our ideas and hopes for ourselves,
our relationship to the people closest to us, and the ways in
which these hopes for ourselves and our sense of how we live
up to others' hopes mesh to give a sense of either fulfilment or
disappointment. We try to understand our adolescence, or our
children's adolescence through the detail of personal transac-
tions, personal responses, personal needs and claims. It is only
through these immediate interactions that the larger, social story
becomes real.

In beginning the story of the girl's adolescence with the
early story of puberty I am not merely noting "objective"
physical changes, for it is the impact of these changes—the girl's
response to them and her impression of what others make of
them—that has the significant impact. The young developing
girl confronts a shift from childhood, from a time in which
others' responses to her had been on a plateau (and being fa-

miliar, had seemed reasonable and just) to a time when she inspires changes in others which she understands as little as she understands the changes within herself. Frankie's "summer of fear" shows that she is terrified of her appearance, that she has the sense of being taken over, of becoming a monster, of having things most strange mingled with her most familiar and personal self. Nothing is more common among adolescent girls, and indeed developing women of all ages, than to accentuate physical dissatisfaction, to feel they would be much better off if only certain things about their appearance were different. Even a young woman who may, in certain circumstances, glow with the pleasure of her own beauty, will have a private list of corrections she would like to make upon herself. Young women tend to give up the visionary quest for physical transformations only when the marks of age and childbirth make them appreciate what they once had, so that at last they look back upon a former physical self with some admiration.

This concern for the superficialities of appearance is not for the adolescent a superficial concern. Linda, a 13-year-old English girl who had a wide range of interests and abilities (she in fact had been the youngest to pass an advanced music exam) was speaking to me in the kitchen when her attention wandered to some neighbours playing in the garden. "Oh, look at her hair," she sighed, and her attention remained fixed on some vision of beauty beyond the window, "it's so blond, so smooth." At first I was amused by this raw, unnecessary envy. I asked her what she thought having such hair would give her. My initial question must have contained a hint that I was teasing, for she looked both hurt and uncertain, so, in a more even tone, I asked, "What would it mean to you to be able to mold your physical self any way you wanted?"

"Oh, Lord! To be whatever I wanted. I don't know. I'd make myself beautiful. Really lovely, so I could always have— well, it would be like a base—you know—something to feel sure about. Blond and pretty—I could go anywhere, do anything, and sort of feel safe. I'd feel all right, in myself. I know looks aren't everything, but you could do more, think better of yourself if you didn't have to feel you looked so dull. Not ugly, really. I know I'm not ugly . . . But if I were prettier—if I could magic myself into being as pretty as I wanted—then I'd just be better off, in myself, somehow."

A young girl's satisfaction with her appearance is linked to overall satisfaction with her self. It isn't just that teenagers are so vain that to be satisfied with their looks is to be satisfied with themselves. It is rather that the teenage girl stresses dissatisfaction with physical appearance when she has some general dissatisfaction. What first struck me when I listened to the list every girl was all too ready to give me about what was wrong with her appearance, was that each girl's idea of what she should look like, was bound to be different from what she in fact looked like (or supposed herself to look like) not only because—as I had originally assumed—that dissatisfaction was built into the adolescent girl's attitude, but because she had no idea of how she should look. The developing girl has no sense of an appropriate, or normal physique for her age. Her conception of normal development is askew. If adolescent girls are confronted with a pile of photographs—all depicting adolescent girls in various stages of development—and asked to sort them into age groups, they will show a complete absence of skill. They simply do not seem to know how to distinguish between early, middle and late adolescent development. Some girls expect an early adolescent to be as well developed as a girl in late adolescence, but the greatest number of errors involves placing a photograph of an early adolescent in the late adolescent group.

Boys, when faced with a similar task of sorting out photographs of adolescent boys into early and late puberty, will do a good, sensible job. Boys seem to know what a typical middle adolescent boy looks like, and what a boy in late adolescence looks like. They are even good at spotting the awkward, in-between stages, when a boy may still be very short, but nonetheless different from a much younger child of the same height. Boys, too, get confused when they try to sort out photographs of adolescent girls. Though not as inept as girls themselves in this ability, they frequently place very thin, small-breasted girls of 12 or 13 in the older adolescent category. Slightly more developed girls, in mid-puberty, were also placed as belonging in the late puberty category. Only well-developed girls, of late puberty, were placed correctly.

The task in this study was not for adolescents to place photographs of other adolescents in specific age groups. Adolescent development—especially physical development—cannot be neatly tracked by age. Some 13-year-old girls are in a mid-adolescent phase, and some are in an early developmental phase. So the task was to place the photographs in groups marked by developmental phase—by early, middle and late adolescence. Photographs of girls in early and mid-adolescence were routinely placed in the group marked "late adolescence." This bias signals many problems a girl has with her own physique. She may complain about being too small, too slight, too short, but she suffers far more when she feels she is too large, too fat, too prominent. In placing photographs of early and mid-adolescents in the group belonging to late adolescence, she shows a bias towards the less developed, and a lack of acceptance of normal female maturity.[5]

A girl's physical development can be highly ambiguous and confusing. She may want to put a halt to it, or indeed feel like screaming out in protest against it. Her resistance to physical development does not come simply from a misconceived ideal of the mature female body. It is linked to the effect her development has upon others.

Physical maturity in a boy has unambiguous prestige. As a boy grows taller and stronger, adults grant him approval and freedom. This is not a matter of older boys being granted more independence, but of taller, stronger, older-looking boys being granted more approval and more independence than their less well developed peers. He tends to respond well to the approval and expectations he arouses in others. For it has been found that the early maturing boy is more relaxed, less dependent, more self-confident and more attractive to both peers and adults than a less physically developed boy of the same age.[6] There are, for boys, no drawbacks in looking older, in gaining physical maturity, in exhibiting the marks of manhood. But as I spoke to girls, and observed them at home, in school, in recreation, it became painfully clear to me that responses to their maturity were far from straightforward, that maturity itself was a very mixed blessing.

Being mixed, there is some good to it. The adolescent girl wants to develop into a woman. If she is an early developer, that is, if she shows breast and body development ahead of her peers, she usually gets some prestige from it. The girl with well-developed breasts at 13 is noticed, and is often more popular. She may not be better liked, but she gets more attention from boys, especially older boys, and being singled out by an older boy often brings prestige. But the early maturing girl is also more self-conscious, and what was clear as I spoke to these girls was that there was a very direct relationship between self-consciousness and self-dissatisfaction. Amy, at 15, was an ebullient Californian who breathlessly offered a strange combination of self-assertion and nervousness. She chewed on her nails as she spoke, and her voice often shook with incipient tears, though her language appeared deliberately comic and forceful. She made a long list of physical complaints with the vehemence and finality of someone ripping a piece of paper to shreds. "My nose is too thick. My arms are too thick. My thighs are far too wide. My skin is blotchy, sort of doughy and blotchy. You know how some girls have this real smooth tawny skin, or a wonderful glistening black skin? Well mine's like old pizza dough! And whenever I stand up and talk to someone or walk into a room, I'm sort of standing in the thick of this thick body, and the people I'm talking to or the people watching me really make me sweat. The ugliness outside me is like a heavy ball inside my stomach, like I'm looking inside myself and seeing the ugliness that's outside folded up inside. I can't break through this awful cloud which just smothers me when I feel someone looking at me—you know looking at me and thinking about what I look like."

The more a girl thought about her appearance, the more unhappy she was. The more unhappy she was about her appearance, the more she felt forced to think about it. "My greatest dream," a 14-year-old admitted, "is just to be able to forget myself. Well, it's not a dream, really, that's not what I daydream about, because when I daydream, I can make things all right. But when I have the most fun, is when I forget about how I look. And then it all comes back to me, that someone's looking at me, and it's like I'm trapped again. My stomach will turn over, and I'll think, 'Yeah, I'm back here again,' but it was so nice, just to be free of it for a while."

Early developing girls do not simply see themselves to be ahead of others, they see themselves as abnormal. They are not just early, in their own view, but wrong. Of course teenagers have a petulant sense of timing. They often retain the child's need for a desire to be fulfilled now, not later. To be assured that in a year or two they will be physically on target often means nothing to them. Seeing herself as "over-developed," she sees herself as a freak, and is convinced that she will always be so.

As girls begin to show signs of physical maturity, they look to friends and peers as measures of how they themselves should be, but their concern is not simply to be at the same stage of development as their peers. There are important differences between a girl who is less developed than her peers—a late maturing girl—and a girl who is more developed than her peers—an early maturing girl. The issue is not simply being on target, being the same as the other girls, because a late maturing girl, who is also not on target, will be much more content with herself than an early maturing girl. She may complain. She may make jokes about herself. She may suggest a bleak view of her sexual prospects ("If I don't get bigger by the time I marry," said one 15-year-old girl, "I'll die of embarrassment"). Yet the attitude of the late developer lacked the awkwardness, even the shame, of the early developing girl. She moved differently, with greater freedom, often with some coyness, and often with clear pleasure. She also laughed at the outrageous things she said about herself, as though there was a comfortable distance between her self-criticism and her complaints. If her delayed maturity was extreme, she often saw it as a challenge, as an opportunity to surprise people with her intellectual precocity—not necessarily by trying to do well in school but by making quick, pert remarks, by startling one with her "knowingness" and her independence.

In contrast, the early maturing girl suffered the same lack of self-confidence, the same wish to bury herself that one would expect to find, for example, in someone badly overweight. Indeed, according to one study, the early maturing girl was found to be so withdrawn, and so low, that she actually does less well in her schoolwork than her less well-developed peers of comparable ability.[7]

"Every time I meet someone—every time I see someone—I feel their eyes right on my breasts," explained a 13-year-old girl, who considered herself "over-developed"; though physically well-rounded she was clearly within the normal limits of weight, height and sexual development. "It isn't that everyone is rude. I know they don't want to stare, and sometimes they just look for a minute, but I know they notice." I asked her whether she did not sometimes find this a sign of admiration. "Well, I guess. Sort of. But even if they're admiring it—well, it makes me feel there's something wrong with me, and I just can't get by it. It's always there, somehow stacked into the notion of 'me,' so whenever I hear anyone say my name, I think they're thinking that too, I mean thinking about my body, and I just wish I could cut it off from me."

Inside almost every well-developed girl, there was an anorexic lurking, someone who wanted to "cut off" her sexual characteristics from herself, and find a "clean" unencumbered self. The young girl, and especially the early developer, feels the tug towards a sexual identity at the same time she is working very hard to establish a broader, personal identity.

I had thought that this pressure of ambiguity might find some relief through friendship, since all girls, whatever their phase of development, are in some sense in the same boat. They all confront similar issues—and anxiety about their appearance, the new, disturbing separation between what she wants to be and how people are now responding to her, the surprise, excitement and terror of the swift physical changes. Also, this is a time at which friendship takes on a new, very strong significance, when the accent on loyalty between friends might indicate the wealth of secrets shared, and the upsurge in articulacy and self-reflection might provide opportunity for supportive discussion. But, particularly in regard to physical development, there is not much solace for the early maturing adolescent girl here. Other girls are too much at sea about themselves to give them support. The most common way I found girls in early puberty dealing with their confusion was in exploring one another's bodies. They play hilarious sexual games which they present as "pretending to be boy and girl," elaborate versions of the childhood game of "doctor" and, because they are more sophisticated, they are better at keeping these games a secret. Since these are quite young girls, about 11 and 12, many of them try out positions with one another, wondering how the sex act works. A little later, as they approach 13, these games give way to fake sleaziness, so that the girls play stripper for one another, or play strip poker. In this way they are able to compare one another, and often within groups of girls there are ratings of who is biggest (that is, who has the largest breasts) and sometimes who is prettiest (whose breasts are prettiest, that is). But this kind of "support," this method of investigation, does not include those girls who feel themselves to be badly off target, especially if they are early developers, because these girls would feel too out of place in such a game, and would suspect that their role was to be ridiculed. (In fact, the less developed girls were actually aroused by the more physically mature girls, and wanted to look at their bodies to get a better idea of what they themselves would become.) Though there was some variation in physical maturity within a group playing such games, the variation was not broad, since only girls at a similar developmental level could admit their curiosity of one another. As soon as the group as a whole became physically mature the games stopped.

Repeatedly I found the support of friendships, certainly during early adolescence, had been greatly over-rated. "Sure I'm glad to have friends," said 13-year-old Chris. "You walk into school, and you need to know who you're going to talk to. I'm not sure I have a best friend. The girls who are real close are into boys in a big way. I'm not. I'd rather be home, just with my Mom when she gets home from work, or by myself, I don't mind. That's really the basis of those friendships—how I see it, anyway, they're always gushing about boys or clothes or hair. I always sit at the same table in the lunch room. I have steady friends in that sense. But important things—no, I don't think I've ever talked about important things with my friends."

The girls Chris saw as "real close" were circumspect about their intimacy. "Yeah," laughed Chris's schoolmate Lee, "I go wild with my friends. We make a show of it. Ruth Ann's been my friend for years. She lives right next door to me. I don't have to tell her much. She knows me. Sort of. But I tell her something, and she laughs so I laugh too, and feel silly, keep it down then. Or sometimes, like when I told her I got the curse, she said, 'Me too,' but I didn't know whether to believe her." Friendship does develop, especially among girls, to include new capacity for intimacy, support and loyalty, but it is not as inclusive as it may appear to adults looking at it from the outside. Nor did girls tend to share among themselves the anxiety and curiosity they felt about menstruation, which was quite a different landmark from secondary sexual development—growth of breasts and widening of hips which do not mark, but are associated with, sexual maturity. The girls did not exactly avoid the subject, but most said they did not discuss it with anyone other than their mothers until they had been menstruating for several months. "I thought I might be teased," explained a 12-year-old girl from Washington, DC. She was so slight that she looked about 10, and the way she pressed the palms of her hands together, and pressed them between her knees when she spoke, reinforced this childlike impression. Her thin shoulders raised up in an "I-don't-know" movement before answering each question. Though she had been quite open and calm about other matters, this topic was hot with embarrassment. "I mean, I know a good friend wouldn't tease me about it when I told her, but she might tell someone else, or she might say something at school, and then—" She moved her thumbs apart and stared at the palms of her hands. "It just seemed better not to say anything. I told Mom, and she got me the things I needed and that was okay."

Some girls were excited by the onset of menstruation. I

was shown a diary by a 13-year-old from Chicago who had written: "Today is the day I became a WOMAN!!!" She seemed to relive the initial excitement as she showed it to me and laughed with pride. Some girls said they had been appalled, usually because the onset was unexpected and caused embarrassment. "I knew all about it—what it was and all that—but it came when I was in school. Boy, did it come. And I had to tell the teacher, and I had to go home. I was a mess," explained one girl who had begun menstruating at 12—not a premature age, but no girl can be prepared the first time menstruation occurs. By far the majority claimed that it had no great impact. I met shrugs of boredom, of lack of interest when I asked about their feelings. "Well, it happens. Big deal. It's just one of those things," or "Yeah, I have my periods. You get used to them. They're all right." However, one psychologist has noted a phenomenon which she called "pubertal amnesia," the syndrome of forgetting how a girl felt when she first discovered she was menstruating.[8] For when a girl claimed that the onset of puberty had little impact, she would then go on to describe scenes or details clearly expressing anxiety about it.

One girl who said that she had not responded in any strong way to the onset of menstruation, explained that the only effect it had upon her was to put a stop to daydreaming. This was a pastime which previously she had enjoyed. Her customary daydreams involved her walking along the street with a group of girls, when they would meet a boy she particularly liked. All her friends would see how he singled her out and smiled at her and went up to talk to her. But after she began menstruating her pleasure in the daydream was destroyed, because every time it came to the point at which she met the boy and he was about to walk up to speak to her, a sanitary napkin would fall from between her legs onto the pavement, and everyone would see the streak of dark blood, and the wrinkled pad, and she would freeze in terror. It was to avoid the excruciating embarrassment she suffered even simply in imagining this scene that she determined to relinquish any daydreaming whatsoever. She was haunted by the possibility of "exposure," so shameful and strange did menstruating seem to her.

When I heard so many similar anxieties from other girls, I wondered whether there was not some connection between the terror of potential embarrassment and the frequent complaint that they had not been adequately prepared beforehand. At the same time a girl would tell me that she wished she had known more about menstruation before she herself had experienced it, she would also admit that she had known "pretty much" about menstruation before, or had been "pretty well" informed—almost always by her mother. "Yes I knew what it was," Amy insisted impatiently as I tried to discover the reason for her regret that she "was thrown in at the deep end without knowing how to swim." "Yes, I knew women had periods and I knew the blood was from the breaking down of the uterine wall when there's no use for that wall, and I knew it means that you were now capable of bearing children. And I knew about those nickknacks you need—the pads and the plungers and so forth. But I guess I didn't know all the techniques. I mean the pads get squashed or the press ons don't stick, and who's going to sit there and go through a tampax course with you? I mean—. This is stupid. Why are we talking about this? I knew enough, but I didn't feel prepared."

The much shyer, more reflective Chris said, "I can't say exactly. My Mom's always been good about telling me what's what. She's very matter-of-fact. You know, some girls are given books by their parents and that's how they learn. But my mother told me, even showed me what it looked like on a pad. But it took me a while to put certain things together—like sometimes I feel real jumpy, like I'm afraid, my heart's beating and I don't know why, and now I recognize that as how I'll feel just before it starts. But I don't know—I guess I didn't expect it, or recognize it, and maybe it's just me anyway."

Whatever information a girl had been given, she felt ignorant about some aspect of menstruation. Either she felt she had not been given enough information about the underlying hormonal process, and complained about the length of time it had taken for her to associate mood swings with menstruation, or she felt that it had come much sooner than she expected, and that she had not been told it could normally start, say, at twelve, or she felt she lacked practical information—how to avoid blood spots on clothes (there was a great deal of worry about spots on underwear; spots on actual clothes, such as skirts or trousers, was thought to be the ultimate humiliation), or how to get a tampon "all the way in," that is, in the right position, and how you could tell it was right.

Other girls focussed not on the fear of exposure, but on fears of what menstruation revealed about their physical well-being. One girl said she was frightened when she saw "those little blobs" on the pad—that is, the small clots of blood; and another said that she believed her menstrual blood "smelled unhealthy, like there was really something wrong inside."

Since most of these girls had learned about menstruation from their mothers, I asked them why they did not then express their fears. The explanations for not laying these fears at their mother's doorstep were that they "didn't want to worry her," or "didn't quite know how to put it." They seemed ashamed of their own anxiety. Much older girls were able to discuss their first reactions to menstruation with friends who were also menstruating. But they were able to discuss these matters among themselves, and pool information, and have relief through communication, injecting their anxiety with some humour, only after they themselves had got used to the experience of menstruating. During the first year of menstruation, when they probably needed help the most, they were least likely to seek it from anyone.

Sometimes a girl felt unprepared for the onset of menstruation because she did not put together the appearance of blood with what she had learned about menstruation and, as a result, she explained her bleeding with bizarre and anxious stories. Gerry, who was 16 when I spoke to her, described a disturbed but not atypical response. When she first saw the brown liquid on her pants, she felt it, and it was sticky. She thought that it was dirt oozing from her. She had been accustomed to masturbate in the bath by letting the water run full force on her genitals. She thought that some of the water had gone in, and that it had mixed with something inside her, and was now coming out. She thought it would "get better." For several days she bided her time. Still afraid that her mother would see through this "symptom" to her private fantasies and indulgence, she turned to her as "a last resort." In a state of acute anxiety, she handed the problem over to her mother, "like blood on a platter." "Oh, that," her mother said—she mimicked her mother, making a swift hitting movement with her hand—and the meaning of the blood changed as it was finally linked to the familiar explanation.

Many girls said they "didn't know what it was at first," even though they knew what menstruation was, and had even seen their mother's blood at some stage. Their inability to connect the appearance of blood to the normal occurrence of menstruation already signalled their sexual ambivalence and anxiety. The most frightening part was the shame that went hand in hand with ignorance. Each girl was only too quick to assume that either the blood, or some aspect of the bleeding, was peculiar to her, and that the explanation was beyond a common language.

SELF-CONSCIOUSNESS AND SELF-DISTORTION

The disruption of the familiar self, the self that has been taken for granted, is what most girls accentuated when they spoke of the feelings of separation, or alienation that suffused them during puberty. It was separation from their childhood, not separation from a parent that made them feel isolated, frightened and alone. "Most of the time I'm fine. I don't want you to think that I feel this the whole time. But it's always there, and sometimes it just surges up in me, this great feeling that I'm moving further and further away from everything that I've known. Like I jerk awake and realise I'm on some super modern train and I don't know where I'm going." Laurie was 15, and puberty had come upon her late and sudden. Already, at this early age, she was looking back to her Edinburgh childhood as an idyll. Her parents had loved her, been proud of her, and "gone easy on" her. Now she and her mother looked at one another uncertainly. Even before each spoke one began answering the querying glance of the other, but failed to answer it properly, and so they fell out, or gave up on one another, each blaming the other, each blaming herself. It was a poignant nearly wordless exchange of hope and disappointment. "Eh?" "What?" "Oh, nothing." "What?" "Not a thing." The changes which were rupturing the even, familiar tone of conversation (and it was clear from their nervousness that this was new) did not cause points of contention but areas of bewilderment. "I see her looking at me," Laurie continued, referring to her mother, "and it's like she's asking 'What's happened?' and when I get up in the morning I reach for my old clothes which maybe I haven't worn for a month or two, and it's like they're somebody else's. I remember as a wee lass going back to school and thinking, 'Why, this tap's not so high after all.' But this isn't fun. I mean you can find it dead funny. But it's not fun. I'm used to giving my Mum a cuddle now and then—you know, a right big hug. Well, I'm afraid to now. I don't know if I'll fit." At the approach of adolescence, at puberty, the attitude towards growth becomes ambivalent. A child is keen to be older, to be taller, to be more grown-up. The typical adult response to a child—"My, how you've grown!"—registers, not perfectly but fairly accurately, both a parent's and a child's pride. Growth is progress and growth is pleasing. The child's sense of what she is, links positively to a sense of what she will become. But a child's sense of her future is vague and undemanding. It is safely relegated to fantasy, and she is protected by a child's body. But during puberty maturity invades her. The growth is pleasurable, but it is also frightening. So even before the real battle begins—the battle for recognition of a new self—there is more primitive, less rational, less articulate tension as a heightened self-consciousness and self-uncertainty emerge. The special new need for friendship and the need for self-explanation, or self-definition, are felt here, but not quite developed. It is only a little later, when the physical changes take on an aspect of normality, that the intimacies of friendship and the self-exploration of diary or poetry writing become common.

The self-consciousness of early adolescence is very close to

Erik Erikson's description of "shame" experienced at a much earlier phase of life, shame which he sees as rage turned against the self, but actually directed at others who are looking at oneself. The real impulse is to scratch at the eyes of the world. But, unable to do this with any effect, the shamed person seeks her own invisibility. "Shame," writes Erikson, "supposes that one is completely exposed and conscious of being looked at: in a word, self-conscious. One is visible and not ready to be visible; which is why we dream of shame as a situation in which we are stared at in a condition of incomplete dress, in night attire, 'with one's pants down.' "[9] Though Erikson is not here describing the tension and obsessions of adolescence, his description reveals precisely the torment of early adolescence, wherein the girl's increasing cognitive abilities which allow her some understanding of others' views and a greater awareness of others' responses, turn back upon herself. She becomes acutely aware of herself as a being perceived by others, judged by others, though she herself is the harshest judge, quick to list her physical flaws, quick to undervalue and under-rate herself not only in terms of physical appearance but across a wide range of talents, capacities and even social status, whereas boys of the same age will cite their abilities, their talents and their social status pretty accurately.

The world of the adolescent girl is not always obsessed by doubt and confusion, but it is always haunted by ambiguity and uncertainty. The early maturing girl has the roughest time because she is different, markedly different not only from what she herself was a short time ago, but also she is different from her female peers. Doubly different, she lacks the support both of familiarity (which the late developing girl will have, even although she too may be different from her peers) and of similarity.

This pressure of self-criticism—so common, so rampant that it seems tinged with self-loathing—is linked to the well-known problems adolescent girls have in dealing with their weight. Most of the girls I spoke to—indeed all but two of the American girls I spoke to—saw themselves as too fat. If a girl was clearly very thin, she would still believe that her hips were too large. For all the changes two decades of the feminist movement have made (and in regard to girls' assessment of their career lives these changes, especially in America, are considerable) little dent seems to have been made in the modern bias for pre-pubertal, or very early adolescent physique as the ideal. Indeed, pre-pubertal girls were more tolerant of plumpness or roundness, but eighteen months on, similar amounts of body fat were considered "gross," "disgusting," "brutish." In noting this prejudice, some researchers have analysed leg length and breast size in fashion drawings, adverts, and magazines to cite these as the probable cause or the certain perpetrator of the bias towards the late maturing or early adolescent figure, but whatever its foundation, it is certainly not a male conspiracy, for men are far more generous, far more catholic in their tastes of women's bodies than are women of themselves.

When I suggested to these complaining girls that they should be encouraged to accept a more flexible view of a good figure, they all agreed, and all said that as long as a body was healthy it should be considered good looking, yet each girl claimed that if she had a choice, she herself would be very slim, long-legged, with narrow hips. The only issue on which the ideal varied concerned breast size. Some girls thought it would be wonderful to have large breasts, and just as many felt they would be content with small breasts.

I was somewhat concerned that the frequency with which early adolescent girls complained about their appearance was somehow manufactured, that it was the social norm. They were clearly preoccupied with their appearance, and wanted to talk about it. Perhaps the easiest way to talk about it was to complain about it. In this way, might they not seek reassurance, even flattery? How sincere—or how severe—are these relentless self-criticisms? Certainly some girls, some of the time, complain in order to be reassured and flattered, but the astonishing number of eating disorders confirms the depth of their sometimes flip self-criticisms.

There is a disease known as anorexia nervosa which is almost exclusive to adolescent or very young women. It is linked to the desire to lose weight. This sometimes fatal disease is really compulsive dieting in a context in which the girl wants to abolish all body fat, and sees any fat as excessive. So warped is her self-image that however thin she becomes she sees herself as fat, and she sees the process of eating as a punishable indulgence. Her illness is generally understood as the result of her inability to accept adulthood and in particular, adult sexuality. Her illness solves this problem for her, not only because her extreme thinness may make her appear much younger than she is, but also because the lack of nourishment retards or stops menstruation and fertility. Also, by suppressing her appetite for food the anorexic girl proves that she is in control of her appetite, and therefore in control of her desires. She may deny that she has any appetite—she simply does not feel hungry, nor does she feel hunger for anything. So the disease "solves" all her problems: being so thin and growing thinner each day, the girl does not look like a maturing female; being so undernourished, she does not menstruate and therefore further suppresses sexuality; and finally, being so "strong" in her refusal to accept food, she takes control over her own impulses, denying the sexual appetite that might otherwise overwhelm her.

Mara explained that she had been "inspired" to diet after viewing a video of *To Kill a Mockingbird*. She was 15, and had in the past two years, gained nearly thirty pounds, ten of which she had gained in the two months previous to her diet. None of the clothes her mother had bought her for the school term fit her, and she wore a baggy sweatshirt over jeans to hide her enlarged stomach and hips. She claimed that no one had known just how fat she really was. The first time she watched the film she was with a group of friends "eating popcorn with lots of butter." When the credits began she was struck by this tiny girl who could curl up inside the tyre swing. "She could fit right into it, her stomach and legs were so neat. Everything was so simple, so honest about her. I guess what I thought was that she somehow was protected, that no one could see her as ugly."

"But wasn't the girl in the film," I ventured, "6 or 7 years old? How could that be appropriate for you?"

Mara shrugged, and her eyes lost their distant, admiring focus. There was a pause before she continued. "I watched the

video at least seven times. I would take it out myself, my weekend treat. And when I saw that girl I wanted to fly out of my
body into hers. The first time I watched the film, after eating
all that buttery popcorn, I went into the bathroom and stepped
right on the scales. You see, even though I knew I was fat, I
didn't want to know my exact weight, and I could fiddle by
stepping on the scales very slowly. I'd do that maybe seven or
eight times, to get the best possible weight. And that could
take five pounds off the total. But this time I was so angry with
myself I didn't want to protect myself. I just got on the scales,
just like that, and it was a hundred and thirty-seven. At 13 I'd
weighed a hundred and five! And I was so fed up with myself
that I scratched my stomach raw, and I looked at the red marks,
and I worked on them till they bled, and I thought 'When the
scars go away, I'll be thinner.' It was that certain—as certain as
the scars going away, and I felt much better. I bargained with
myself that I would only weigh myself once a week—usually
either before or after I watched that film again. And when I
saw how much I was losing I was so excited, so pleased. I could
soon get by with a boiled egg and celery sticks and nothing
else all day. Or sometimes I would divide the egg into quarters,
and have four meals that day—you know, each quarter of the
egg would be one meal. I took off those sweatshirts, and I felt
I was being open and honest for the first time in over a year.
There was no looking back. I still get a thrill when I stand on
the scale and look down and it shows under a hundred pounds."

A related eating disorder, again found primarily in adolescent girls, is bulimia, which to my amazement was practiced
widely, at least to some degree. This illness is characterised not
by the refusal to eat, but by alternating eating "binges" or mas-
sive intake of food, with "purging" or vomiting the rich, sweet
food so quickly consumed. It is associated with anorexia in that
the obsession is with weight loss, but here the girl indulges in
food. She does not control her appetites but feels she can indulge in them without facing any consequences, without being
punished for her indulgence by gaining weight. The bulimic
girl feels that in some way she has "beaten the system." She
has found a way round the retribution for her desires, and this

provides her with special smugness, a sense of freedom, a sense that she is "getting away" with something. It is a dangerous habit, since the alternative gorging and purging can lead to such extreme enzyme imbalance or dehydration, that the heart can simply stop functioning. Also, the activity of frequent vomiting increases the chances of asphyxiation—from inhaling vomit.

A severely bulimic girl will construct her lifestyle around her disease. Usually her gorging is in private, as is the purging, so that her "needs" will require more than the usual amount of "privacy" or seclusion. Like an addict, she will always keep these needs in mind. "I have to spend a lot of money on food," 14-year-old Lena explained. "I like ice cream and sodas—they come up easily, and help other things along too. Chocolate is a disaster. It really sticks inside you. I have to choose my times really carefully, because if my mum heard me in the bathroom, she'd start asking 'Are you all right? Are you all right?' And then I need time alone for a while, because afterwards, you know, your eyes are all red, and you just look odd." Lena was not too thin, and she seemed completely normal. Only a few dots of broken blood vessels around the eyes betrayed her habit, which, after we spoke, she admitted could be gauged as "severe." Often a raging headache would plague her as an after-effect of vomiting, and she would wake up in the night, parched and nauseous, but like any addict, such setbacks did not dissuade her from her habit.

Like anorexia, bulimia is considered to be an illness, but it does not have to be adhered to so strictly in order to be effective. I think for this reason it is far more common. Some girls alternate between anorexia and bulimia. The underlying dynamics are quite different—a determination to control all desire in anorexia, and an angry delight in "beating the system" of her own appetites in bulimia—but a weight obsession binds these two conditions together. Bulimia is more widespread because it has greater flexibility than anorexia. A girl cannot be occasionally anorexic. If she simply fasts for a while, and then begins to eat, she may be over-concerned with her weight, but she is not suffering from an illness. It is possible to practise gorging and purging occasionally, however, and many teenage girls see this as a safety valve, or safety measure, an insurance against the consequences of being unable to control the amount of food they eat. Some girls found any mention of the practice disgusting, but many admitted they would like to develop the "skill" of disgorging after feasting, just as the Romans did on special occasions.

Psychologists have never been kind to the mother. Among the crimes laid at her doorstep are these eating disorders. Conventional analysis claims that the girl's ambivalence towards her sexuality, which she attempts to control or deny with these self-endangering techniques, is a response to the mother's control, intrusion, or envy. Anorexia, that desperate attempt to restrain all appetite, is thought to be the daughter's bid for control over her self. She needs this super-control because her mother is trying to gain control of her. Anorexia is a means of taking charge. By rigidly containing her own desire, she is protected from intrusion or rejection. Generally the anorexic adolescent, who now causes her parents such concern, was a good, obedient child. Her will was her parents' will. Therefore, to assert her own will, at such a relatively late and crisis-ridden stage, she must take drastic measures and make clear proofs. Yet the first psychoanalyst who concentrated on adolescence, Anna Freud, saw asceticism as a general, defensive feature of adolescence. Her interpretation of this phenomenon as an attempt to deny, or to defend against, the upsurge of feelings associated with adolescence, had no mother-blaming centre.

The ascetic adolescent—and anorexia is certainly compulsive asceticism—is afraid not just of this or that impulse, not just of sex or maternal control, but of impulses in general, because suddenly impulses have a new and frightening strength. The daughter's obsessive fight for control over her impulses may not be directed against the mother at all, but against the complex upsurge of feelings within her, which seem both foreign and undeniably part of her. If her mother then enjoins her to eat, the battle will reign between her and her mother who then becomes an advocate of those impulses she is trying to suppress. If her mother either approves of or resents her sexuality, the daughter will find her mother's attitude intrusive, simply because it touches upon that aspect of herself she is trying to deny.

Before we look too hard for unconscious reasons for these common disorders, however, we should appreciate the conscious ways in which these controls may make sense to an adolescent girl. In her determined and destructive clinging to starvation, the anorexic actually looked for approval. Every anorexic had been under pressure to lose weight. A 15-year-old ballet student, who attended a boarding school for the arts, and for whom weight was a constant issue among her peers and her teachers, saw anorexia as the best way of achieving the physique that was required of her. In opting for anorexia she was complying with the wishes of her teachers, one of whom had humiliated her in front of the class by walking up to her and, without a word, pinching the flesh at the bottom of her rib cage. He held it hard, for several minutes, and every time she breathed in, she said, it seemed that he began pulling it tighter. "I should not be able to do this," he told the class. "There should be no flesh to pull away here." This became her gauge for the "proper weight." When no one could tug any flesh away from the base of the rib cage, then you were thin enough. Her humiliation in the ballet class became a source of determination—and anger. She would show him [her teacher] and she would redeem what she saw as her pride.

All one had to do to get any girl in a tizz about her appearance was to cite a standard, however ridiculous. It could be the ballet teacher's test for excess fat along the rib cage. It could be a magazine article giving clues for whether or not your legs were in great shape. I was told of one test for leg shape involving standing with your legs together and seeing whether there were three "windows," one between the ankles and the calves, one between the calves and the knees, and another between the knees and the crotch. If there were less than three windows, then there was some "excess" fat somewhere. The anxiety was so pervasive that there was really no such thing as a girl secure in her appearance. She did not know what she should look like—and many of them felt they could not predict what they would look like tomorrow.

Eating disorders in adolescent girls must be set in the context of uncertainty, ambiguity and anxiety with which girls in general tend to view sexuality. The mother's influence is great, but the crucible of its power is the girl's own uncertainty and fear. "It wasn't models or movie stars that made me feel fat—it was my mother," insisted Heather who, at 20, was still obsessed by minute variations in weight. "The first thing I've learned to notice about another girl is how thin or fat she is. People who are thin inhabit a different world. I'll meet someone with a lovely figure and once we start to talk I'll always bring the conversation around to weight. I want to know how she stays so thin, but even when I'm asking her that, I'll know that whatever she says won't help me. If it were simple advice then I'd already be thin! What I really want is a glimpse into that other world, where you try on clothes and don't buy an outfit simply because it makes you look thin or where you don't have to worry about what you look like from behind when you're standing up and talking during a cocktail party. I talk about it as a way of reaching out and trying to grab that thinness from her. While I'm thinking all these silly things, I'm also thinking how pleased my mother would be if her daughter were that thin." "That's ridiculous!" interjected Heather's mother. "You're fine. How many times do I have to tell you that I think you're fine?" But for Heather, her mother's "fine" was a compromise, a position of disappointed acceptance. Behind the insistence "You look fine," lurked shadows cast by her own anxious vision, and by her continuing need to have her mother's admiration retain the rich physical love which characterises a mother's love for a young child. "It was a surprise," admitted Heather's mother, "to see my tiny little girl get so big. She had a terrific growth spurt between 11 and 12 which knocked the wind out of us all. At 9 you would have thought she was going to be a lithe beauty. By 12 she was chubby. And at first I worried that she wasn't eating right—what child does? I tried to get her to diet, and I know her dieting made things worse, because she'd starve and binge, but

I'm used to her now, and I never hear the end of how I was the first one to tell her she was overweight."

If a girl is dissatisfied with herself, and if her mother at any time in their joint history has reinforced this dissatisfaction, then the girl will use that point of intersection as a hook on which to hang the cause and content of her self-doubts. The mother's significance becomes her liability. Where the daughter is so uncertain, she regresses to her view that the mother's duty is to admire her completely, and she tends to blame any lapse, any blip in this duty to her continuing problems.

Even when the eating disorder is not so straightforwardly related to the desire to be thin, but is more clearly related to self-anger, or self-dissatisfaction or fear of rejection, a focus on the girl's difficulties with her mother seems to offer a crude or blurred picture.

An anorexic 17-year-old felt under great pressure from the excellent academic records of her five older brothers and sisters, all of whom had attended Oxford or Cambridge, universities which were beyond (though not considerably so) her current level of academic achievement. Feeling unworthy, she felt she did not deserve nourishment. Denying herself food was an ex-pression of self-anger, though its effect was to force the family to acknowledge her self-assessment and to take blame for it, and eventually to offer her the assurance which corrected the previous assumption. To isolate a mother/daughter conflict here, is to ignore the general problematic context in which the girl passes through puberty and adolescence. The anorexic girl does show a complex fusion of wilfulness and compliance. The bulimic girl shows an angry, secret compromise of indulgence and control, but to see this as primarily mother-related is to forget the way in which, during adolescence, the girl is forced to look outward, or rather, is forced into recognition of out-ward people looking in upon her. Ambivalent about her sex-uality, and feeling separated from her self, no longer able to sense continuity in growth, no longer able to understand peo-ple's responses to her, she stands apart from her physical self, suffers a new self-consciousness very close to shame, and she often seeks ways of hiding herself, disguising herself, transforming herself, perhaps into something she is comfortably aware is not her, thereby protecting herself from others' eyes.

Most girls suffering to any degree from bulimia saw their habit as one of convenience, and nothing else. They were not aware of this syndrome as a well documented disease. Many of them had heard about anorexia, but few recognized the term "bulimia." They believed it was a practice which they personally had developed, ingeniously, to meet their own needs. Even girls like Lena who were clearly locked into an addict's mentality saw the disease as a sensible solution to their eating compulsion. Yet Lena explained that when she was eating, and when she was purging, she often had thoughts which were usually kept at bay. She had angry thoughts—"well, not really thoughts, kind of images" and when she described them, they turned out to be scraps and fragments of angry images, of her mother shouting, of her older sister "not doing anything, really, just kind of standing there, like she does, knowing everything, being so self-satisfied and superior." The eating and purging seemed closely linked to this orgy of anger, for when she was finished, she "lay down on the bed, exhausted, and just thought of nothing." In another case of bulimia a 16-year-old girl admitted that she suffered severe self-loathing when she "pigged out." She felt huge, fat, disgusting—"masculine"— and she felt that no one would desire her, that she was ruining her chances for a female sex life. Her rage against herself turned into an orgy of eating, yet in vomiting, in making this into a bulimia syndrome, she was trying to save herself at the same time.

Bulimia has previously been seen as a rejection of sexuality, but as far as I know this peculiar link with anger has not before emerged, when eating takes on a devouring rage, and then purging replies with a means of freeing oneself from the rage as well as from those objects (those ideas and images of people close to us which form part of our mental furniture) on which the anger is concentrated. Nor has the way it appears to the girl as a safety net been appreciated. For Lena at least, this was a way of controlling not only her appetite for food but her anger as well. She could focus it, and indulge it, without hurt-

ing the people on whom it was focused, people she did not
really want to hurt, because however angry she was, she also
loved them, needed them and, what is very important to remember when looking at adolescents, valued her attachment to
them.

The eating disorders so common to adolescent girls touch
common adolescent issues. They reveal problems not only in
those girls who suffer from the disorders, but in many girls
who suffer conflict and fear over their changing physique. The
difficulty most girls have with maturity, with sexual growth
and change, with the diffuse shifts in maternal identification
(which are present throughout her life, but which emerge with
special sharpness in early and middle adolescence) is highlighted in these bizarre syndromes. Sensitive primarily to one
aspect of this set of problems, psychoanalysts and psychologists
have used their malleable tools to shape the mother's blame.
The customary way of analysing these disorders as a result of
the mother's intrusion, of the mother's attempts to gain unhealthy control and the daughter's virtually helpless resistance—blocks out the general ambiguity and confusion of
female sexuality. There is no indication, for example, that the
greater stress suffered by an early maturing girl has anything
whatsoever to do with her mother. It is not her mother's response to her maturity that leads to preoccupation, distraction,
and a (temporary) suppression of achievement. The girl's battle
to control her impulses can be recognised as a common response to the upsurge of sexual energy in adolescence. The role
the mother plays in her daughter's physical, sexual and emotional maturity—and it is an intimate role—requires a more
flexible definition, which has proved particularly difficult to
come by. From all sides of adolescence there are veils: so blinkered is the child looking upon her own maturity; so blinkered
is the adolescent looking upon her mother; and, strangely, so
biased, so seemingly innocent of her own adolescence is the
mother as she looks upon her daughter.

MATERNAL AMNESIA

As a child what I remember most clearly is the way I looked upon adults as members of a different species. They were encased in the glass of Cinderella's slipper, just as mobile and just as magical. Adults had stepped beyond the hot touch of embarrassment, beyond the grip of retribution, and indeed beyond self-criticism. For everything they did there was an explanation. For every choice they made was a justification, as neatly and securely wrapped as a department store package. Where my world was formless, haphazard, and with unspoken meaning, theirs had shape, direction, and a name for everything.

For children, the secret of the adult world is not, as classical psychoanalytic theory sees it, sex,[10] but certainty, and the child's amazement about sex is not so much what it is, but how it manages to fit in with everything else. For adults it is very difficult to look backwards, undoing the puzzles they spent their own childhood and adolescence constructing. I remember listening to stories adults told of childhoods, and thinking of things seen from a far distance, of colourful but diminutive creatures acting in a world with more definition, and more shape than any child's world. I am still convinced that some truth lurks in this childish puzzlement. Adults relegate childhood memories to some other self. Even the pity or humour felt towards the previous self is experienced indirectly. Only intermittently and haphazardly do adults link up memories of their own childhood with the experiences of their children.

It is not however, adulthood itself, but parenthood that forms the glass shroud of memory. For there is an interesting quirk in the memory of women. At 30, women see their adolescence quite clearly. At 30 a woman's adolescence remains a facet fitting in to her current self. She still sees her mother with remnants of the adolescent's clarity. Her adolescent vision is not intact, but its meaning remains fresh. At 40, however, memories of adolescence are blurred. Women of this age look much more to their earlier childhood for memories of themselves and of their mothers.[11] This links up to their typical parenting phase.

When a woman's children are young, she loves them in a highly physical way. Mothers of young children frequently say their children give them "everything"—which is not to say that these women have no needs for other things, but rather that there are few chinks in the area of themselves that children can't fill. There are exceptions with very difficult infants, who may make the woman feel inadequate as a mother, but since she usually goes on to have another child, and is unlikely to have two children with very difficult temperaments, she will still find something very close to perfection in the early relationships. During this early phase of mothering a woman may still retain a keen memory, and even bitterness, about her adolescent battles with her mother, without these memories casting doubt upon her own role as the mother for a very young child. She may still suffer that anger and tension informed by attachment and humiliation, involving a need for her mother to appreciate her as she is, and resulting in humiliation because this need is not perfectly fulfilled. Her own confidence as a mother is not yet undermined by her daughter's struggle against her. The new mother may resist her own mother's authority and power more than ever now that she is in a position to effect her own. This is power not in the sense of domination, but in the sense of competence. It is control not in the sense of will, but in the sense of mastery, which we need to see ourselves as agents of our own lives. The mother of young children still feels involved with adolescent battles for self-validation, and is capable of great irritation when her mother does not offer it up, and she feels her own superiority as she so successfully and continuously offers validation of her own young children. She may, in her thoughts and judgements, make free and easy use of the problems she and her mother had during adolescence. She may now, without any touch of self-doubt, cite her mother's failings, supremely confident that she will not share her mother's guilt.

Nothing shakes a woman's clear commitment to and confidence in motherhood as her children's, especially her daughter's, early adolescence. All studies I know show and repeatedly confirm that mothers and daughters during early adolescence endure increased stress—and there is more tension between mothers and early adolescent daughters than between mothers and early adolescent sons, or between fathers and either early adolescent sons or daughters. For as a woman sees her children enter new phases of development, seeking from her new, more flexible and often less rewarding forms of validation, she must reassess her own skill as a mother. As the daughter becomes a harsh judge of the mother's "mirroring" or validating responses, the mother feels herself under attack, and in her defensiveness she can no longer uphold the previous views of her adolescence. She can no longer see her adolescent self so clearly in the right, and her mother as clearly wrong. No longer convinced of the validity of her adolescent anger, she no longer remembers it clearly. As her assessment of that time changes, her memory dims, since the memories no longer make sense to her. Her memory makes amends to her own mother, blurring their battles, and finally erasing the wounds. If such memories do linger, they are a source of pain, for she glimpses through them to her daughter's future complaints about her, complaints she knows she cannot and should not avoid. In self-protection, and to retrieve her past with her own daughter, she looks back to earlier times with her mother, when the attachment was easier, less critical.

The mother of an adolescent daughter, therefore, sees her own adolescence very dimly, and no longer understands it. Her own daughter's new demands are both familiar and unrecognisable. She knows she and her mother went through this challenging choreography, yet she no longer understands why, since she can no longer understand it in the terms she gave it an adolescent herself. Now, through her daughter's adolescence, she must learn these terms anew. She may "learn" by stereotyping them, or she may "learn" by denying them, or she may simply try to conquer them with anger and will power. For the most part, however, she learns the good and hard way. She learns by responding to the demands and confidences and needs of her daughter, and she learns because her daughter ruthlessly corrects her responses. She learns through the terror of maternal protectiveness, and through her recognition that she still has an enormous influence over her daughter but lacks control to direct that influence. The following chapters tell the largely disregarded story of the positive side of this exhausting procedure.

NOTES

1. McCullers, 1946, p. 16.
2. Frank, 1953, pp. 116-17, aged 14 years, 6 months.
3. Mead, 1930.
4. Margaret Mead, Anne Petersen, Daniel Offer, Eric Kaplan, Philip Katz, Heather Carruthers, Timothy Forrest, and Nancy Sheper-Hughes are among the few who have investigated cultural differences in adolescent development.
5. Brooks-Gunn and Petersen, 1983.
6. Clausen, 1975.
7. Bardwick and Douvan, 1975.
8. Tobin-Richards, Boxer and Petersen, 1983, pp. 127-254.
9. Erikson, 1965. pp. 252-3.
10. Ernest Jones sees the child's curiosity itself as based upon curiosity about parental sexual activity.
11. Rosenthal, 1963; see also, Prieu and Vincent, 1978.

Chapter 2

THE MYTH OF
SEPARATION

I was introduced to adolescence as a demon, and as a mother's curse at a very early age, an age so early I cannot begin to name it. My mother, a medical professional, was an innocent devotee of psychoanalytic theory, and faced me with the following prediction:

"You won't listen to a word I say. You'll think everything I do is wrong."

"When?" I demanded. But she was not describing me. She was describing an earthquake which would change the natural order. She was predicting a catastrophe which would leave me unprotected. I imagined the strange grey landscape that would impress itself upon me as I looked upon the world without maternal intervention. I imagined the confusion that would numb me as I confronted choice without her direction. The world beyond my mother's convictions and preferences was a world without intelligence or meaning, and she was telling me that one day I, by my own will, would dwell within it.

"When you're 14," she concluded after a moment's pause, during which time she had raised her chin thoughtfully to look at that future which seemed to be residing just above my eye-level.

Yet in fact the terrible event struck earlier than even her dire predictions. It came silently, and privately, causing her no immediate harm and effecting no enormous change. It simply drove a tiny wedge between the way I had agreed to look upon her, and the way I soon discovered she could be seen.

I was 10, and had been playing that afternoon at a friend's house. Diane and I had one of those relationships that are probably quite common during childhood, but seem strange and uncomfortable considered in retrospect. We were friends, though I felt no affection for her—in fact she tended to alarm rather than support me. But we were friends because somehow or other we found ourselves at one another's houses. I liked visiting her because I liked the food. There were frozen hamburgers, already in patties, easily put on the grill by her large black babysitter. There was a huge tin of Jay's potato chips which was always put out, right in the middle of the kitchen table, when her older sister came home from school. But after the ritual snack, we were sent to play in the attic which had been "re-modelled for the children," and there, with the low ceilings, the warm wood floor and the old furniture, time would chill, and each moment would mark the endlessness between now and my mother's presence.

It was hard work for my mother, doing all that "chauffeuring" when I went to visit a friend after school. From school I could walk home myself, but at 5.30 p.m., I could not find my own way home from a friend's. So, on her way home from work, with domestic obligations awaiting her, she had to make an extra trip for me. The least I could do, I was told, was to make her job a little easier. I could be ready on time. I could be outside, waiting. She was prompt. I should be prompt.

"All right, already!" Diane exclaimed when, for the fifth time, I said we should be outside, on the porch, waiting.

"There she is." I was utterly relieved, for we stepped onto the porch just as her car turned the corner.

"No—that's—" Diane grabbed my arm and laughed wickedly, "I thought that was a man."

I stared at the familiar figure through the windscreen. Her close-cropped hair, covered by a tight-fitting mink hat, presented to neither of us the aggressive chic to which my mother aspired. Instead, I saw what Diane saw. I saw a determined, masculine-like appearance, someone distracted, someone unprepared and unwilling to welcome a child. I felt the magnetic tug of her anger. It persuaded me to bide my time, ticking through the silence until hostility eased. But for the first time my awareness that there was more to the maternal bond than the security and love which we all as children heard so much about, rose to the surface of my mind. I felt ashamed for us both, ashamed for her alienation from the maternal role, and ashamed of myself for siding with Diane, for spotting some breach in the contract of our love. I knew I wanted to protect us both from this shift in the "we" that had once, in my mind, been us. I wanted to smooth the rough edges of her anger, and to fold up, unobserved, the blueprints of my judgement.

For in feeling myself become separate from her, in seeing that I was separate, that the childhood closeness was no longer to be counted on, I scanned her face for some other opening, some other assurance, whereby I could remain attached, and attach anew. I needed some recognition from her that this change did not set me adrift. And though she offered no acknowledgement then—her face hard set against getting through the dinner hour—I remained at my lookout post, snatching every opportunity (many of them inappropriate, a few of them successful) to show her this newness, this difference, which was still to me all confusion, but which, by showing it to her, would take shape. Hence we fought. The scent of my difference made her nostrils flare, and she would shriek like an infuriated mare at my transgressions. I must have shrieked too, but I only remember the sound of her anger. Mine seemed bottled inside me, unspeakable, unheard, bursting with the righteousness of the silent complaint. I lost my childhood concentration on her rules and values. I would lapse into a world of my own enthusiasms, my own set of things to envy, and would be distracted from the track she had set for me, the track on which my older sister was so smoothly coasting. I acted independently without even being aware that this was what I was doing, and I failed her. My judgement was bad because it differed from hers; often it made no sense to her. I was out of her control, out of her grip, doing the opposite of what she would have me do, even as I tried to please her. I was very bad at guessing what would please her, and she saw me as trying to distress her.

We continued to battle, but the battle became a kind of dance, the steps of which improved tremendously when my sister left home and left my mother free to me, free for my self-presentations, in which she eventually began to take delight, as I think I knew she always would—or at least felt, she always should.

THE TRADITIONAL VIEW OF ADOLESCENCE

Adolescence has been called a "second individuation phase," whereby the child prepares for adulthood through psychological separation from his parents.[1] The maturing child is thought to devote adolescence to severing his emotional bonds with his parents. He is thought to clear the decks of infantile attachment and idealisation, thereby making room for a mature sexual bond to someone outside the family. The adolescent's task, it is thought, is to construct a self unhampered by his childhood identity, which was so tenderly and intricately linked to his parents' wishes and values. Hence the adolescent sets himself not only against his parents but against the parental images and ideals that reside within his mind and heart. He fights his parents in order to fight his childhood love and dependence and attachments. It is within this conflict between separation and attachment, between habitual dependence and the desire for independence that the rebelliousness, the rudeness, the criticism, and aloofness that is thought to be typical of adolescence must be viewed.

The key word "second" individuation phase signals that this theory of the adolescent's proper task or typical aims rests upon other theories about a first individuation phase. This first individuation phase has been thought to take place during infancy, as the infant awakens to himself as some being separate from the mother. At the very start of life, it was once thought, the infant does not differentiate himself and his mother. His experiences initially are of one being in various states of contentment or despair. Subsequently, there is a "hatching" into an awareness of an individual self. This awareness issues in a desire to preserve this self, with its boundaries, from the infantile submersion in the mother. At the same time, the child remains dependent upon and attached to the parent. He now works with the concept of separate people being together, interacting, being deprived of one another, and threatening one another's identity. This view of the infant's emerging awareness of the self, combined with modified interpretations of the Oedipal situation, form the basis of traditional theories of adolescence. These traditional theories remain current, although it is generally now agreed that they each require extensive modification.

The newborn infant in fact responds to the mother in an interpersonal way. His first responses indicate an aim to get the mother to respond to him. He is therefore responding to her as a distinct person. The mother and infant immediately begin a long, complex and flexible series of interactions, of contact, stimulation, delight, followed by intervals—some only a second long—of withdrawal, or "solitude" or distance, like steps in an intricate, sensitive and well-managed dance wherein the partners get to know one another, and get to know themselves through one another. Such interactions of attention, stimulation, response, withdrawal, are the building blocks of a relationship, which is generally thought to be formed well before the end of the first year of life.

So, it seems the once widely accepted belief that the starting point of relationships is symbiosis, unity with the mother, and that a relationship develops as the infant resists a primitive unity, must give way to a view of development which begins through relationships. From the start, the infant is willing to "work at a relationship." The infant tests the responses of the person close to her, learns how to respond and how to elicit the responses she requires. The infant is born into a relational world, not a world of Eden-like wholeness, not an undifferentiated unity of self and mother. Of course the infant's "self" is not fully developed, but nor is it fully submerged within the mother.[2] The infant already shows a need to connect and then withdraw. She turns away from her mother, refuses eye-contact, stares at a part of her own body (or, when the mother fails to respond to these signals, cries in protest from the excess stimulation, or goes limp). Therefore the fight towards separation may not be as mammoth, as against our first impulses, as previous theories make it seem.

The child is born with some degree of psychological separation, but at the same time is keyed to relationships, and comes to be aware of herself as she becomes aware of herself with another person. Also, the child develops a sense of her independence and character by, as it were, seeking the mother's permission. She discovers the meaning of her actions and the extent of her skills by reading her mother's face and voice. She is encouraged by her approval or quailed by her anxiety, her anger, or her fear. Trotting away from the mother towards the swings, the infant turns back to her, offering a grin, expecting a grin, and then delighted by the mother's delight at her independence, her growth.

This process of looking to the parent for approval of growth, of independence, is called "mirroring," for the child is looking to the parent to see the meaning of what she herself is doing. She finds in that mirror of the mother's face either pleasure or anxiety, and here too are her attitudes towards her independence formed. "Mirroring" can take place only when the child has a clear sense of the mother as being separate from her. The important role it plays shows how the child needs an audience, since approval becomes an important issue, just when autonomy and independence are possible. But though it may have a particular importance in this early phase, it continues to have importance in the development of the child, and retains its importance throughout adolescence.

Few adolescents do not care what a parent and, in particular, what a mother thinks about them, and when an adolescent does not care (as she sometimes does not care what a father thinks) it is because the parent has rejected or abandoned her, or because all mirroring is negative or distorted. It is in the context of the child's continuing need to know what the mother is thinking of her, and how the mother is responding to her, that we must view the child's development. It is in the context of our growth and independence, and our sense of it as good or as dangerous, of our tendency to see ourselves and our development with at least one eye firmly placed on the responses of people close to us, that we must look at adolescent development, too.

The second thread from psychoanalytic theory that binds the traditional theory of adolescence is woven from the Oedipal phase, or rather a recurrence of this phase. The first Oedipal phase is thought to end around the age of 5 or 6. This first or primary Oedipal complex was described by Freud, who took as a prototype the psychodynamic development of the male child. It occurs when the boy's passionate love for his mother, and his sexual desire for her, comes into conflict with both his love and loyalty to his father, and his fear of his father, a fear which Freud saw as linked to, or underlying a very basic, primitive and universal fear of castration—as punishment for sexual desire of the mother and as punishment for vying with the father. The young boy emerges from the Oedipal phase by making the following compromise. He will not act out or further pursue his desire for his mother himself. Instead, he will identify himself with his father. He will see himself as being like, and part of, his father. Instead of competing with his father he shares, vicariously, his privileges and power. He no longer pursues his sexual desire for his mother; he heeds his father's prohibitions, and contents himself with the masculine identity that is conferred upon him through his identification with his father. One day, he sees, he will be a man like his father, and he will have the sexual satisfactions and the social standing masculinity confers upon the adult.

The young boy's sexual urges, after the "resolution" of the Oedipal complex, are thought to lie latent for several years. The latency period is that period of childhood when things seem relatively stable, when no new drives emerge, and when the child's character is more than less predictable, more than less calm, more than less accommodating. Adolescence is the storm after such calm. With the upsurge of sexual feelings, the child is again threatened by Oedipal attachments, longings and fears of retribution. Indeed, this new upsurge of feelings is more violent, more threatening than the infantile feelings that precede them. Accompanied as they are by sexual maturity and physical strength, the fantasy is far too close to reality, the unconscious wishes in danger of consciousness and action, and hence must be swiftly and thoroughly repressed or diverted. The task of adolescence, then, is seen as giving up these incestuous love objects—giving up the desire for the mother, and seeking love attachments outside the family, thereby leaving, if not the love then the passion, for the parents behind.

The struggles of adolescence were seen to be struggles of the ambivalent: the growing child wants to be independent, but also has a pull towards dependence; the growing child idealises his parents but also wants to give them up as ideals. Giving them up, he feels depleted. Part of his own ego structure is crushed, so he fills himself instead with idealisations of friends, and idealisations of himself. When he fights his parents in the here and now he is really fighting his own internal representations of them, his own childhood love and confidence in them.[3] His shift in mood, his shifts in maturity, though apparently hinging on trivial issues, actually involve passionate tensions. He wants to be separate but he fears separation. He wants his mother to let go, but he is terrified of abandonment. Hence, one common image of adolescence is as a time of mourning, mourning for these lost love objects, for as they were relinquished, they were as lost as if dead, and thus the common depressive feelings, the melancholy of adolescence was explained. Adolescence, as a time of growth, was seen as a time of loss. Still current is a view of growth as a series of losses, as though growth is naturally felt to be negative, and our maturity is a school of mourning.[4]

THE FEMINIST REVISION

When feminism expanded from a political creed to a study of female psychology there was a shift from denigration of Freud as male chauvinist to attempts to extend and salvage from prejudice the great value of his work. When the initial, pioneering anger of feminism subsided, some took the opportunity to build from within Freud's work, to use his concepts to construct a more solid and telling story of female development than Freud himself, well aware of his limitations if not his bias, was able to construct. Among the most influential theories of female psychological development is that presented by Nancy Chodorow in *The Reproduction of Mothering*,[5] which extensively reworks the dynamics of the female Oedipal situation.

Freud viewed the female Oedipal phase merely as a defective counterpart to male identity and conscience formation. He concluded that girls, never having suffered the boy's fear of castration, lacked the fear of retribution which was the foundation of a strong moral conscience. He believed that girls, as they establish their gender identity, had to come to terms with a deep resentment of the mother. The girl, in a development which parallels that of the boy, desires her father and fears her mother. When she relinquishes her desire for her father, however, she has no compensating masculinity. Instead, she harbours a resentment for her mother. She blames her mother for her "castrated" state, for the defect of her feminity. Freud believed that the girl, during the Oedipal phase, turned against her mother and towards her father with the same clarity of desire as the boy turned towards his mother and away from his father.

The enormous influence Chodorow's reworking of the female Oedipal phase has had is a result not so much of a reconsideration of the way in which a girl desires her father, or a phallus, but the way in which she remains connected to her mother as she forms her identity—in particular her gender identity, her sense of herself as a female. We can see how, for a girl, the "relational self" dominates a distinct self, and leaves women more inclined to seek, need and value attachment to others.

The boy, in forming a gender identity, sees himself like his father and unlike his mother. As part of his bargain in giving up his desire for his mother, he has identified himself with his father. The boy defines himself in terms of his separation from the person to whom he has from origin been most attached—his mother. To preserve his sense of self he suppresses those feelings he associates with that first attachment. To protect his masculinity, he denies as part of himself those feelings which he associates with his first and primary caretaker—that extreme dependence, that union, that state of flux between himself and his mother. Hence, in defining and preserving a self, he seeks boundaries, not attachments. This identification protects him from those confusing desires towards his mother, but also offers him a masculine identity, whose outlines are those of a clearly bounded self. Close attachments to others may therefore always threaten him with loss of self-boundaries, and hence he may guard against intimacy.

The girl's development of a self and self-boundaries is very different because of the different ways in which she resolves her Oedipal feelings and develops a gender identity. She does not need to turn away from her first and most powerful figure of attachment—the mother—in order to preserve a sense of herself as female. Nor do her early desires for her father over-power this primary attachment to the mother. For her, the Oedipal story is less drastic. As the very young girl turns with love and desire to the father, she does not fear her mother, or resent her mother to the extent that the young boy may fear and resent his father. Freud's story only makes sense in the masculine version because, in the domestic setting he envis-aged, the boy would never have been as attached to his father, trusting him with all feelings in the way both he and his sister had learned to trust the mother. As the sexual desire for his mother emerges in the boy and he comes to fear, dread or re-sent his father, he retains the primary and the strongest attach-ment of his early life. It is unreasonable to suppose that the girl, as she experiences the upsurge of Oedipal feelings, turns away from her mother as easily as the boy is thought to turn away from his father. That primary attachment to the mother, for both boy and girl, remains very strong. The boy, in the tradi-tional Victorian household, can plausibly turn against the fa-ther, because the attachment was not profound in the first place. The girl, in the traditional household, cannot be supposed to turn aside from her mother and towards her father. The do-mestic reality of care and love make such a picture highly im-plausible.

The girl, in her Oedipal passion, does not turn to the father as strongly and compellingly as the boy turns to his mother. She does not fear her mother's wrath or her mother's vindic-tiveness. Her fear is less not because, as Freud assumed, she had less to lose (already in his view being "castrated," that is, de-void of a penis) but because she trusts her mother with both her love and her rage, and because however strongly she may desire her father, the desire does not outweigh her need for and value of her mother. As the girl turns towards her father, she maintains a loving trust of her mother. Even during the Oedipal phase, when she desires and is fascinated by her father, the first emotional bond she formed with her mother remains intact. During this Oedipal phase, she adores and idealises two people, and comes to learn of her self as a being in various relations to others.

This ability to develop a sense of herself and of a female identity while keeping faith with that first dependency and love, grants her a head start in skills of intimacy, in attentiveness to others' needs. Unlike the boy, she is not threatened by attachment, for she emerges from childhood with a strong relational self. She will feel comfortable and confident amid intimacy, and she will be bewildered by separation. She does not see the point or purpose of firm self-boundaries, and is far more likely to neglect her needs for self-definition and individual fulfilment than to ignore others' claims upon her. The boy, on the other hand, developed his identity by seeing that he was different from, and separate from his mother. Intimacies that in any way imitate the first intimacy and union with his mother, threaten his self-boundaries. He knows his way comfortably around the landscape of separation. It is intimacy which threatens him, because it threatens the boundaries through which he came to know himself. He is more likely to place his own needs for development first. He is more likely to see others' claims upon him as secondary.

Thus it is that mothers produce girls who are mothers, and boys who are not. For mothers produce girls who develop a self-identity that is highly relational, and boys who develop an identity that demands strong control over those early merging feelings. And thus it is that, if separation is the adolescent's task, boys and girls will approach their teenage years from a very different position. For a girl undergoes the first separation/individuation phase without actually separating, without drawing distinct self-boundaries, especially boundaries between herself and her mother. This closeness will be aggravated by the fact that her mother, a woman and a daughter, will not draw clear boundaries between herself and her own daughter. Thus the daughter confronts not only her own fear of separation, but she also confronts her mother's fear of separation. Therefore, it is supposed, "the girl struggles with object relations more intensely during her adolescence: in fact the prolonged and painful severance from her mother constitutes the major task of this period."[6] Boys, however, have a head start, and more often "complete the adolescent task successfully" for they enter adolescence with firm self-boundaries. Thus they are well prepared for what has, since the beginning of adolescent psychology, been seen as the explanation of adolescent turmoil—the desire to establish a separate, autonomous self.

Independence and autonomy. Self-identity and self-direction. Erik Erikson, so influential in the way we view development and our developmental needs, saw steps to maturity (with the exception of the infant's learning of "basic trust," the foundation on which future development was built) as steps toward autonomy and separation. Development through adolescence has been seen as a rejection of childhood loves, and this rejection has been seen as healthy, as necessary to maturity. We build up ourselves, first. We establish an identity in relation to social goals and values. Then, as full-fledged adults having discarded our childhood bonds we are able, perhaps, to achieve intimacy, an intimacy whose purpose is generally seen as reinforcing self-identity. But the modern day gods of autonomy, independence, and separateness are as limiting and restraining as purity, abstinence, and politeness were in the previous century. Now, many analysts feel, it is not repression of sexual impulses and desires which throws such a wrench in the working lives of people today, but repression of relational needs, repression of attachment to others, limiting of the ability to make those adjustments—often today called "compromises"—which are necessary to the development of the relational self. It is, I believe, from this bias that the traditional theories of adolescence as a phase of separation has arisen. Given this bias the giants of adolescent theory—Anna Freud, Peter Blos, Erik Erikson, Heinz Kohut—neglected female adolescent development and in the end, told the story only of one type of masculine adolescent development.

To understand female development, to understand the wide range of male development, and to draw into our understanding of adolescence what we already know of our continuing attachment to parents and continuing concern for our children, we need to look at theories that stress relational capacities and experiences. In particular, we need accounts of adolescence which accommodate this continuing bond, in which independence is not seen as rank autonomy, in which growth and development are not viewed as destructive of previous bonds, in which growth itself is not seen as something which we resist, in which development is not always experienced as a mourning for the previous stage, and in which self-interest is not at odds with binding attachments, and rejection of parental values is not necessary to the discovery of what one values oneself.

THE HISTORY OF STORM AND STRESS

We all confront our children's adolescence with the well-entrenched assumption that this phase is peculiarly troublesome. Since the very first published work on the psychology of adolescence this view has been unchallenged. In 1904 Stanley Hall published two heavy volumes called *Adolescence: Its psychology, anthropology, sociology, sex, crime, religion and education*, in which he showed himself to be a follower of Aristotle and Shakespeare, both of whom see adolescence as a period which reveals enormous possibilities of growth, and encompasses a variety of contradictions such as hyperactivity and lassitude, happiness and depression, egotism and self-abasement, selfishness and altruism, gregariousness and shyness, sensitivity and cruelty, radicalism and conservatism. Caught within such changes and ambivalence, the adolescent is bound to feel "storm and stress." Anna Freud concurred, fifty years later, when she insisted that adolescence is necessarily hectic, stressful, a naturally violent time, since the adolescent suffers from a host of new and violent impulses, which he must confront in order to mature. Erik Erikson, too, speaks of adolescence as a time of "normative crisis"—that is, a time in which a sense of crisis, or significant and stressful change, is not a sign of abnormality, but of normality. During adolescence the usual gauge for normal behaviour must be discarded. Instead, we are led to suppose that we must expect bizarre, inconsistent, "abnormal" behaviour.

Several years ago a challenge was put to his stereotype of adolescents as necessarily—or even normally—stress-ridden, full of conflict, and rebellious. Was there any evidence that most adolescents actually rejected their parents, or their parents' beliefs and principles? The evidence for the stereotype was piecemeal, made up of anecdotes and images which might well be biased by our expectations. Professional analysts continued to support the stereotype of adolescence as a time of noisy desperation, but analysts saw adolescents with problems. Analysts saw adolescents who came to them for treatment. Perhaps adolescents who sought help from analysts suffered from certain types of problems, problems that result from confused, strong impulses, from a sense of being controlled by incomprehensible feelings. But it is one thing to see adolescents with problems as having a typical range of problems, and quite another to see the adolescent as typically problematic. Normal adolescents had not been studied. It seemed possible that storm and stress theories arose because the people who put forward the theories worked with exceptionally distressed adolescents.

In challenging the stereotype, Daniel Offer studied normal adolescents. He studied male adolescents only, for, according to rumour, he and his colleagues could not obtain a grant for studying female adolescents. In contrast to Anna Freud, who insisted that lack of stress during adolescence was a sign of abnormality and hence a cause for concern, Offer found that many normal children charted a smooth, untroubled and even happy path through adolescence. Certainly some adolescents were troubled. Some were unhappy. Some suffered stress and cast up the waves of their own feelings upon innocent parents. But Offer's study showed that many perfectly normal adolescents are also perfectly free from turbulence.[7] At about the same time, though in a less well-publicised study, Giselle Konopka and her researchers spoke to 2,000 teenage girls throughout America. Konopka's interest was not so much in the adoles-

cent's emotional temperature but in her intellectual proximity
or distance from her parents. She wanted to discover whether
the girl's moral precepts and values tended to differ widely from
those of her parents. She found that, to a very high degree,
girls adhered to their parents' beliefs, and valued their parents'
views.[8] Adolescents also value their friends' views, and discuss
matters of ethics with them, and allow their beliefs to be influenced by their friends. However, this peer group influence does
not create a distance between an adolescent and her parents
because she tends to choose friends who are like her parents.
She accepts her parents' values, and puts those values to use
when she chooses friends with whom she feels she has values
in common.

Most mothers I spoke to expressed surprise that their
daughter's adolescence was not as tumultuous, difficult or
alienating as they had been led to expect. They found it "exciting" or "interesting" or even "entertaining." Yet no one would
deny that parents face problems with adolescents which they do
not face with children. Some parents' confidence in their ability
to shape and support a child plummets during their child's adolescence. Some parents are "terrified" of what their children
are doing to themselves. In many families a child's adolescence
puts an end to domestic peace. It may stimulate anger and dissatisfaction in all family members. It can "force" a parent into
a role she cannot recognise as belonging to her. Some parents
find all interactions with their children become either aggressive or defensive. Some parents look upon their children as
strangers, while their teenage child reciprocates with angry
cries, "You don't know me. I don't know you. We have nothing to say to one another."

We need to understand adolescence in a way that will make
sense of these battles, but we also need to make sense of the
child's continuing bond to the parent. To do this, I think we
have to be sensitive to the very different meanings of "separation" that are often blurred in psychological theory, especially when the theory involves mothers and daughters, and
especially as it is used in the theory of adolescent development.
We have seen how the notion of blurred self-boundaries in

infancy gives rise, through different paths of Oedipal resolution, to the supposition that girls have less distinct self-
boundaries than do boys. We also know that nearly all theorists
of adolescent development speak of the need for separation in
two ways. First, there is separation as individuation—the development of a distinct self, a sense of self-boundary enabling
one to distinguish one's own wishes, hopes, and needs from
those of one's parents. This separation, as emergence into a
distinct self, is always a matter of degree; it is never final. We
look to others to see what we are. We modify our own feelings
through our responses to others. We forever hear the echoes of
our parents' desires and expectations. Yet within the vast spec-
trum of individuation we have a good sense of what we are
aiming at. The second sense of separation is like a divorce. It is
breaking the bonds of affection with the parent, turning away
from the parent, choosing other objects of affection, replacing
the parent. We must distinguish between individuation as self-
identity, and some sense of self-determination or self-agency,
and between individuation as a means of separating from others, cutting bonds of affection. We must see how a developing
sense of self is not necessarily at odds with responsiveness to
others' needs or wishes. Most important, I believe, we must
understand that we develop within a family, that we develop
through our relations with people, not by turning away from
people, or discarding them. The interesting story is how an
adolescent girl develops within her family. Having, in general,
less distinct self-boundaries than a boy, she negotiates her individuation differently. To emerge as a self, distinct from other
family members (particularly her mother), she does not cut herself off from them. Her individuality matures with a constant
reference to them.

Adolescents do not have a relationship with "parents" but
have highly distinct and distinctive relationships with a mother
and a father. However united the mother and father are in terms
of discipline and values, the adolescent has very different relationships with the mother and with the father, and seeks from
each different things. To understand the adolescent, and the
adolescent's behaviour within the family, we have to under-

stand the dynamics of these very different relationships, not only the unconscious feelings governing them, but the highly observable ways these different relationships function. We have to understand what the adolescent is seeking, what are the aims of her battles, and we must not lose sight of the way she continues to focus on her mother and father—especially her mother—even as she fights her. Often her fights are attempts to gain recognition, attempts to get her mother to recognise the different person she is becoming. She continues to care very much what her parents think of her, and how her parents see her. The quest for individuation is a quest not for separation but for a different balance with her parents.

WHAT DOES THE ADOLESCENT WANT?

Adolescents transform—they do not abandon their relationships with their parents, particularly with their mother. Only if they are unable to find some way of making this relationship flexible, only if they are unable to find any validation of their changing self, only if the once nurturing love turns to strict confinement, only if they are unable to work within the relationships they so clearly value, only then does an adolescent seek to break the childhood bond to the parents, only then is there an attempt to abandon the previous internal representations we all carry of our parents. Only then does the adolescent see her task as one of separating from her parents.

To understand adolescence, we must draw a very clear distinction between individuation and separation. Being an individual distinct from one's parents does not imply the absence of a strong and binding relationship to them. There is no doubt that one of the adolescent's continuous aims is to construct a new sense of self, a self different from her childish one, a self through which she can relate to others, make choices, and have ideas which she feels, and which others see, as stemming from that highly valued though vaguely conceived notion of personal identity. Hence Erik Erikson saw adolescence as a "normative crisis," a crisis of identity wherein the adolescent is given special time out for deciding and constructing who he is, what his goals are, how his abilities and interests can blend with, serve and find rewards within society. Erikson, looking at a masculine formation of identity, sees the work of individuation and identity as quite separate from relationships. In Erikson's highly influential view of identity and intimacy, the adolescent must know "who he is" in order to choose a marriage partner. The adolescent decides "who he is" and "where he is going" before he decides whom he is close to, who will be important to him. He leaves his parents behind as he seeks himself. Having found himself, he is then able to link this new, polished, independent self to others.

No one would want to challenge Erikson's reputation as a great contributor to human psychology, but this "masculine" type model of development is wholly inadequate to female development. Recognising this, Erikson suggests that girls, because their identity is more relational, put the primary adolescent task of identity formation to one side. Girls, he believes, leave identity issues unresolved until they meet someone—a prospective husband—whose identity will help them make sense and shape of their own. Hence girls do not achieve true individuality, but a borrowed one. Thus Erikson's theory of adolescence enforces this stilted perception of individuality, intimacy and independence. He sees intimacy as something which can be achieved only after independence and autonomy. The girl's story is an aside. She needs intimacy for identity because she has no other road to identity.

It has been assumed that to become individuated, the adolescent must separate from her parents. Further, it has been assumed that since the daughter has less distinct separation boundaries, she is less well individuated. But in fact, being an individual and being in relation with one's parents are not oppositional. Being individual and being in relation represent two sides of a single whole. The adolescent needs a relationship with the parents to achieve individuality. It is through this relationship that the adolescent can hope to get validation for a concept of self. In particular, the girl turns to her mother for self-confirmation. She fights with her mother to gain validation. She expends much energy, she plots silently and continuously, to wrest from her mother the recognition she needs. She is prepared to shock her mother into submission. She will behave outrageously in order to get a sharp response—no matter that the response is a protest. She will challenge her mother so as to upset any complacency the mother may have about her daughter. She will goad her mother into taking a newly appreciative look at her. She will try to destroy her mother's previous images of her and to impress her with a new adult self. At the same time, in spite of all her bravado, she feels herself unformed, unproved, easily shamed. She insists her mother does not understand her—does not even know her—because her mother refuses her this enthusiastic appreciation she wants and knows she does not deserve. She is touchy, critical, sulky, rejecting. Her battles for her mother's support and admiration are frequently too bizarre to reveal their aims.

But why does the adolescent girl focus on her mother in this way? Why are the mother's responses so important and under such pressure? Adolescent girls continually complain about their mothers, and in particular express dissatisfaction with a mother's attitude to her. I heard endless complaints about mothers, complaints involving anger, bitterness, resentment, vindictiveness.

"My mother views my life as though it were a little side show of her own," explained 16-year-old Donna. Her voice had that ambivalence typical of adolescent girls listing complaints about their mothers: she tried to sound perky and confident, as though she were tossing off a description of which she was sure; but beneath this bravado was an anger, frustration, or disappointment that made her voice shake with tears. "Every time I tell her something about myself, she says something like, 'Well, I felt that way,' or 'When that happened to me I did this or that.' And I just want to tell her that things might just be different with me. You know, if she could just stop seeing me as though I'm *her* twenty years ago." Donna's assessment of what her mother did "every time" was certainly incorrect. I saw her explain to her mother what she had said to "some guys who kept bothering [her] and saying things to [her]" while she was getting things from her school locker, and her mother worked very hard to discover what had been going on, why Donna was upset, and how she had "handled the situation." Throughout the course of the day and a half I spent with them I never heard her mother present any of those "identification clamps" which Donna believed were set "every time." The tactics which, presumably, were used sometimes, were so outrageous that Donna enlarged them in memory. There was a desire for the "crime" to fit the punishment which it brought.

"My mother told me I couldn't go out with him anymore." When 16-year-old Meg told me this, her tears totally submerged any confidence she hoped to find through her sense of injustice. She had complied with her mother's insistence that she tell her boyfriend "that I couldn't go out with him anymore." The mother's objections were rather peripheral, but strong; and, in seeing them together, I had no doubt how strong the mother was. Her will had a chilling authority, and once uttered, her directives were not negotiable. What was clear was that she saw any attempt to negotiate as an attempt to manipulate her. Meg both feared and honoured her. In other respects she was self-confident and sophisticated. She attended a large state school in Chicago. Both her parents were professional people—her father was a physician and her mother was a dentist. There was every reason to believe that the family would function in an "open" or tolerant way, but the power of her mother's personality was such that Meg felt the pressure of her relationship with her mother in every aspect of her life. "I was torn," she explained. "—I just didn't know what to do. I mean, at the time she convinced me that he really wasn't treating me right, that he hated women, that he was using me. I wish I didn't feel so sad about it now. Didn't she see what she was doing? I mean, didn't she care I'd be this sad? And she thinks I'm being sad in order to get back at her—as though it's not really making me unhappy, but that it's all directed at her. I can't make her see what I really feel, or how I think things really are. She takes some behaviour as an 'indication' and then blows it up all out of proportion, and I can't show her how things are really balanced—I mean from my perspective. And why can't she just let me figure things out for myself? I know she's had more experience, but it's as though I'm not getting my own experience. And why was she able to get that then? She learned things when she was my age. I feel like such a schmuck when she tells me what to do. I feel all spongy—like nothing—inside. I start to make a decision and I just want to talk it over with her, and suddenly she's screwing it up in a ball and throwing it away."

Within these complaints was a continuing need, a continuing battle for recognition, for help, for appreciation. These girls seemed to be fighting against a mother's interference, because her interference showed lack of faith in them. The mother's interference was not resented because it meant the mother remained too close, but because it meant that the mother did not appreciate the daughter's skills in making decisions and choices. Adolescent girls were fighting a mother's interference because they wanted her to acknowledge their independence. Whatever resentment they had was not towards a mother's excessive concern, or even excessive control, but towards her inability to see, and appreciate, their maturing identity.

"I hate my mother like poison," Marian told me. At 17 her confidence had swallowed the tears, and the anger became a feigned dismissal. "I come home from school, my mind buzzing with a stiff essay I'm composing, and she wants to chat over milk and cookies. 'Mu-um, I've work to do,' I say. Any book is more interesting than a little chat with her. She says 'Oh, I'm interested in what you're working on,' but whenever I try to explain it her face goes all blank, and she has to work so hard to keep up a polite expression. I can feel her toes squirming under the table. She thinks my books are like toys— little dolls lining my walls. She tidies them. Can you imagine? I have some opened to special pages. I have them arranged in order of importance, so she goes and tidies them. She has no sense of what I'm doing with them. She thinks they're a small part of my life. She cannot appreciate my commitment." In the bloom of late adolescence she wore her blue-stocking personality proudly, taking a stand as someone her mother would never understand. Therefore, her interests were self-discovered, self-made. Their value was self-constructed, and was all hers.

She was steeped in her individuality, and wanted to offer it to her mother, the gift of a valuable self. To show her appreciation the mother was expected to be bowled over by this new personality. The "poison" was the mother who wanted her daughter to be something else. Or, more accurately, the poison was the mother who would not have minded if Marian had become something else. Proud of her new found interests and skills, to which she determinedly linked her identity, she could not accept that her mother did not value the particular direction she was taking above all others.

"I'm proud of her. So what does she want of me?" Marian's mother inquired without any expectation of an answer.

Debbie, in mid-adolescence, had no specific handle of identity. She was not aware of any positive claim she might make to get her mother to see her as sparkling, as special. She dressed like what in Berkeley High School is called a "Dead head"—that is, she posed, in terms of dress, like a high school druggie and pusher, mimicking not the behaviour, but the appearance, of those who behaved as her parents would least want her to behave, mimicking it to shock them. Not knowing what she would become, or what she wanted to become, she nonetheless wanted to burst the mould of childhood expectations. She wanted to shock her mother into the recognition that she was unknown.

At a much earlier phase of adolescence, Margot, as yet with less well constructed defences and strategies, was like a patch of dry timber eagerly awaiting any word from her mother to burst into flames. At the slightest correction or direction she sobbed pitifully like a child, and screamed, "Leave me alone. You never leave me alone. I feel you're trying to get inside me." The stimulus for this outburst was her mother's instructions about using the cassette deck. She was to put the tape in that way—no, the other way—but not to forget to rewind the other tape—first!—and put it away, and before setting the timer should make sure the revolution setting was at zero. The continuing list of instructions seemed mild enough to an outsider, but to Margot it was clearly a barrage against her self-esteem. Her mother's outraged confusion turned into a desire to punish the daughter for her extreme response: "Put the tape away! Don't touch it!" The daughter's predictable protest, "But you said . . ." was countered by, "I've changed my mind. You can't use it." Margot was willing to placate her mother ("All right. Show me what to do.") in order to make use of the machine, and in order to quell her mother's anger at the outburst which now frightened her too; but she seemed to be tucking away the insult for another time, when she might have further "say" in the matter.

These girls, who much of the time bewildered, and indeed terrified their mothers, were working very hard to gain recognition from them. They were bitter and vindictive to the extent that they felt they would not gain such recognition. Their anger and frustration measured their doubt as to whether they could urge her to take a new look at them, and see them anew. For no matter how often girls complained about their mothers, they almost never said they did not care what she thought.

"I hate her," Marian explained more fully, "because she won't understand how deeply these new opportunities [at university] mean to me. It's as though she's saying 'Well all this is very nice, but when are you going to get on with the really important things in your life?' She will not see that to me this work is what is really important and the rest—all that stuff she thinks is the nitty gritty of a woman's life—family and a home and all that—is secondary. No, at this point it isn't even secondary, it just doesn't come into the picture. And she refuses to understand that."

"When I see my mother coming towards me," Debbie said, "I feel her eyes boring into me. You know, it's as though she'd really like to drill holes with those eyes, and just destroy everything that's there. She won't see what I am, so—what the hell—I make it real hard for her, and make her see something that's worse than I am. I don't know what she thinks, but sometimes, I guess, she thinks I'm just what I pretend to be, and boy, does that upset her. I mean she should know better than that. She does know better than that. But sometimes she doesn't know, or isn't sure."

"My mum wants what's best for me, I know," admitted

Margot. "But there's this—" she paused and made fists with both hands, "There's this need to direct me—not so much what I do, but what I should think, and how I should feel about things, and how bad I should feel if I don't care about something, or someone else, or if I don't understand how things are with her, and she has worries too. So she makes me feel mean when all I want is for her to see how it is for me, but she won't, because there's always something wrong with the way I'm looking at things."

Over and over again, the violent complaints, bursting with frustration, were about what the mother would or would not see, about what she could "appreciate" or "understand". Though in some sense such complaints were typical—you could recognise them a mile off as a teenage girl speaking about her mother—these complaints were embedded within an atypical, or unexpected content. Most girls said that the person who understood them most was their mother. Most girls said that the mother was the person they were most likely to confide in, the person they were most likely to bring their problems to— problems about school, friends, siblings and fathers. Most girls said that they would trust their mothers with their confidences. "The worst she will do," one 14-year-old admitted, "is tell my father what I've told her. That will make me angry, and if I find out about it, I'll give her a hard time—she doesn't have the right, not if I've told her not to. But it's not as bad as laughing at me behind my back, or telling someone else, at school."

MY MOTHER, MY FATHER

The worst she can do is tell my father.

Usually we think of adolescents on the one hand and parents on the other. Then we speak of an adolescent's relationship with parents, and the problems she has with them. But these adolescent girls clearly had two very different relationships with their different parents, one with their mother and one with their father.[9] These differences covered every aspect of the relationship—her feelings, her sense of trust, and her sense of self. For what was remarkable was how she saw herself to be different in the company of each parent, and how she proved herself to be different by exercising a different level of maturity in the way she viewed each parent.

The range of differences began at a very simple level. Most girls enjoyed doing different things with their mothers and with their fathers. With their mothers they preferred unstructured activities, vaguely described as "doing things in the kitchen" or shopping—which most girls thought of as an extra special treat, "like just the two of us taking a holiday," or "being able to get her attention, without her always thinking about dinner or my little sister or when my Dad's coming home." They also liked "just sitting and talking." When adolescent girls described what they liked doing with their fathers, however, they did not emphasise activities which offered opportunities for conversation, but activities which involved a specific task. Usually they liked the father helping them with something, or they liked him to teach them a certain skill. Girls spoke fondly of fathers helping them, or teaching them how to connect a plug safely to the wires, or how to mend a chair with doweling and glue, or how to fasten a door on its hinges. Most girls enjoyed their father teaching them a sport. Most girls had been taught to ride a bicycle by their father, and they all smiled as they said this. They also enjoyed a wide range of recreational activities with him, such as camping, or hiking.

Adolescent girls clearly value time with both their mothers and fathers, but they seek—or expect—very different things from each parent. Not only was there little emphasis in talking to the father, in confiding feelings and sharing ideas (except if the ideas were shared in a structured argument, as they would be if they would discuss politics or social issues) but whereas girls often said their mother was the person they would most likely confide in, many of them said that their father was the least likely person they would confide in.[10] "Are you kidding?" was the amazed reply when I suggested that if the mother were not available, they might turn to the father. "I'd die before I told my father about my boyfriend—I mean about how I really feel." "Oh, sure," 14-year-old Mary muttered sarcastically, "Can't you see us sitting down to have a heart-to-heart with Dad? About sex!" she screeched. She had that irritable petulance common in mid-adolescence. She gave the impression of feeling that she was overweight, and her hairstyle showed she was not yet used to her plumper and larger face, and she slouched like a tired 9-year-old, except for the disconsolate look she cast upon her developed body. "Can you imagine it?" she demanded of her older sister, who laughed easily, unperturbed by the younger girl's irritation. "He'd be as uncomfortable as we would. He'd say 'Yeah. yeah,' squirm in his seat and change the subject." The father as confidant did not merely pale beside the mother, the father was someone they would positively avoid, the person they would turn to last. The father was not so much feared or distrusted in this role. He simply was thought to look ridiculously inept.

These very marked differences in what a girl likes to do with a mother and with a father are merely the more obvious of an entire range of differences. A daughter not only plays with her parents in different ways, she argues with them in different ways. She has different expectations about the course and resolution of the argument. She uses different tactics for resolving a quarrel, and harbours a different sense of who is to blame. It is far easier, apparently, to bear a grudge against the father than the mother. "He knows I'm mad at him, so he won't expect much more than sulking for the next few days," Jenny explained. Believing that her father expected her to hold a grudge, she thought it was all right, or even necessary to do so. At 16, Jenny had that spark of many young black girls— keen, sly, wry and hopeful. She lived with both parents in an Oakland house which, like many houses built just after the big earthquake in 1906, was spacious, elegant, and so under-insulated that, "My Dad only has to sneeze upstairs, for us to jump in the kitchen." The notion of space but no insulation was clear in her description of her fights with her mother. "Mom and I had a terrible fight. We were both torn up about it. But it's hard to stay angry. Well, no, it's easy to get real angry. But even when I'm panting in my room, I feel like she's

near me. I know she's panting—crying inside, really angry—
on the other side of the door, and it starts ticking over in my
mind, 'How are we going to get over this. Who's going to
make the first move?' Not that either one of us will admit we're
in the wrong," Jenny added with a smile.

Most girls had a very different sense of how to "make up"
with or "make amends to" the mother and father. To make up
with the mother, they might say "sorry" or try to "talk things
out." "I know I hurt her," a classmate of Jenny's admitted,
"when I get mad at her. Even when I'm spitting out all those
rude words, I'm thinking about what's at the end of this. And
I know there are some arguments she'll listen to—she's a real
sucker for me saying it's all her fault. You know, I'll say, 'The
reason I did this was that you let my brother do it,' or I'll say,
'But you do it to me, and I'm not supposed to mind,' and that
will sort of distract her, so she'll stop and think, and when she
does that I know we can begin to ease off each other, because
she's not so sure anymore and I don't feel so beaten." "I can
always just say 'I'm sorry,' " a third classmate, Alecia, boasted.
"Even if she gets real nasty with me and mimics me—'You're
sorry, nah, nah,'—I know the fight's over."

Few girls assumed that they had this reciprocal power—to
hurt and to heal—with their father. Instead of meeting the
problems arising from a quarrel with her father head on,
daughters were inclined to wait until things "cooled down" or
"calmed down" and then just "pretend nothing happened." "If
I said 'sorry' to my dad," Jenny explained, "I'd be giving away
too much." "I sometimes apologise to my Dad," Alecia said.
"But every time I do it, I'm sorry, and I say to myself 'I'm
never going to do this again. Never-ever.' He sniffs—." She
gave a wonderful imitation of a complacent snort. "You know,
takes it like that, like I'm saying he's right and I'm wrong. I
only mean to say 'I'm sorry we're fighting.' But he doesn't take
it like that." "Yeah, that's what my Dad does," Lydia concurred. "He's sweeter than that. I mean, he can go all soggy
when I say I'm sorry, and then he says 'That's all right honey,'
but it's that same thing. It's thinking that 'I'm sorry' means 'I
was in the wrong and you were in the right.' So I don't apol-

ogise any more—not unless I'm feeling real sneaky, and want something from him. I just go away, and let the pot cool."

Girls did not always want to mitigate the effects of a quarrel, or their anger. Sometimes they wanted to punish a parent. They wanted to see a parent hurt. They wanted to show a parent how much they had been hurt. And just as they would make up in different ways with a mother and with a father, they would use different methods to punish a mother or a father. "Getting back at mother" was very different from "getting back at father." In some sense the mother had the worse of it, with more "back talk" or "disrespect" or "shouting" as her punishment, whereas the father was ignored, and would "just get real brief answers." The adolescent daughter would attack the mother directly. She would "punish," or try to hurt the father by giving him the silent treatment. She was hot in her anger towards the mother, and icy towards the father.

Adolescents, for all their self-involvement, are emerging from the self-centredness of childhood. Their perception of other people has more depth. They are better equipped at appreciating others' reasons for action, or the basis of others' emotions. But this maturity functions in a piecemeal fashion. They show more understanding of their friends, but not of their teachers. What is even more striking is that adolescent daughters view their mothers with more depth than they view their fathers. Daughters see a mother and a father in different ways, and have a different relationship with each of them. That is not surprising. They are two very different people. But not only do they respond to the mother and the father in different ways, they view them with different levels of perceptual maturity.

Parents and children always have difficulty seeing one another clearly. Objectivity does not thrive within the family. But girls saw their mothers with far greater clarity than they saw their fathers. The generosity and empathy they easily expended on their mother was hoarded like a miser in relation to their father. An adolescent girl tends to be remarkably good at seeing things from her mother's perspective. She can explain why her mother behaves as she does. "She's worried sick about cars and car accidents." "She's always more edgy when my Dad's away." "She doesn't want to have the trouble with me that she did with my sister." "She thinks I'm a little lazy, and always need an extra push." She can explain why her mother reacts as she does. "She's flustered because we're having guests this evening. That's always a bit too much for her." "She can't stand it when I have to work out at the gym all weekend. When I come home in the evening all she can do is snap, just because she missed me." These girls could take a mother's perspective, in the sense of understanding it, even when they did not share it. It seemed that they were reciprocating what they felt to be her greater ability to see things from their point of view. For however much a daughter complained that her mother "did not see" or "would not see" what she was, she also judged her mother not only to try to understand her, but to be generous in this understanding—in contrast to the father's tendency to "lay down the law."

Girls see their fathers as exercising authority over them. Even when they consider their fathers kind and supportive, they describe their relationship with him in terms of control. Yet daughters describe their interactions with mothers in terms of intimate exchanges. It is not that the mother has no authority, it is that her authority is transformed by intimacy, or utilised in intimacy to support these exchanges. The mother listens, comforts, offers advice. The way she exercises authority is by "insisting on knowing what is going on." What threatens her power is ignorance of her daughter's feelings, whereas the father wants to control what she does without this close reference to the daughter's feelings. It isn't that fathers do not care what their adolescent daughters feel. It is that they do not go about finding out how they feel. They do not tend to engage in the kind of exchanges whereby they would have the opportunity to sense the ebb and flow of feeling. They do not have the information—about school, friends, hopes, anxieties—which would allow them to link moods with deeper emotions. Lacking a rich contextual picture, the father's understanding is less intimate and less elastic. He is concerned for the daughter's well-being, but the daughter interprets this concern in terms of control, whereas the concern coming from the mother is experienced first as emotional involvement, and only subsequently, if something goes wrong, as control or intrusion.

Accompanying the different views of each parent, and the different depth of the views, was a difference in how they tried to be nice or "good" to each parent—should they happen to want to be so. To a mother, a girl was likely to help her ("make her life easier") by "telling her I love her," whereas to a father she would reciprocate, or show gratitude, by "keeping out of trouble" or "doing well in school," especially if he was paying for school. These girls were aware of a financial debt to their fathers, but they saw the way to make their mothers happy, or to be good to them, was to reaffirm their closeness.

This reaffirmation came easy for them. Here I was, speaking to girls in mid-adolescence, which is a time that is generally thought to be characteristic of the greatest conflict between parent and child, and most girls said the person they felt closest to, the person they felt most loved by, the person who offered them the greatest support, was their mother. She was likely to be closer to her mother than to her friends, and closer to her mother than to any other member of the family; if there was an exception to this the closest family member would be a sibling, most often a sister. "Sometimes I feel closest to my sister. We can talk about anything, and we don't mind feeling ridiculous. It's more serious, though, with my mother, and I know she'll listen—well, not every time. She can be busy—she's often 'too busy right now'—but when I talk to her, I feel she's 'there' for me, and even when the things I say make her cross—like I'll tell her what I said to my boyfriend, and she'll say, 'You shouldn't have said that! What is he going to think of you now?' or I'll tell her what I did with some friends, and her eyes will pop out of her head. You know, she's still surprised that I can take the lead with my friends, and sort of form groups, and get them to do things. But if she gets cross when she hears things, I just wait it out—usually—and then she'll calm down, and give me advice, and—I don't know, sometimes it's real funny, and I wouldn't follow it—no way!—but it somehow helps, anyway." In contrast, the father seemed to have "no time" or "no patience" or "no interest" in the girl's feelings—at least this is how the adolescent girl tended to describe her father, who never admitted to the charge of "not caring" or "not wanting to know." But, according to the daughter, her father "just doesn't try to understand me. He comes in and says what he thinks, or what I should do, and that's that. I don't get a chance to give him my side. So I just stay out of his way." In addition to the father not hearing what she had to say, or refusing to see her point of view, she complained that he actually did not see her. "He doesn't see how much I've grown up. He still treats me like a little girl. I feel myself clamming up when he's around."

Because the father would not listen, because the father would not see her, the adolescent girl who had a fair degree of control over her actions, and a keen sense of strategy within the family, would avoid the father, either by "keeping out of his way" or "clamming up," that is, not necessarily avoiding him, but keeping a lid on self-expression and self-exposure. Such tactics were not simply defences against being ignored or misunderstood or misperceived. This was a form of deliberate punishment. If her father did not listen to her, then she would in some way hide from him, disguise herself in his presence. The daughter would punish her father by not giving him any part of her. Because he lacked the flexibility to listen and to see, she would cut herself off from him. Separation was brought about by anger. It was induced as punishment for not allowing her to grow close.

Adolescent girls are not close to their fathers. They often increase the distance between them in order to punish the father. They tend to be less close to their fathers during adolescence than they have been during childhood. It is terribly difficult to understand precisely what is going on as the girl draws away from her father. It is tempting to see this failure of intimacy between father and daughter during adolescence as some repercussion of an earlier state, when the father simply let the mother do most of the caring and even much of the loving for him. The distance between father and adolescent daughter made me wonder whether they had ever been very close.

In the early stages of the women's movement, the institution of parenthood and the traditional divided roles of mother and father came under criticism and scrutiny. The emphasis at that time was on parenting of infants and very young children. Since gender identity emerged in very early childhood, it seemed reasonable to look to early child-rearing practices to explain different gender characteristics. The infant's initial bond with the mother was thought to be responsible for gender identity as we know it. The girl's early identification with the mother would set her on course as a female who would find meaning through attachment to others. The boy's early identification with the mother would always haunt him, so that to preserve his masculine identity he would seek control over strong emotions, close bonds, and tender merging. If this theory were right, then gender identity could be changed. If the father were to care for an infant in the same way a mother did, or if the father had an equal share in caring for the child, then the gender stereotypes would be destroyed. The infant girl, cared for by both the male and female parent, would not see herself so closely bound to the mother and so separate from the father. The infant boy, being cared for by both female and male parents, would (it was predicted) not associate those early feelings of boundless love, attachment and dependence with a purely female phenomenon. His masculine identity would not be threatened by deep feeling, for he would direct such emotion and receive such emotions from his father as well as his mother.

Many parents, believing that the traditional institution of motherhood is beneficial neither to the parents nor to the children, shifted the old balance of parental responsibilities. The shift is not so easily put into effect, however. Parenting can be established as a time-share job, but mothers are less good at "switching off" their parent identity and turning to something else.[11] Many women envy the father's ability to set clear boundaries between home and work, between being an on-duty and an off-duty parent. But few women envy the father his emotional distance or psychological disengagement from the child.[12] Women work very hard to maintain a closeness to their child. Fathers value intimacy with a child, but often do not know how to work to maintain it.

In the past fifteen years, women have increasingly extended their roles outside the home, but their roles within the home have not drastically changed. Most of them do continue to be the primary parent, the primary caretaker. However determined both mother and father may be to share the parenting load, the woman is more likely to do more because she is quicker to see what there is to be done and quicker to respond to the child's demands. She has the opportunity to teach her husband the skills she is naturally better at and for which she has been more intensively trained, but often the task of teaching him is too costly. She feels that in reminding him she is "nagging." She feels that in correcting him she arouses impatience and irritation. It is easier, and safer for the marriage, to take full domestic responsibility than to engage in the reminders, the teaching, the insistence that may be necessary to change a father's domestic and parenting patterns.

However, some couples do stick with this determination to share, fair and square, early parenting tasks. Many of the adolescents I spoke to, both in England and America (though the majority were in America) had, as infants, a larger than typical share of father care. The differences to the adolescents, however, were far more marked among boys than among girls. It was boys who had been close to their father during infancy, and boys who remained close to their fathers in adolescence who were "better" at friendship—that is, they valued friendship highly and sought self-exploration through friendship. The boys whose fathers participated fully in their care (that is, who did about fifty per cent of the parenting jobs) saw friendship as more than a means of getting buddies or "mates" to do things with, more than a companion or accomplice. Boys whose fathers had spent more time caring for them had more sophisticated aims in forming friendships with girls. They did not seek girl friends simply for the purpose of having someone to go out with or make out with, but saw relationships as having developmental potential.[13] They wanted to "get to know the girl," but also to get to know themselves through the girl. Dating itself was seen as an opportunity for psychological intimacy. For whatever the reason—whether boys with fathers who devoted more time caring for them simply had fathers

who were more expressive and warmer than boys whose fathers
maintained a traditional paternal role, or whether the father's
time and care itself made the difference—these male adolescents
were different from the stereotype of the male adolescent. They
valued intimacy more, and they saw relationships as an important facet of their identity. In this respect having two parents
caring for them, having the father assume many maternal tasks
was highly effective in shifting the stereotype. But dual parenting does not seem to have the same effect on girls. However
close the father's participation in caring for the girl, her aims
and self-image during adolescence remain indistinguishable
from those of girls whose parents have stuck to the traditional
division of labour.[14] The primacy of the mother/daughter bond
is such that it is not altered by the close, caring presence of a
father during infancy, and in fact, the father is often crowded
out during the girl's adolescence.

The strange, disturbing and sad picture of father and
daughter seems to be that during the daughter's adolescence,
the distance between them increases. Most fathers become extremely attached to an infant daughter. This closeness is usually
sustained in early childhood, but thereafter gradually diminishes. Girls who are very close to their fathers in early childhood, are less close at 9, and less close again, at 13. They confide
in them less, spend less time with them, enjoy their company
less, receive less encouragement and support from them. Frustrated, hurt and angered by this distance, an adolescent girl will
"punish" her father for his lack of empathy, for his unwillingness to understand her, by aggravating the separation between
them.[15] Thus she aggravates the separation for which she is
punishing him.

THE BATTLE FOR RECOGNITION

If she gives up on a father's understanding or empathy, a
daughter will avoid discussion with him. She lowers the level
of conflict by avoiding contact. Seldom, however, does a
daughter avoid a mother, even to diminish conflict. She tries to
avoid conflict with her father because it is unproductive. She

may find conflict with her mother painful, but she does not avoid it. She seeks out contact to analyse, explain and even expand conflict. Being closer to her mother, she has far more problems with her.

The adolescent girl repeatedly complains about how the mother sees her. She engages in vigorous argument to correct and redress and defend her mother's image of her. She fights not so much for freedom as for her mother's belief in her judgement and trust in her independence. These are not the responses of people trying to separate from one another. These are the responses of people who remain preoccupied with the relationship, and who are hoping for something to happen within the relationship. For girls in mid-adolescence are looking for and trying to elicit new responses from their parents. Earlier, in the first stages of adolescence, girls suffered a keen sense of separation, but this was separation from themselves—from their familiar world of childhood. Their loneliness was confusion about the physical and hormonal changes taking place within them. They were thrust into a world where change differed from the innocent, exciting growth of childhood, when development was greeted with unambiguous delight. Instead, at puberty, they met with mixed responses, and saw that their development, though containing some good, some excitement, some promise, also changed the network of responses and expectations. The girl who develops early, before her peers, suffers a special loneliness and a special self-consciousness. With the high visibility of her physical maturity, she sees herself as awkward, abnormal, ridiculous. She is a girl trapped within a woman's body and no one will hear her protests that she is still a child. But in mid-adolescence there is a catching up of the will, a catching up of understanding, and a push of the self away from childhood. The self wants new boundaries, and seeks confirmation of these new boundaries from the parents. The adolescent girl sees her mother as willing to listen, and willing to see.

"I try to explain things to my mother," Amy declared. "I try and even before I start talking I know she's going to drive me up the wall. I say, 'I'm changing my subjects because of this and that,' and sometimes I get an 'Oh, no you're not,' but that'll be just the start. Then I explain how it will help me with my other work, or with what I think I want to do, and usually she'll come down off her high horse. She'll start giving me reasons why it's good. We start out on opposite sides of the fence, and before you know it she's sitting next to me giving reasons for my own arguments, like two people who keep piling layers on the same sandwich."

"No matter how tough my mother is on the line she's taking, I know it's not the last word," Gail, a fellow student of Amy's at Berkeley High, concurred. "It's always worth having a go, anyway. I say something, and you can see her stop and think a bit. She doesn't say she's thought of it all before. Oh, sometimes she'll say, 'This is a no option situation,' like when I had to go and be interviewed at this school she had her eye on. But it's not like that with my Dad. I know one girl who can wrap her Dad round her little finger. When her Mom says 'No' she calls up her Dad at the office. Well, when my Dad says 'Boo' I can just forget about my arguments. I open my mouth, and then I think, 'Forget it. Maybe I'll get Mom on her own.' With her mother she can renegotiate her relationship. The mother is more flexible than the father, and better equipped to shift her responses. She is better equipped because she is more sensitive to her daughter's own self-image. This shift from responding to her daughter as a child and as an adolescent is seldom smooth and easy. The process is complicated, and it proceeds piecemeal. The daughter matures piecemeal, too. All mothers were aware of how an adolescent daughter would be very grown-up one day, and infantile the next, or how she would be sensible about one thing, and impulsive as a 2-year-old about another. Daughters, too, believed their mothers were sensitive and sensible on some issues, and "hopeless" on others.

Many girls joke about what their fathers do not notice about them. "He was surprised—no, he couldn't understand what had happened—when he saw my bra in the laundry. 'Whose is this?' he wanted to know, holding it up like it was some awful foreign thing. My mother had to tell him, and when he said, 'Oh, you've started wearing a bra,' my Mum laughed and said 'She's been wearing one for more than a year.' I was dead embarrassed, but I was pleased, too, because he was embarrassed." Another girl described how, when she was wearing a swimsuit, her father looked directly at her eyes, kept eye contact "as if the rest of me wasn't there, didn't have a right to be there." But it must be difficult for a father to do the right thing, for another girl complained that her father did look at her when she was wearing a swimsuit. He demanded, "Just where do you think you're going dressed like that?" as though her figure were itself indecent, and to reveal it was an offence. But however angry a girl was with her father because he "won't see," or "refuses to listen" or "can't understand," she fought more heatedly and spent more time fighting with her mother. She fights with her mother because she wants, and believes she can, make her mother see and make her mother listen.

It is the greater hope of getting the right response from the mother, receiving the validation and confirmation—the new, more sophisticated versions of "mirroring"—that spurs the teenage daughter on to persuade her, coerce her, tease her into recognition of a new self. And it is through this persuasion, coercion, teasing, that the daughter often learns how to define herself. She learns to correct her mother's assumptions about what she is now. She learns to define a self emerging from her childhood self, and she learns to cast away some childish identity. But to do this, to individuate her maturing self, she wants to remain close to her mother, not to separate from her. In contrast, her relationship to her father is more brittle. She does not put the same effort into correcting her father's view of her. She does not have the same strong confidence in her influence over him. She does not believe he can be made to see and to listen.

Given this fragile bond between father and adolescent daughter, it is not surprising that the daughter's loyalty, when tested, lies with the mother. When her parents are divorced, the adolescent daughter almost always lives with the mother. Partly to compensate for her loss of the father, and partly to compensate her mother for the loss of her husband, she remains extra close to her mother.

Chris's mother and father were divorced when she was nine. Her mother worked as a secretary and personal assistant at the Securities and Exchange Commission in Washington DC and her father still worked locally and she saw him "about twice a month." "I think my mother's great. She's real strong, and she has a lot of common sense. I see some of my friends' mothers who have husbands right at home and they don't give their children half what she gives me and my brother. She's cheerful. She works hard. She provides this nice home, and frankly, I've never missed my father much. I see him, but every time I meet him it's as though I'm meeting him with a smaller and smaller part of myself. You know, when Mom comes home from work, I feel this—yeah—this sort of hugging thing. I don't rush and jump up all over her, but it's like I'm giving her a big hug. When I see my father now, I guess nine-tenths of me goes blank." Girls in Chris's position judge a father as knowing them hardly at all. Not only does he (in the daughter's view) know little about her, she "could not care less" what he thinks of her. Yet no daughter, in any plausible way, claims she does not care what her mother thinks of her. She generally criticises her mother's view, and complains about it, but she cares about it. Even when a girl is not close to her mother, she very clearly cares about her, cares what her mother thinks of her, and cares what she thinks of her mother. Whenever a girl is not close, or thinks herself insufficiently close to her mother, there is a decisive, dramatic reason. The most common reason involves some impairment in the mother's ability to respond to her. The most usual way in which the mother is "incapacitated" or rendered unavailable, is by dependence upon alcohol. And even then, the daughter does not give up on her mother.

"I get real tired of people getting on my mother's case," Tracy complained. I had met her though an acquaintance of mine who was a social worker. Tracy had been keen to talk to me because I might "tell the real story." She was 15, lived in Washington DC, and had been referred to the social worker by the juvenile court for passing a bad cheque with a stolen bank card. Her mother was not diagnosed as an addict or alcoholic, though it was suggested in the social worker's report that drugs and alcohol diminished her capacity to control her children. Tracy was quite unprepared to allow her delinquency to be mitigated by the mother's failings. "I mean," she demanded, "who knows the whole story? Me or them? Me or her? Even I don't understand everything, because you have to take into account her whole situation. It's like she has to put together her day—day by day. She's suffered so much, and she has all those worries—things like you don't even have to think about. I mean, those bills, and our food, and whether our Dad's money is going to come through this month, and a whole lot of other things that no one knows about because she tries to be strong and protect us from them. I know I don't always help her. I know I just add to her problems sometimes, but no matter what I do, she's there to help me. Everyone makes mistakes. Some people come in this house and forget that. Well, everyone makes mistakes, and that doesn't mean she's not a good mother or that I'm not a good daughter." It is extremely touching how a girl, deprived of her mother's attention and care, will see her mother's faults, and hate the weakness underlying the faults, yet wish to salvage her opinion of her mother and protect her from others' criticism. She refused to see her mother's poor condition as permanent. The more grotesque the mother's failings, the more temporary and peripheral the girl was likely to judge them. Often the daughter saw herself as her mother's potential saviour.

"I know that one day she'll get over this problem," insisted 16-year-old Kathrine whose mother was an alcoholic. "It's hard now, because we kids aren't old enough to help her, but I know next year my sister's going out to work, and I've promised to finish high school—I know I will—and that will really please her, give her confidence, show her that one of her children has the power to keep at something. That will make her so proud. I've seen her look at those graduation pictures in other people's houses, and I know what mine'll mean to her. And it isn't as though her problem is so big, either. Most of the time she's fine. She really is. It's just sometimes that she goes under—. But you know she was there every day to pick me up from school when I was younger. She didn't miss a day. Now how can you call someone like that an alcoholic? Anyway, my sister'll be working next year, and I'll finish high school and maybe even go to college and get a real good job and if she needs help we can send her to a clinic."

Under the severe pressure and deprivation of not being able to think well of the mother, the teenage daughter works very hard to see things from her mother's point of view and to make excuses for her. "She's had a hard life." "She's had nothing but one disappointment after another." "She's done a good job, and she really keeps things together with hardly any money, and she just needs something to help her relax sometimes, but she just can't handle it, and it isn't her fault." Girls with healthy, caring mothers were free and easy with their criticism of her, but if a girl had true and just cause to criticise her mother, she refrained. Certainly a girl whose mother is an addict will be angry and frightened, but these emotions were not expressed, or even felt in the typical adolescent way. The girl who could not depend on her mother's strength and care appeared to skip several steps in development—she would forgo her need to be understood by her mother, and would instead try to understand her mother and rebuild a good image of her, either by making excuses or having fantasies about one day being able to "help her see it all through," or "pay for some real good treatment, like I know you can get in a private clinic," or, more vaguely, "set her a fine example, and make her proud, so that she'll feel better about herself, and see what's possible for her."

The happier girl's responses are tougher on the mother. When the daughter sees her mother as strong—which is how she wants to see her—she can bounce impressions off, shake her up, shock her, to make the responses she needs come forward, keep her on her toes with outrageous surprises, so that the mother will be threatened with as many changes in her perspective as her daughter feels taking place within herself. Confused herself, the daughter wants to shake the mother's complacency and assurance. Yet however hard she works at this, she wants to think well of the mother. She is so keen to think well of her that anything about the mother can be taken

as cause for admiration. Like a lover seeing virtues in the be-
loved, girls cite an enormously wide range of reasons for admiring their mothers: she is a good homemaker, career woman,
supportive. They admire her for making life enjoyable. They
admire her for making them "work hard" or "see what life's
really all about." They admire her for creating "a kind of centre
to the family." They admire her for making them comfortable
with so little financial support. They admire her for not giving
them too much so that they realise the value of things. The
girls admire the mother for "keeping to basics" even though
she had opportunities to be frivolous or snobbish. They admire
her for the way she made the beds, or washed their clothes, or
folded their shirts. They admire her for her ability to cook or
bake to a certain consistent standard. They admire the way she
smiled at them when they came home. Every trait became a
reason for a teenage daughter to admire her mother. However
much many of these girls admired their fathers (and some of
them saw their father as the best, most admirable person they
knew) their admiration was more abstract. They admired him
for being clever, and competent and successful or working hard.
He seldom supplied the emotional stability, the meaning of their
daily lives, as the mother did.

The modest but permeating dependence on her mother's
availability was straightforwardly described by a 16-year-old
girl whose mother worked varying shifts in a hospital, and
whose schedule she was not always sure of. "When I come
home," she explained, "as soon as I open the door, I want to
know whether or not my Mum's home. And if she isn't, then
everything seems different, sort of flat, and I go to the kitchen
and I start my homework, or maybe help start the dinner. I
just need something to do. It's not that I'm afraid. I'm not
afraid of anything. I know what to do if anything happens, and
we have wonderful neighbours. I'm 16. I know my way about.
But somehow I feel like I would feel if I were afraid: So as soon
as I walk through the door, I shout 'Mum?' and I hold my
breath until there's an answer. If she is home, I just hang around
her for a while, maybe help her—if she's doing something I can
help her with—and we talk for a while."

A startling discovery was how much more attached these girls in mid-adolescence seemed to their mothers than did girls a few years younger. At least they felt more dependent upon the mother's company. One girl of 13 described a situation similar to the 16-year-old's homecoming, but with contrasting wishes and hopes. "I feel like jumping up and throwing my books in the air when I come home from school and my mother's out. It's like—I don't know—it's like suddenly finding that you're free. There's no one pushing at you, telling you to do your homework, asking you how the maths went today." Yet this girl's secrecy centred around her eating habits. On the way home from school she would stop to buy several bars of chocolate, and would then have to get them from the door, from her coat pockets, under her pillow. She would eat them at some private time, usually before (or while) she was doing her homework.

The need for privacy was a need to indulge in something mildly illicit. Faye, another 13-year-old, described a sense of pleasure, of "space" when she brought a friend home with her and discovered her mother was out. "We just sit in the kitchen and there's this wonderful feeling of space flowing around me. I get up and do things myself—fix a snack, open a soda—and I don't have to worry about what I say, or how loud I say it, and I don't have to wonder what my Mom is going to say about this friend of mine. She always has her views, and they're always changing. One day a friend will be a 'real nice girl' and then the next time she comes Mom will say, 'I don't like the way you sound when you're with her.' So sometimes I'll be in my room, talking to a friend, and then think, 'Oh, no, did Mom hear that?' or I'll worry about what we sound like. When she's not home, as long as I leave the kitchen clean, I'm okay."

It could be that older girls take more pleasure than younger adolescents in coming home to find their mothers in because they have more freedom anyway. Mothers of very young adolescents do tend to be intrusive, and to give "advice" in order to control. Young adolescents have a distinctive way of responding to such control—a still childish, irritable response, very close to a younger child's tantrum, but with the anger swallowed, bitter and cold, so that it seems the child is not lashing out, but writhing from within, and the mother in contrast is calm in her anger, self-righteous, confident. This gives one the very awful impression of something about to explode, yet it is usually self-correcting. Typically the mother cannot "hold on" to her self-righteousness or confidence, and see-saws between taking the daughter's point of view, or respecting it, and trying to reach a compromise.

"What are you doing, having a friend over, when you have your geometry test on Friday? What about all this studying you said you were going to do? And look at this kitchen! I have to start dinner in a few minutes. Is it going to be ready for me, or not?" demanded Faye's mother as she swept into the kitchen, shattering the friends' solitude. Faye made a conspiratorial face at her friend, a kind of sneer which she did not bother to hide from her mother. "Faye!" her mother shrieked, and the daughter's face went red, her legs kicked the underside of the table, and with deliberate exaggeration, she breathed heavily. "We're going to do geometry. We're going to do it together. That's why she's here. But we were just having a snack. We've been at school all day. And we're tired. All right?" Faye's mother watched the puce face, the tearful eyes and the grim line of her daughter's mouth. With a slight "giving up" laugh she says, "All right. But now is the time to get started, and Kim goes home at five."

Since both aspects of the intimacy—the sympathy, understanding, knowledge on the one hand, and the advice, guidance, support, control on the other—are necessary to the daughter, there can be awful clashes, wherein the daughter feels conflict within her own needs, wherein her own needs seem to get twisted about. She hands her mother information to get support or sympathy or self-validation, but instead may meet disapproval, correction, shock, anger. This happens to every close mother and adolescent daughter at some time. Often they can untwist, separating strands of self-validation, of criticism, of disappointment, though this may take many arguments, and much time, whereby the mother and daughter can expand their views of others, and cease to see one another as objects to gratify either needs or hopes, but as people with differing needs and perspectives.

Maternal intrusiveness, which over the years has got such bad press, is always linked to sympathy and concern, but is simply a distorted or hardened version, wherein the mother grasps clumsily for the control she believes will benefit her child. During the many changes of early adolescence the mother can begin to learn to expand her sympathies, though at this stage the daughter is unable to help her, and the work often seems exhausting and unrewarding. If the father misses out—as he often does—on this painstaking discipline of letting anger and self-righteousness ebb and sympathy flow, then he will have missed out on the elementary steps of dealing with an adolescent daughter, of helping her grow, of providing her with self-acknowledgement that goes a little beyond the present self, thereby providing her with her confidence to keep going, keep moving towards a viable self. Even fathers who have been close to a very young daughter seem to opt out of this painstaking process of parenting an adolescent. Hence they gradually lose the closeness they once so enjoyed.

One of the most frequent complaints against the father was that he simply ordered her around, told her what to do, thereby "pulling me back" one girl said, "stripping me down," taking away, that is, the very delicate growths of adult self that had to be respected before they took shape. The adolescent girl's attitude towards adults in general was shaped by the way in which she was seen by them. When asked what they did not like about adults—what would make them dislike an adult, or what they thought was unlikable in adults—adolescent girls repeatedly complained about adults' tendency to disrespect them, their refusal to listen to them, their quickness to assume they were superior to the adolescent, their assumption that the adolescent was "not good enough for them." They complained that adults did not trust them to do anything on their own, that they did not trust them to have good judgement. They disliked adults who were automatically unfriendly to them, who would scold them for little things "as though they expected me to have the wrong attitude" or "bad attitude." They disliked adults who seemed to have no time for them, who were never around—and at the same time they disliked adults who were "nosy," who were always suspicious, always thinking they were up to no good and butting into their business or interrupting their play or their privacy.[16] They disliked adults who laughed at the things they did, and who looked down on them. All the complaints about adults were complaints about how the adults tended to see them.

Adolescents seek a kind of respect, or a preparedness to respect them. They need a parent to have confidence in and to enjoy their awkward maturity. But one common misconception is that adolescents want to be treated as equals. The mid-adolescent girls in my study were close to their mothers and enjoyed being with their mothers. They enjoyed unstructured activities, which offered the opportunity to talk, and talking with a mother was one of the things they most enjoyed. But they did not seek the reciprocal type of conversations that would be characteristic of friendship. They were uncomfortable when a mother did converse with them as an equal. They liked to talk to a mother to get her advice, to hear her views, to explain to her how things were with them. For the most part it was a one-sided exposure, a relationship of confidence and response, and this is what they sought.

UNHAPPY CONFIDENCES

Because this asymmetrical emotional intimacy is so important to the daughter, because this intimacy develops in mid-adolescence, when she has a greater ability to express herself, to think about herself, think about her thoughts, and construct a sense of self, the adolescent girl has a new need for the mother to sustain empathy towards her. This new need is heightened by her new capacity for suffering humiliation. A child may feel crushed, may burn with embarrassment for reasons which an adult would never guess. Even praise, in the wrong tone of voice, even friendliness, if somehow inappropriately measured, can strip the child's ability to cope socially. She will then retreat behind a curtain of tears. However cruel the child's bewilderment and panic and rawness are, they are nothing to the sharp, icy, desperate humiliation adolescents are capable of suffering. For in adolescence, the new capacity to assess the self, to view the self as having a continuing identity, make slights against it difficult to bear and difficult to forgive.

Even apparently tiny slights can be resented for a long time, and linked up with a mother's general failure to offer self-validation. Many, much larger issues of conflict between adolescent and parent come down to a problem of humiliation. When the issue seems to be one of control, the underlying problem may be one of humiliation: the control is resisted because it is humiliating. "I left home—and I stayed away, I mean I really stayed away from them for over a week—because they kept getting at me, wouldn't let me say anything, and made me feel like shit. I mean, I wasn't a person. I was only this lump to be moulded to suit them. And every time I stepped in the room, there was this 'nag, nag, nag' about how I was dressed, how I was doing at school, or how late I'd been in the night before. I couldn't breathe, because they were on at me, until I felt I was this tiny pinhead they were just kicking about." It was the criticism, the constant disrespect, the constant attack upon her self-esteem that sent this young girl away from home. In the condition of constant humiliation, intimacy makes no sense, and has no purpose, for one of the main functions of that special asymmetrical intimacy between mother and adolescent daughter is self-validation and the building of self-esteem.

The intimacy between mother and daughter has a built-in push towards conflict, though this argumentativeness is generally geared for growth. However, a daughter may meet real disappointment as she confides in her mother. The mother's very sympathy for the daughter or empathy and confidence or trust in the daughter may make it difficult to hear what her daughter is saying. Many mothers find it difficult to deal with a child's unhappiness, and when a moody adolescent tries to explain her feelings, the mother may deny this unhappiness. "She tells me that I'm so much better off than lots of other people. 'I should be grateful,'" Jayne mimicked her mother angrily. Then she sighed. "It's not that I'm not grateful for what I have. It's just that I can't go around being happy, just because other people are unhappy." Another tactic a mother may use to deny the reality of her daughter's dissatisfaction, is to blame her for it. The anxiety about her daughter turns to anger: "If you only spent more time on your school work and not so much time thinking about boys, you'd be better off." The mother here is surely trying to fight on behalf of her daughter. Her denial of her daughter's unhappiness is an attempt, however ineffectual, to overcome it. Mothers used these methods of denial when they felt helpless in the face of the daughter's new moodiness or despondency. She could either stick with these methods, and lose her daughter's confidence, or accept that she had to listen to her daughter, and once again, live through adolescent anxieties. This was not easy, because a mother's sympathy can be an exhausting burden. "I see my daughter's moodiness. One day she came home and took down all the photographs we have of her and turned them face down. 'I can't look at them anymore,' she explained. 'They're so ugly.' It went through me like that—," she drew in her breath sharply, "like, 'Oh, no, it's happening.' I've only just outgrown it myself," she laughed. "Now I have to go through it again. And I think this time it will be worse. I think of all that love I gave her, and how I was really building up something as I loved her, and now it seems that everything has to be built up again. I know how difficult I made life for my mother. I don't really mind that. The worst thing is that I'm not sure I can do anything."

Whereas a father would be criticised for being "too strict" or "too rigid" or because "he won't let me do what I want," a mother would be criticised for "only seeing things her way," or "twisting things to her meaning" or "not being able to keep out of my life" or "being one of those people who has to run other people's lives." The criticism stresses how the mother intrudes, how she controls through intrusion, not how she controls through authority or strictness.

The atmosphere of confidences and intimacy and mind or emotion sharing is delicate and volatile. Often, under stress, things get jumbled. The mother may turn to the daughter as an ally when her marriage is breaking up—indeed, the mother and daughter tend to gravitate towards one another, thereby further blocking out the father. The adolescent daughter, during her parents' divorce, usually decides to suppress, temporarily, or "put on ice" her own need for a confidant in her mother. "She has enough on her plate now," a 16-year-old girl explained. "I don't tell her as much as I used to—well, how is she going to listen to my boyfriend woes, when my Dad's treating her like this?" Few girls complained when their mothers turned to them as confidant during a particularly stressful time. They were happy to rise to the occasion, to adopt a "maturity" or a guise of maturity, yet independent studies show that girls who are used as confidants in such cases do less well in terms of emotional adjustment during or after a divorce. For though girls in general weather their parents' divorce better than do boys, girls who are used as confidants by their mothers, show less independence, less individuation, and less self-confidence, even though, temporarily, self-esteem may be boosted.[17] The best way to weather their parents' divorce is to separate from it, to find some part of oneself that is aloof to one's parents' problems—and this involves not taking sides, and hence not having to deal with problems of conflicting loyalty. It involves being able to shut oneself off from one's parents' anxieties. The girl who is used as a confidant during this difficult time may be seen as a wonderful friend, and may be thought to have "matured wonderfully" but she is unable to protect herself because she is unable to remain separate from it, and from her mother's needs.

This flip side of the mother and daughter intimacy is of course an extreme version, when the mother's capacities for validation and empathy are curtailed by her own anxiety and fear. In such cases the daughter's sympathy with her mother puts criticism at bay, just as she is willing to put to one side her own needs for her mother, for her greater need is to see that her mother is "all right" or "set on her feet again." When the relationship between mother and daughter is less severely distorted, the daughter is more inclined to complain. "I get the creeps when she tells me about her and Dad. I mean, I don't want to know about their sex life. And it doesn't seem fair. I mean, he's not going to tell me his side, is he?" Here the mother was expressing some dissatisfaction in her marriage, or with her husband, to her daughter. Since this complaint was not uttered in a context which would entrap the daughter's sympathy—the mother was not undergoing a separation or divorce; she was simply expressing long-term disappointment—the daughter had the chance to step back and to criticise the mother's attempt to involve the daughter in her own problems. Daughters, who have a choice, resist a "friendship" or an equal sharing of confidence with the mother. This resistance, however, is over-ridden when the daughter sees herself as stronger than the mother, or when the daughter, fearful for her mother, tries to become stronger.

Though this resistance to a reciprocal sharing of confidences is fully understandable, what surprised me was the way girls were irritated by almost any confidence from their mother. "I know how you feel. I felt the same way," was not what a girl wanted to hear from her mother. Perhaps she herself wanted to be the star. Whatever the cause, she expressed impatience with the notion that her mother had once been an adolescent, experiencing the same feelings and conflicts as herself. Many mothers advised their children in various ways not to "be like me." Usually this involved career decisions, or particular hopes from marriage. "Don't expect marriage to solve all your problems." "Don't expect the excitement to go on forever." "Don't give in to him [a husband] too much." "Don't lose sight of your own goals." Or, indeed, girls were also told, "Don't expect to do too much. You sometimes have to decide between your work and your children." "You'll need to find different ways of surviving in the work world than I did. Don't try to fight it all the way." But whereas the child loves to hear her mother's "stories from when you were a little girl" and asks about her mother's hopes and plans, and even wants to know the names of her friends, "when you were 9 years old," adolescent girls do not want to hear such things. They are in love with a vague future and a potential self. They see the object of their love as unique, and beyond comparison. They want the mother to share this love. Any comparison with the mother's defined and therefore limited self, is felt as a slight upon their romance.

However, constantly in their thoughts, when they look to their future and plan their future, is their mother. They will either do as she has done, or not do as she has done. They will not try to combine a career and motherhood because she has worn herself out doing so. They will not depend on a man for economic support because she has, and has either learned that such dependence is unreliable or has resented it or simply regretted it. They will give a great deal to their children because their mother did, and her children benefited. They will not try to give too much to their children, because their mother did, and in trying to give she became intrusive. Whether as a positive or negative model for her future, for her goals, for her hopes, her mother is already the measure, and will remain so, to some extent, throughout her life. She will be face-to-face with her mother as she grows, yet the demands which stem from this confrontation, and the resistance she must make against enmeshment, against the sense that her mother is projecting ideas, thoughts, feelings, patterns upon her, and meshing with or even invading her, can cause intense irritation. When the mother herself brings the two of them together, or draws inferences about what the daughter is, from information about what she is, the daughter feels closed in upon herself.

In adolescence comparison between mother and daughter can be so painful that to avoid it the daughter will stand comparison on its head and opt for counter-identification, for proof that she is unlike or opposite to her mother. Girls work to school themselves to be different. These 15-year-olds slide easily from maternal to self-criticism, from maternal criticism to self-determination:

"My mother's approach is too narrow. She sees only the tiny details of things. I can see myself about to think the same way—well, I was wondering whether to take up this job as school news editor. And I started fussing over all the details. Would this mean I'd come home too late from school? My little sister would have to make her own way home. Would I have time to do my homework before supper, the way I like to do it? And then I thought 'I'm thinking like my mother. I'm worrying over every detail until the whole thing seems impossible. But this is something I want to do, so I'll give it a try.' "

"All her life my mother has sided with my Dad. It's as though they speak with one voice. God, it gives me the creeps. When I'm with my boyfriend I pounce on everything he says. None of this 'Yeah, I know what you mean' business. I don't accept what he says just because I'm—well, for now—his partner."

"She's always thinking about herself. How does she look? Did she say the right thing? She comes home from work, and she takes her day apart bit by bit. I want to get involved in something bigger than myself, so I get away from that kind of pettiness." A girl may then be launched on the task of proving what her aims themselves disprove. Her determination to be different from her mother reveals her fear that they are alike. She tries to escape this fear by using her mother as a measure of opposites: what her mother is, she will not be. Yet still her mother's life patterns and personality configuration are lodged within her and remain her measure. Still identification with the mother remains the force behind her determination, her opposite identity. Even as she tries to prove she is "completely different" she lives with her mother as a model.

NOTES

1. Blos, 1962.
2. Stern, 1985.
3. Blos, 1966.
4. See Viorst, 1987, for the most recent presentation of development as a process of mourning for previous stages.
5. Chodorow, 1978.
6. Blos, 1966, p.66.
7. Offer, 1969; Masterson, 1968.
8. Konopka, 1976.
9. Steinberg, 1981.
10. Youniss and Smollar, 1985, make extensive comparisons between girls' and boys' attitudes towards mothers and fathers.
11. Ehrensaft, 1987.
12. Apter, 1985.

108 — ALTERED LOVES

13. Cooper and Grotevant, 1987, pp. 247–64.

14. Earlier writings indicate that women who become professionally successful have a closer bond to their fathers than their mothers. See, for example, Hennig and Jardim, 1977; 1978. I did not find this true for a later generation of professionally successful women (cf. Apter 1985). Nor do current studies show this for adolescent girls (cf. Cooper and Grotevant, 1987).

15. Youniss and Smollar, 1985.

16. Konopka, 1976.

17. Johnston (research in progress).

Chapter 3

VALIDATION VERSUS INTERFERENCE: THE CHOREOGRAPHY OF IDENTITY

One of the main tasks of adolescence is to achieve an identity—not necessarily a knowledge of who we are, but a clarification of the range of what we might become, a set of self-references by which we can make sense of our responses, and justify our decisions and goals. It was Erik Erikson who first centred the psychology of the adolescent with this bias, where, for the most part, it remains today.[1] Erikson saw the teenager's task as meeting the challenge between "identity" and "identity diffusion." In leaving behind childish roles, adolescents are thought to become preoccupied with finding for themselves a satisfactory answer to the question "Who am I?" and to find this answer they may "try out" a variety of identities. It is self-exploration through experimentation. But because this self-exploration involves anxiety and uncertainty, some adolescents settle for an immature self too soon. Just to get an answer, just to avoid the anxiety of not being sure what he is, he takes up an identity before sufficiently exploring his potential. Erikson calls this "foreclosure": the term for a bank closing on a loan is linked to a psychological decision, or set of decisions, to give up prematurely the adolescent's time loan, to give up experiment and exploration because he cannot keep up the pressure payments of uncertainty. A pre-formed and limited identity is chosen because the experiments and creativity are too costly.

At the other extreme, an adolescent may fail to choose, or establish, an identity until too late in his development. He will be unable to make appropriate decisions because he lacks the context in which to make them. Without self-clarification, he has no basis upon which to choose a career, or take steps towards a profession, nor can he form strong, healthy bonds with friends, since—for Erikson—a sense of self-definition precedes intimacy. Such absence of self-definition is thought to give rise to depression and despair, to a sense of meaninglessness and self-deprecation which Erikson labels "identity diffusion."

Adolescence is society's permission slip for combining physical maturity with psychological irresponsibility. During this time the adolescent confronts as part of his normal development an "identity crisis," whereby he turns away from the childhood orientation towards parents, to an engagement with his peers, through whom he absorbs a new sociability and competitiveness. It is in this context that he gets the push towards a new, adult self-definition, into choices and decisions which will "with increasing immediacy, lead to a more final self-definition, to irreversible role patterns and thus to commitments for life."[2]

This is how most of us still view the adolescent—as someone turning away from his family, and using a peer society to help formulate and validate his goals. The early relationships with the parents are seen as a foundation upon which he builds something quite different. Though these early relationships continue to influence us throughout our lives, parents themselves soon lose that special influence over us. Parents seem to accept this, too, and ruefully parents of children as young as 14 speak of themselves as "superannuated." Repeatedly parents said, "I know they have to separate," or "I should be helping them separate," often adding apologetically, defensively, "But I just don't think she's ready yet." The mother of 15-year-old Amy expressed this conflict:

"I want her to be her own person—I really do. And she is. She always has been. 'I'll do it myself' must have been her first words. But what am I supposed to do? You tell me what I'm supposed to do. I'm supposed to let her be herself, help her feel good about herself. I know all that. Fine. But what do I do when she spends the entire day moping and telling me what's wrong with her and why everyone is better than she is? What am I supposed to do when I find her in the living room sitting all day picking the callouses off her feet? Am I supposed to say, 'Okay, this is the person you are—a callous-picker?" Well, maybe I'm supposed to, but I don't. I still have a say in what kind of person she's going to be. She has a lot of potential, but there's also all this crap in her. If I don't help her sort it out, who is?" No wonder mothers were so confused by the peculiarly insistent demands their adolescent children made on them. No wonder they felt such a strange split between what they had been taught their child needed, and how they actually responded to them.

Erikson's theory, which is in many ways so accurate, and so sensitive to the thrust of the adolescent's challenge, leaves out of account the continued development through the parents, and also turns its back on the fact that parents and children need one another, care for one another, and work so hard (though not always effectively) to get things right between one another, try to make things work between one another— usually throughout their lives, but certainly throughout adolescence, when the bond remains very strong. It also shoves aside issues of female adolescence, which, in Erikson's theory of adolescence, gets a very poor hearing. Girls simply do not break those affective bonds so cleanly, nor do they develop a personal identity which precedes a capacity for intimacy.[3] Indeed, Erikson treats the female adolescent as a special, parenthetical case: she retains a plasticity of identity, waiting to be moulded by her choice of a husband. While her brother works hard at self-creation, she awaits a mate around whom she can fashion her "inner space."

This highly biased view of adolescent development ignores not only the positive dynamics of female development, but also ignores the way in which we all become individuals within a family. It goes against what we know about our bonds to others to think that to mature is to break those bonds, and to the extent that we do not break them we remain immature, even infantile, thwarting ourselves and our development. Adults maintain a sense of intimacy with their parents, their siblings and their children throughout their lifetimes. They work hard to establish an individual identity, and value individuality, but they also value attachment and connection to others. What remains to be explored are the dynamics that keep these relationships functioning so that the people involved can steer a path between disengaged separateness and cloying enmeshment.

WHAT DOES AN ADOLESCENT NEED TO DEVELOP AN IDENTITY?

The adolescent does not develop her identity and individuality by moving outside her family. She is not triggered by some magic unconscious dynamic whereby she rejects her family in favour of her peers or of a larger society. She develops, as we all develop throughout our lives, in relation to other people, learning to see herself; to make sense of experience and establish a stable (or fairly stable) view of reality and the self within it. In particular, she continues to develop in relation to her parents. Her mother continues to have more influence over her than either her father or her friends.

Identity is always changing—or always susceptible to change. It is a process, not a thing, though certain things, certain relationships, certain experiences become a permanent part of it. But in order to establish an identity in any meaningful sense, the developing child needs to integrate her thoughts and feelings into something like a stable, or continuous whole. She needs to have reached a certain stage of ego development, wherein what she does and feels counts, because she has some control, some sense of responsibility and the capacity to act responsibly. This does not mean that she always acts sensibly, but that she has some understanding of how her actions are linked to consequences. She sees herself, and understands herself as an actor within the world. A personal identity emerges, too, as she comes to know herself as a person with various needs, and levels of need. She then has some capacity to negotiate conflicting needs, to ask "What do I want more?" or "What is more important to me?"

Personal identity requires a certain level of what psychologists call "ego development." This development is not measured by actual behaviour or by the content of a child's thoughts. Rather, it is measured by how she thinks about her behaviour and how she perceives other people. Ego development involves the ability to assess and integrate her own feelings and thoughts. It also involves her ability to see things from another person's perspective and to make inferences from behaviour to feelings, or from feelings to behaviour. It involves her ability to understand what another person is feeling on the basis of his behaviour, or how another person is likely to behave, given how she knows he feels.[4]

Ego development is not fixed, and is never final. We continue to make gains and losses throughout our lives. But during adolescence various stages of this development can be recognised and measured. An early adolescent is, typically, at an early stage of ego development. She is able to understand that other people think about themselves and their place in the world about them, but she is unable to separate her own concerns from those of others. During this early stage, she understands that different people have different thoughts, but she assumes that they think about, and are preoccupied with the same things that interest and preoccupy her. Since she is concerned about her appearance, she believes that everyone else is too. She cannot believe that a dress or hairstyle is unnoticed. She cannot believe that any feature which dissatisfies her is invisible or unremarkable to others. Since she sees her parents' behaviour as irritating or demeaning, she assumes that everyone else sees it in this light. Hence she is embarrassed by everything her parents say. Even the way they dress, or comb their hair, implicates her in some bizarre identification, which she believes others must see. Believing that others share her irritation, her embarrassment is increased. Later, perspective-taking becomes more sensitive, and she is better at picking up cues about the extent of others' concerns. She is able to see that something of great concern to her is of inconsequence to someone else. She is able to see that most people do not view her parents as a 13-year-old views them.

Other issues of ego development involve self-control: is she impulsive, has she any concern, or any measure for the outcome of her actions? Is she capable of independent thought? How confident is she of her own ideas, or how dependent is she on ideas of others?" How immediately does she accept a parent's beliefs? How does she go about reinforcing or reconsidering her beliefs? We can measure ego development, too, in terms of the content of thoughts, or the quality of preoccupations. Are her thoughts most commonly about cartoons, toys, impressing people, being cool, being sharp, being popular in various ways, fitting-in—or have more rewarding goals overtaken these?

The lower stages of ego development are characterized by impulsive, exploitative and dependent orientations ("I must do this because I'll be punished if I don''t''), the middle levels are characterized by conformist thinking ("This is right because Mom says so"), and the high stages are characterized by the cognitive complexity which emerges in adolescence. Some years ago Piaget noted and named formal operational thinking, where in reflection upon oneself and upon what one thinks, abstract and logical thinking becomes possible. The ability to think in abstract ways affects the adolescent's view of herself. She is able to review her past, and to look critically upon the childhood habits and habitats she once accepted without question. Now questioning, revising and criticising become a way of life. As these intellectual skills become possible, adolescents work very hard to master them. They exercise their new skills upon the parents, who find the constant criticism and objections and general challenges totally exhausting. Yet parents must accept, and even validate these new skills, for they form an enormous part of the adolescent's development.

WHO HELPS HER GROW?

The growth of an adolescent has many frames of reference, and individuation involves all of these, for in individuating herself, in coming to sense self-boundaries and self-difference, the adolescent girl must also have some sense of her independent thinking, and must therefore also have some sense of others' beliefs and feelings. These capacities are developed within a family, fostered by certain family dynamics and inhibited by others.

For adolescent girls, the dynamic push towards individuation and ego development comes primarily from the mother—not simply because the mother tends to spend more time with her, but because the mother's behaviour simply has more effect upon her.[5] The girls seem to understand this, and often fear the power their mother has, and will continue to have, upon them throughout their lives:

"Sometimes I'm walking, or sitting on a bus, and I feel her voice inside me. It's like my own nerves are twanging, but making the sound of her voice. And I get so angry—I know it's funny—she isn't even there—but I say to her, in my thoughts, 'Leave me alone!' She says, 'Think for yourself!' And then somehow she gets inside me, like this," admitted 16-year-old Lindsay who smiled away the conflict with her distinctive calm English manner. The older the girl was, the more aware she became of the depth of her mother's influence upon her. At 19, Denise, a third-year student at the University of Chicago, reflected on her past and present responses to each parent: "When I'm angry with my father, I want to punch him; but when I'm angry with my mother it's as though something's ripping me up inside. And then, angry as I am, what I do is try to talk to her. I've been away from home for three years now, but still I'll be holding these conversations in my head, and I'll start getting angry with her—at something I've made her say— and I'll go to the phone and ring her, and then I hear her voice, and I'm not angry anymore. I just want to talk. Sometimes I say to her what I was saying to her in my mind, and she never says just what I thought she would say, but it's still so much her. It's a huge relief, because the anger just goes." The mother's actions and responses to the daughter have more effect upon the daughter than do the actions and responses of the father towards either a daughter or a son. The mother's behaviour is more sensitively registered on the daughter than it is on the son. From all psychologists know about ego development and its measurement, it emerges that the mother and daughter bond dominates the daughter's development at the very stages during which she is rapidly forming an adult-like identity.

Earlier I spoke of the "battle for recognition" which involves a daughter's vigorous attempts to force her mother into recognition of her new self. As much as she may insist upon her right to privacy, she will be infuriated if the mother does not want "to go into things," if the mother wants to avoid difficult issues. Whereas children tend to take cues from their parents about what is acceptable for conversation and what is not, adolescents test the ground more courageously and more maddeningly, teasing their parents into acknowledging topics or issues with which they themselves feel uncomfortable. Adolescents can tease, persist, and cast a general, unforgiving gloom when they are trying to get a parent to confront them, to meet a need or request. I found girls highly ingenious in the way they would coax their mother into acknowledging them in various ways. Sometimes they were satisfied simply by making the mother worry about what they had done or might do, or what they really thought about something or someone.

"What I think, Mum, is that we should let her have her own way." Elizabeth, 16, was advising her mother how to handle her younger sister who was now 14 and was causing a mild ruckus about her desire to go on a weekend boat trip with a boyfriend and his family. Elizabeth and her mother were in the kitchen together as they spoke. They were not facing one another, because Elizabeth was slicing vegetables while her mother stood by the hobs, beginning to cook supper. Elizabeth kept turning towards her mother, taking surreptitious and half-amused glances, while her mother's increasing discomposure was expressed in frowning absorption with the level of heat beneath the saucepan.

"I can't just let her have her own way in everything, dear. I don't know his parents. I don't know the boat. I'll talk to your father about it."

"I think you should let her go. You would have let me go."

"Well, I don't know."

"Oh, yes, I would have made up a good persuasive story."

"Elizabeth!"

"Oh, yes, Mum. I'm much better at presenting things to you. [My younger sister] always gets me to ask you for things when she wants them."

"She doesn't. And it wouldn't make any difference. We treat you both the same."

"Oh, no you don't. I know how to hide certain facts. Like

I'd say it was a nature trip and I was going with a family. I wouldn't be stupid enough to tell you I wanted to go with some boy."

When the mother was reluctant to look into the new personality of the daughter—the new individual who was becoming aware of her wide-ranging responses and feelings—the daughter might be satisfied just to shake up the mother, stir her into discomposure.

Here, we can go one step back, and see how the mother's own penchant for aggression, and her tolerance of differences can actually help the daughter, since the daughter, with her special tendency to remain attached, needs an extra push towards individuation. Normally we think of helping our children, and giving them confidence by being supportive, and no one would advise withholding support.[6] But it isn't calm, unobtrusive relations between mother and daughter that give the daughter the strength she needs. It is a good fighting relationship, a relationship through which the daughter can define her differences.

The expression of disagreement from the adolescent to the mother is positively correlated with self-exploration. That is, the more the daughter disagrees with her mother, the more intelligently reflective she is able to be within herself, the more she can turn inward and see what is happening to her, and to think about what she herself wants and thinks and feels. As a matter of fact, not only does some aggression between herself and her mother (in particular, her aggression towards her mother) help her out, but what also helps her, are sharp exchanges between her mother and father. The more arguments they have, the more clearly the mother expresses a different opinion, or a different view from the father, the more independent she is. Parental arguments, it seems, set the daughter a good example.[7]

But what impedes the daughter's ego development? This has been a hot issue in feminist theory, and has been shaped by the strong and sincerely felt bias against mothers—or, rather, against the "mother knot," the engulfing connection which seems to forbid individuality and separation. The main problem between mother and daughter, and the main impediment to the daughter's development, either sexual, intellectual or professional has been seen to be permeability—the blurring of boundaries between mother and daughter.

In observing adolescent girls with their mothers, however, there was little evidence of this type of bond. If the mother did pave the way for such an interpersonal flow of thought or feeling, the daughter was quick to resist it. Tag queries from the mother such as "Isn't that right?" or "Isn't that so?" or "Don't you think so too?" or the leading questions, "Don't you think?" "Isn't that nice?" were almost always rejected. Even by the age of 11, girls were adept at slipping beneath this communal net. By the age of 15 or 16 they perfected a "ping-pong" effect, whereby anything a "tagging" mother would say, would be thrust back to her with a tidy spin. At age 10 or 11 a girl was likely to respond to the question, "Wouldn't that be nice?" with "No," or "I don't care if it is nice," whereas her 15-year-old sister would say, "It's nice for you, but not for me, so you can do it and leave me out, if you want it nice all around."

Girls tend to be touchy and sharp-witted with a mother who assumes that they think alike, or that they think as one. The daughter is very good at reminding the mother about self-boundaries, about their different ways of thinking, about the naivety of her assumption that they share ideas, or that each needs to confirm the other's ideas. The animosity that often comes with the daughter's challenge, however, and the skills she works so hard at to counter a blended identity, indicate that the daughter herself feels threatened.

Permeability cannot be measured or guessed by what is going on between the mother and daughter at the moment. The adolescent daughter may put up a momentary fight, only to give way on the larger issues. Also, permeability is reflected in the daughter's responses and behaviour with others, not only in her behaviour with her mother. She may present herself in opposition to the mother, but then, outside the home, in other circumstances, act with a sense of being very like, and somehow constrained to be like, her mother. Knowing this, the adolescent girl begins to fight her mother on all fronts. Even in her absence the mother may present a threat. Unspoken thoughts, easily guessed at, will be argued against. The mother who practises the utmost discretion and diplomacy will discover that her daughter continues to argue against her as though she were outrageously outspoken.

The adolescent, equipped with her new abilities to reflect upon the past, to reconstruct meaning through memory, and to learn to construct (and hence to long for, or fear) possible selves, can imagine, fear and fight battles which the parent cannot fathom. The new rational capacities bring in their wake a new irrationality. The adolescent self has a thin new skin. As her ability to see things from another's point of view improves, she becomes hypersensitive to others' views. Her greater sensitivity to another's perspective leads her to blind angry alleys. Sometimes an adolescent simply has to see a parent to feel that her day is ruined. The comfort of support and familiarity turn into oppression and frustration. The parent's view seems to pull her down, to lock her into the old self she is trying to shed, to inhibit the new self-image so delicately and tentatively forming. Glances, looks, stares, are loaded with projected meanings. These appear with great regularity on the list of parents' complaints about children and on the list of children's complaints about parents.

"I can't concentrate on stage when I know she's in the audience," admitted one 16-year-old acting enthusiast. "I can rehearse at home, with her around, and she helps me learn my lines—I mean really helps me, just feeds them to me until I can spout them off by heart—but if she's in the audience, in a real theatre, I feel so distracted, like something's tickling me or something. I imagine what she's thinking—that she's thinking I'm great, wonderful, marvellous, and I'll hate her for being so excited about the whole thing—or I'll imagine that she's criticising me. All those things are helpful—until the play actually begins. Then I don't want her anywhere near me. I guess that's pretty mean, but I think I can make her understand."

"Just the way she looks at me is enough to make me hate her." "She stares at me, and it's as though she's wriggling right

inside me." "Her eyes seem like peelers—like they're stripping
me down." The mirroring of childhood can become reversed
here—not a confirmation of the self but a denial. Yet in response what do adolescent girls do? They do not hide—they
show off, they fight, they criticise, they try to coax, cajole, or
beat their mothers into a better, more complete view of themselves. They seek to correct her misguided image. And hence
they fight with her. They fight with her to get the confirmation
and validation they need. And they are highly particular—quite
unlike that toddler described by Heinz Kohut who is filled up
by his mother's smile as he runs away in the playground. This
toddler is anxious about leaving his mother. Will he be all right?
Will he harm the relationship by running off? As he walks towards the swing he looks back to his mother on the bench. She
is smiling. She is delighted by his independent movement. He
is blessed with pride and confidence. His mother offers him
love as a gift for his independence. He is growing up, but not
growing away from her. His growth is a gift not a threat.[8]

For the adolescent, the mirroring is never so straightforward. Approval and disapproval cannot be wrapped in the same
bold patterned paper as used for a child. Adolescents are ever-
watchful, ever-critical, and have the emotional and intellectual
energy to pounce upon a response which isn't just right. They
uncover a wealth of imagined responses and criticise each in
turn. Their need for that validation is just as great, but their
need is far more complex, and far less intuitively managed than
that initial "dance" of input, response and repose of the infant
and mother—it is less intuitive, somewhat less rewarding, but
equally necessary.

When we know a person very well, her presence is sufficient to call up a host of feelings. Whether in love or in hatred,
the intimacy comes to us ready made in the other's presence.
This is why the company of someone we love is so pleasurable
or comforting, and why the presence of someone we hate can
be so exhausting, demeaning, and infuriating. This is why the
embraces and the fights begin almost before words, before we
discover the pretext for either the celebration or the battle. The
adolescent often responds to the parent's simple presence—

or to any reminder of the presence like breathing, a familiar mannerism, the sudden sound of swallowing—with rage and frustration. She suffers a maddening ambivalence as these non-articulate sounds bring her back to a previous self viewing her present self. She feels trapped—both by the comfort she is inclined to feel in a parent's presence, and by her wish to expel the previous self which welcomes the comfort.

Alongside these subterranean history lessons between mother and adolescent is a troubled script that involves the issue of agency. When the 2-year-old expresses outrage at being helped with some task she cannot yet perform—such as buttoning a shirt, tying her shoes, or unlocking a door—she finds her parent's intrusive help as a criminal reminder of her own incompetence. An adolescent's frustration at intrusion or "interference"—another word the adolescent girl uses freely in describing what is wrong with her mother—is similar, but significantly different. The task or lesson with which the parent offers help is not something which the daughter cannot do. She does not lack the motor skills or the physical coordination. She does not lack the strength or the height: she is not too weak or too short. Her indignation at a parent's "intrusion"—which can be anything from a word of advice to an angry prohibition—comes from an ambivalent intimacy. She knows the mother so well, and is so accustomed to thinking within the boundaries of her values and biases that the mother's voice has an unfair power within her. Her own inner voice seems small by comparison. Thus any word, any sound can be felt as an intrusion, as something that breaks the thread of thought or ripples the certainty of a decision. A mother's shrug can remove all joy from some precious anticipation. Her doubt can crumble self-confidence. Her fear can put an entirely new face on some activity. The teenage girl, keen to act according to her own wishes and will, suddenly finds her will defeated by a click at the back of her mother's throat.

"Stop asking me that!" an 18-year-old girl shouted. "I can get to the airport myself. I don't need you." Before going off to college, several hundred miles away, the mother was willing to let her daughter make the journey alone, but kept asking,

"Are you sure you don't want me at least to come to the airport with you?" The mother's offer was felt as a chain, which had to be ripped cruelly off. The mother's anxiety enlarged the remnant of self-doubt the daughter was trying to ignore. But the mother needs this flashing resistance. She needs to have her anxiety stamped out like an incipient fire. For she has to learn that her control, which once made her daughter safe, is no longer necessary. Or is it? When can she be sure? The daughter's insistence is not enough. The daughter's confidence is not a reliable gauge. The mother and daughter must fight and challenge, test and question throughout adolescence. The daughter must prove her point before she earns her right to believe in it.

Fights between mother and daughter often arise about very minor things. "Stop telling me what to do." "Can't you let me do it myself!" The protests are often uttered as brusque rejections of minute maternal responses. They may be uttered in response to suggestions in small tasks, such as dressing, cooking, doing homework, organising a day, trying to set the timing for various activities. But however heated these explosions seemed, they were in fact little puff balls. They hurt the mother more than they annoy the daughter. These irritable exchanges do not indicate a rift between mother and daughter. The daughter may be very good at explaining why the mother is so wrong to speak or to look at her in such a way, but she also sees the irritability the words and glances inspire as superficial. "I get angry with her a hundred times a day. That's just the way I am. Sometimes I'm sorry. Usually I don't even think about it." "I get real mad at her. I mean she says such stupid things, like I'm still a child. But it's not like I'm hating her or anything." "Oh, yes, we snap at each other. Lots and lots. But unless it goes beyond a certain point, it's just part of what we do. You know, like I used to always bicker with my sister. It's that sort of thing." For the most part, mothers and daughters are sanguine about their quarrels. For the most part, the quarrels involve tiny issues.

This is not to say that mothers did not worry about large issues—about sex and its consequences, about the formation of adult character and in particular about the child's ability to assume adult responsibility. Mothers can be terrified by a daughter's negative views, especially by a recklessness that seems self-destructive, or a refusal to work for future goals. Mothers did worry enormously about these things, but, with the exception of the latter (the issue of responsibility) they did not often fight about big issues. Rather, when the differences in values persisted, when there was little agreement about future goals, hostility and rudeness reigned in an absence of discussion. Quarrelling, no longer productive, no longer reinforced by the gains that came from them, was abandoned. Bursts of irritation were for renegotiation, not for separation. Separation was defeat. Battles were for winning.

SHE MUST LOVE ME FOR MYSELF

All mothers vacillate between permeability and mutuality, between seeing a daughter as merging into herself on the one hand, and seeing her as distinctive and even strange on the other. Permeability is not a crime which forever thwarts the girl's development, but adolescents tend to be on the look out for it. They often treat it as a crime, because it offends their current aims of self-definition. Even mutuality—the sympathetic understanding of a distinct person—can be treated as a crime because it presumes a certain knowledge of them, a knowledge which they perhaps want to deny. Not knowing themselves, the mother's knowledge seems to give the self a form, to take it up and shape it before they themselves are ready. The mother's belief that she knows and understands seems to take the self from her, and away from her own control.

Since the development of an identity is so important to the adolescent, and since the adolescent girl is deeply affected by her mother's behaviour, and highly sensitive to her mother's views, she will fight to find an appropriate reflection in her mother's eyes. She will fight for validation and, being unsure of herself, she will argue with her mother if she believes her mother has got things wrong. She will argue against her mother's entire view of the world just to correct her mother's view of her.

"My mother thinks she knows me, but really she doesn't

understand anything about me." Or, "My mother would be shocked if she knew how I really felt/what I really did/what I really want to do." Sometimes a daughter feels that her mother is not giving sufficient weight to something, to some aspect of her interests or her identity, and so the daughter overstates it, to get the emphasis right. Sometimes girls will brood over hateful feelings towards their mothers when the hatred is resentment at not seeing her clearly enough, not appreciating her—and sometimes, simply not looking upon her with the appropriate wonder. I heard many adolescents (and indeed many adults as they reflected on episodes in their adolescence) complain about a parent's response to some achievement—to a high grade in a maths examination, to a new job, to a decision to marry, to reporting praise they had received from a teacher. " 'Oh,' my mother said when I told her the exam result. I'd come second. 'Oh.' It seemed she was disappointed." " 'We're happy for you,' was all she said, when I decided to apply for pre-med. She didn't understand it was the most important decision of my life. Then, when I got in, she said, 'You've done very well'—almost as though I hadn't."

"When I told my mother I'd been nominated for class secretary she said, 'That's nice,' and I really felt there was something threatening in her tone, like she didn't believe me, or didn't believe I would win. 'Don't you want me to run?' I asked, and she said, 'It's up to you, but I don't know how it's going to affect your school work.' Well, I didn't know either. I couldn't prove that it wouldn't effect my grades. But she spoiled the whole thing. I couldn't put my heart into it. I couldn't ask her help with my campaign speech or anything."

Parents are never forgiven for not giving just the right response at the appropriate moment. Or, rather, there are particular times in the adolescent's or young adult's life, when a certain response is needed, and this need is not met, and the failure to meet this need is forever remembered, and never forgiven. Usually parents remain unaware of this, because even if the child tells them, the criticism is so absurd that they do not take in the extent of the grudge. "I was pleased. I told her I was pleased," exclaimed a mother when she heard her daughter relate her lugubrious response to her new job. "What am I supposed to do?"

What parents are supposed to do is generally what they often do but the fact that they do it often means that their children can have very high expectations. And adolescents, like children, are good at forcing parents to meet their expectations. Adolescents tend to do this aggressively, thereby increasing the parent's stress of knowing she is not fully meeting her daughter's needs. As in the face of a raging 2-year-old, the mother may be quite bewildered by those needs. The adolescent is looking for a very special set of responses, a preconceived notion of what this new person within her deserves. Repeatedly I heard complaints from girls in mid and late adolescence about their mother's love—not that the mother didn't love them, but that she did not love them for themselves. "Oh, yes, my mother loves me," said 17-year-old Pam. "She loves me, but do you know why? She loves me because mothers are supposed to love their children." "How can my mother love me?" asked Danielle. "She doesn't even know me. I mean, she doesn't know anything about me. She sees me as her baby. What I am now doesn't figure into her love."

Pam came from a lower middle class family, in nearly rural Michigan, but she (and her brother) were very bright, did well in school, and would clearly go further in terms of education than their parents. Pam at that time cared deeply for her ambitions of understanding and creating, for she wanted to become a poet. Her mother's concentration upon her as the girl she had loved as an infant and child slighted Pam's emphasis on her skills and ambitions. Pam identified her self with her poetry. To love her for anything else was to love something that was not her self. Danielle believed that her mother did not appreciate the significance of her maturity. She felt her mother still "spoke to a child." Her complaints, like those of many adolescent girls, were initially outrageous and subsequently circumspect, even fair. She began by making a strong simplistic statement "she doesn't love me" and then modified it, as she thought more clearly about what she meant. "No, I don't hate her really, and I know she loves me—I mean I know she loves me!—but we are ready to throttle one another half the time.''

The complaints about how well she was loved, were linked to how well she was seen. It was accuracy of perception, far more than strictness, which preoccupied adolescent girls. They complained about a mother's personality, about her "hang ups," her limitations, her prejudices—but most of all about her vision. When a daughter did complain about her mother's personality, her limitations, her prejudices, she complained in terms of how these affected the mother's view of the daughter. "My mother is too uptight to see that I can handle my love life myself." "My mother always worries about whether I'm doing the right thing." "My mother always has to offer her advice. She thinks if I'm not acting on her guidelines, I'll go off the wall." "My mother thinks that if I dress like a punk, then I'll behave like the worst person she can imagine." "My mother thinks that if I hang out with those boys then I'll become known as a tart. She doesn't even know what those guys are like. She just doesn't like the way they look."

Daughters also complained about a mother's fears and hopes, or of a stubbornness which made her want to control the daughter. Their use of the term "control" was quite sophisticated. A girl was unlikely to complain of her mother's control over her movements or activities. She was very likely, however, to complain about her attempts to control her thoughts, her emotions, her outlook. "She doesn't tell me what I must not do," explained 18-year-old Lauren as she was preparing her college trunk for her first year at Santa Cruz. "She tells me how I'll feel if I do something—like I'll be glad if I wait a while for sex, or sorry if I don't work hard, or in a mess if I choose the wrong friends." "Sometimes my mother says 'Well, only you can decide'" said Gail, "or even worse—'Only you can know what's right for you'—and I'll stare her down, because I know that she thinks she knows what I should do or 'What's right for me' and she's sort of keeping it to herself for some weird reason. It's as though she has these ideas, and I'm going to get in her bad books if I don't do what she thinks I should, but she's making me fend for myself. I don't know—

it makes me so mad—because I can't believe she doesn't think she knows, and I'm asking her, so why doesn't she say?"

A daughter, when she believes her mother's understanding or attention is imperfect, feels that her mother does not love her as the person she really is, but simply loves her daughter, who has only an accidental, historical connection to the person she truly is. The daughter may then retaliate. She may try to limit her own love for her mother as punishment for her mother limiting her love for the daughter. One young woman, more than forty years ago, wrote about her mother who did not understand her, and of her older sister, who was not at odds with her mother:

> I love them; but only because they are Mummy and Margot. With Daddy it's different. If he holds Margot up as an example, approves of what she does, praises and caresses her, then something gnaws at me inside, because I adore Daddy. He is the one I look up to. I don't love anyone in the world but him . . . I want something from Daddy that he is not able to give me . . . I long for Daddy's real love: not only as his child, but for me—Anne, myself.[9]

This is the hope of many adolescent girls—to capture a parent's heart with love for them as they are, as people. They reject the notion of being loved just because they are the child of the parent. They want the parent to fall in love with them all over again, because being new, they deserve a new love. But to gain this love, to help the parent give the child what she wants, the child herself must develop not only a sense of what this new self is, but also must understand the parent enough to know how to present herself effectively—and she has to be sensitive enough to receive the other's communication of acceptance or admiration. The girl's ability to see her mother as a complex and independent person, puts her in a better position to get the response she needs from her mother. If her understanding is incomplete, if she views her mother only according to her own interests and needs, then her view of the mother will be simple. Her actions will be understood only in this rigid framework. She will not be able to give accurate information about herself because she will not be able to see herself from another's viewpoint. The daughter's mature perspective gives her a round-about advantage. Being more sensitive to her mother, she can present herself better. The more clearly a girl sees her mother, the better she can present herself to her mother. But does it help her if a mother sees her daughter as she really is? This is what she wants. This is what she fights for. But is this beneficial?

"Validation" does not mean "reflecting accurately." Parents think wonderful things of their very young children. They invest them with giant talents and beauty. They see normal development as miraculous. And very young children, it seems, need this irrational appreciation of them in order to develop with confidence and self-love.[10] They need to be fed irrational appreciation in order to gain a normal appreciation of themselves. An adolescent's need, for all her nit-picking honesty, is not all that different. A mother does not validate her daughter by seeing her accurately, as she "really is." Where mothers and daughters are concerned, the more accurately the mother views the daughter—the more objective her assessment of the daughter's abilities, skills, and characteristics—the less she is able to validate her.[11]

Validation of a person involves responding to those feelings and thoughts the person is trying to put forward, whether directly or indirectly. In a sense it is a way of responding which indicates "I hear what you are saying, and what you are saying makes sense to me." It is different from "mirroring" not only because it is more complex—involving more subtle responses than approval and delight, but also because the adolescent does not receive the parent's reflection in the same way a toddler does. Whereas the toddler seeks a very general reassurance, the adolescent requires that the parent understand her and appreciate her through that understanding. She does not need the parent to agree with either her beliefs or her attitudes. She needs to be recognised, appreciated on her own terms. The daughter is asking for recognition of a new self, but that new self is still unformed and untested. The mother has to help give it birth, and she does this in part by acknowledging it. But this acknowledgement, this more sophisticated version of a parent's "mirroring," must also contain that irrational admiration found in the earlier responses. The mother validates the daughter not by responding objectively to what she is, but by perceiving her through her appreciation of what her daughter wants to be. The fantasies, hopes and irrational confidence of the adolescent must be shared in part by the parent. From the daughter's point of view, the mother is never perfect in this task, and the imperfections open the door to criticism. The mother who does not appreciate her is "dense." The mother who does not see the wisdom of her words is "not listening to a word I say." The mother who will not accept her argument "doesn't want to know." The daughter becomes distant and critical, in self-defence, if she feels her mother does not appreciate or acknowledge the person she thinks she is. She may cast aside the mother and turn to someone else, someone who seems more willing to acknowledge her—as Anne Frank turned to her father. Sometimes she believes that another person appreciates her more because she is not so well attuned to the imperfection of his responses. The adolescent daughter has very high standards for the mother. She has learned that these standard are often met. When her mother "fails" her, she feels frustrated and angry. She complains that her mother "does not love her for herself." Yet underlying this complaint, is the need to be loved for something she is not.

IDENTITY THROUGH THE PARENT

We cannot understand adolescents without reference to their parents. We have, however, been accustomed to see adolescents in opposition to their parents. We have been persuaded that the adolescent looks more to peers than to parents for confirmation of the maturing identity. We have even been persuaded that parents have a negative effect on an adolescent's identity, that the adolescent will try to become what the parent least expects and least desires. But this theory, which is in keeping with what many parents feel about their adolescent children and their aims, highlights problems, enlarges them, and then presents them as normal. Adolescent daughters, in particular, want to wrest acknowledgement from the parents. They use negative tactics, or the shock treatments of the rebel, in direct proportion to the failure of their primary aims.

It is the mother from whom the daughter most deliberately seeks confirmation and validation, which amounts to permission to individuate. There is nothing magical about the daughter's concentration upon the mother. She turns to her because her responses bear the greatest weight, and are seen as the most credible. The permeable boundaries between mother and daughter foster the presumption that ideas and values are shared. They remain highly responsive to one another's ideas even as they diverge. But there is another reason why the mother's responses have a special meaning and validity to the daughter, and this involves the power of self-esteem.

Self-esteem functions as a motive. We make choices, we make decisions, we choose friends, we join activities on the basis of how these will affect our self-esteem. We also evaluate and grant significance to other people's responses to us on the basis of how well they think of us.[12] We want to think well of ourselves, and we often act, and even more often try to act, in ways that will enhance our self-opinion. The daughter turns to her mother for self-confirmation because she can depend on her mother to see her with that special importance that will boost her confidence. She finds her mother's views of her credible not because they are, but because they are supportive. Indeed parents of adolescents are well aware how quickly a child will fail to find their views credible when they fail to be supportive. Hence the daughter, feeling her father less supportive, will confide in him less, place less weight on his opinion.

Daughters describe themselves as being "distant," "uncomfortable," "withdrawn," "insensitive" when they are with their fathers.[13] Sometimes they feel argumentative, or guarded, careful about what they say, and hence some girls even describe themselves, as being, in the presence of their father, dishonest (disguising what they felt or thought) or phony—usually in the sense of pretending to be happy, to be relaxed, pretending to feel what they did not feel. The way they describe themselves in the presence of their father is of course related to how they see their father. They describe him as elusive. He does not tell them directly what he thinks or feels. Instead, he expresses a mood which is expected to dominate them. If he is angry or upset, then the daughter believes she is expected to tread carefully, to "respect" his needs. If he is happy then, the daughter believes, she is expected to be happy, too. Many girls believed that a father was not direct or "straight" with them even in administering authority. He would voice his prohibitions or criticisms through the mother. She would then use her tact and intimacy, but voice his opinions. Girls were immensely irritated by this practice, since the father was protected from her counter-arguments by his absence. "That 'Your father says,' or 'Father thinks' or 'Father wants' really gets me," explained 15-year-old Ellen. "I say 'Why?' or 'What does he mean?' or 'Do I have to do this all the time?' and Mum just shrugs, like she's just delivering the message, but she's the one who enforces his rules, because he's not around to check up on me." The father then could use his distance or his absence as an excuse for delegating authority to the mother. Even when parents were divorced the father often left it to the mother to explain what he wanted, why he would not be able to meet the daughter that weekend, or how he wanted her to be dressed and what he was planning to do when they did meet.

What is surprising is not that the girl sees herself as very different when she is with her mother, but that she sees herself more vaguely. Though she often feels less realised, less genuine when she is with her father, she feels more well-defined in his presence. Being "herself," apparently, involves not being too well-defined. Girls often describe themselves, with a mother, as "helpful" or "cooperative," "comfortable" and "loved"— sometimes they feel "selfish" or "judgmental"—but their descriptions are not of the well-defined and self-knowing person she feels herself to be with her father. Her "real" self is really vaguely defined, involving not a definite stance but preparedness for communication.

Only when the daughter feels a great tension between herself and her mother does she see herself with clear boundaries. Then the girl might feel "frustrated—and that's an understatement," or "awkward" or even "ugly." When, in her mother's presence, her sense of self-definition is strong, it tends to be negative. What a good relationship offered was something more diffuse, less well-defined; and yet these girls clearly turned to their mothers for self-definition and self-confirmation. But what this means for an adolescent is that the self is allowed to develop through the relationship, not that it is already defined.

THE MOTHER'S NEEDS

The daughter seeks more contact with her mother and, such is the character of parent/adolescent partnerships, the more contact there is, the greater the conflict. The daughter's high expectations of the mother lead to high demands, to a high level of criticism, to anger when these expectations are not met, to repeated and often stormy attempts to get what she wants, what she expects from the mother; and the mother, getting most of the adolescent daughter's flak, is also more distressed by conflict. "My husband can walk out of the house in the morning and leave this cufuffle behind," said a mother of a 13-year-old daughter whom she described as "lovely" and "warm" but with whom she had "some storms," especially in the morning when "I still have to remind her every few minutes what she's supposed to be doing. He gets as cross as I do at the time. He thinks he has less patience than me. But when he leaves the house, it's over for him. For me, even on those days when I'm at work, I see her cross face, and feel how much she's hating us, and how unreasonable she is and how unreasonable she forces us to be—you know, how you think you're using logic, and then realise you're shouting at the top of your voice. It makes me feel awful, almost sub-human. I'm angry at her for making me feel this way, and I also think that if I knew more, knew better how to handle her, then she wouldn't get so angry with us, and hate us so much. I can get so upset that when she wants to make up, I'm so tense that I reject her. When she was

small and we had these tiffs it was much easier to make up, and
I didn't feel she held a grudge. Now she does, and I worry
things are going to go from bad to worse."

It is the conflict itself, not the increasing individuation of
the daughter, that causes her distress. Though the mother has
been accused of holding onto the daughter and fearing the
daughter's autonomy, she in fact is no more disturbed than the
father by the adolescent's emotional independence. She is,
however, more distressed by the conflict. She more often reports a loss of self-esteem and she is more prone to psychological symptoms of stress.[14]

Mothers are not distressed by a child's greater emotional
autonomy, but they do seem to identify with it, and go through
something similar in themselves. Mothers whose daughters exhibit greater autonomy will fight for greater emotional autonomy themselves. (Yet fathers do suffer from the greater
emotional autonomy of their sons. As the son gains in autonomy, the father feels a loss of power, a loss of that precious
intimacy which does not always come easy to him, but which
comes easier between him and his child, and which remains
easier between him and his son. Often he loses this closeness
to his daughter even before she gains emotional autonomy, but
he retains it for his son, until his son becomes more independent.)[15]

We have to be careful how we view the dependence of a
mother's well being on the good relations between her and her
children. These relationships seem to matter more to her, and
yet we should not, as so many psychologists and psychoanalysts have done, assume that the dependence on the child's well-
being is dependence on the child's need of her. The special
closeness between mother and daughter, and the special problems the daughter seems to have in "separation" during adolescence, have been seen as linked to the mother's own
ambivalence. The mother is thought to be ambivalent about
letting her daughter go. As she sees her daughter reach for
independence, she worries that she is losing her nurturing role.
She also worries that she is losing an ally, a female companion
who protects her from her diminished social status. She feels

ambivalent about her daughter's new sexuality. Her daughter, now (or soon to be) an attractive young woman, reminds a woman that her own sexual charms are fading. Youth is admired; the middle-aged woman does not command the same attention. The blooming daughter reminds the mother that the days of her youth are over. These ambivalent feelings combine with guilt. The mother is thought to become excessively tender and protective of her teenage daughter. Her true feelings, however, are thought to be resentful and hostile.[16]

To see the mother's dependence on her good and close relations with her daughter as a selfish or even self-oriented strategy, is to distort the reference in which this need arises. Mothers are more distressed than fathers by conflict with either sons or daughters. They tend to have more direct conflict with their daughters, since they have more contact. Mothers tend to bear the brunt of conflict. They tend to exercise authority more often. Their authority covers a wider range than a father's. They tend to rule in matters of dress, manners, and in the details of doing school work—whereas the father, however opinionated he may be, and however loudly he may voice his opinions, bursts upon the scene intermittently. The mother's authority is open to continuous questioning. Not only are mothers on the receiving end of far more criticism from their adolescent daughters, their authority is questioned in great detail, and under constant renegotiation. It ranges from their instructions about baking to advice about their future. Mothers tend to be in the thick of conflict, and find it more difficult to escape. Even mothers who work outside the home, and have a highly rewarding or highly demanding profession, find it much more difficult than fathers to switch on and off. They think about their children at work. They worry about them while they work. Thoughts and reflections, regrets and anger linger longer even as they leave the scene of domestic action. Mothers find it very difficult to set their parental identity aside.[17] Also, in her empathy with her children, a mother may suffer not only her own but also her child's stress from the conflict.

Mothers find that good relations with their children are linked to their own well-being. Adolescents, too, see their well-

being as linked to good relations with their mothers. No adolescent claimed both to be happy and have a poor relationship
with her mother, though she could be happy and yet have a
poor relationship—that is, devoid of intimacy and pronounced-
ly hostile—with her father. The mother's and daughter's mutual dependence upon good relations between them adds a
double edge to their quarrels. Hurting one another, each suffers
not only her own pain, but also the other's. When a mother
quarrels with a daughter, she has a double dose of unhappiness—hers from the conflict, and empathy with her daughter's
from the conflict with her. Throughout her life a mother retains
this special need to maintain a good relationship with her
daughter.[18] Her sense of a "good" relationship is highly general. It involves a certain degree of closeness, though many
mothers whose daughters were between 18 and 20, admired
them for "being able to sort things out herself," or "no longer
coming to me with every tiny trouble," or "not asking advice,
now, on every decision." "Closeness" does not mean, for these
mothers, knowing everything about the daughter or being
brought in to every decision, but believing that the daughter
sees her as available. "She knows I'm there if she needs me.
She knows I'm there. That's what all this care I've been giving
her these years is telling her," said a mother of a 16-year-old
girl who, she feared, "was getting a bit deep" with her boyfriend. "If she doesn't know that then I might as well wash my
hands of her, because if she doesn't know that she's not going
to know anything. We have our differences. Every family I
know is full of them. But she knows who loves her and who
will care for her no matter what. She might not be smart enough
to take advice, but she'll be smart enough to come to me if
she's in trouble."

"I don't have to worry about her keeping the worst from
me," a woman said proudly of her 14-year-old daughter. "She's
come home and said, 'Mom, I got this really bad grade' and
when she says this I can see she's afraid of what I'm going to
do, and I'll maybe be more disappointed than her but the fact
that she's told me just takes the fear out of it. So we can sit
down, and think how she can do better next time. I know that

face, when she comes in and is about to tell me something I'm not going to like. She doesn't know this, but it goes right to me, and there's no way I'm going to punish her for something she's told me. It's this kind of thing I want her to have. It's for both of us, I guess. She's not real open, not free and easy with her feelings, but she knows she can tell me the worst and I'm not going to bust up on her." Mothers who feel that a daughter does not trust them are not able to see the daughter herself as happy, or as "thriving"—a concept extremely important to a parent. "She's shut herself off from me. I don't know what she's afraid of, or what she's got to hide." "She's too proud to bring her troubles to me. I don't even want to think about where she's heading." A daughter who does not trust a mother, who will not be open to her, who will not see when she needs her help, is—from the mother's point of view—a girl "headed for trouble" or "skating on thin ice." She cannot believe that a daughter who has deprived herself—deprived them both—of that channel of confidence and trust, is a happy and healthy daughter. Her belief in her daughter's needs is linked to her own needs. The mother is distressed by conflict with either an adolescent son or daughter, but only when the mother is in conflict with the adolescent girl does she also suffer lower self-esteem. She may claim that she blames her daughter. She may say that adolescents are simply difficult. But she takes it to heart, and her self-esteem suffers.[19] Conflict with her daughter (but not her son) reflects upon her value and her competence and her success. If she gives up on a good relationship with her daughter, she gives up on her own happiness.

NEW LEVELS OF PAIN

The conflicts between mother and daughter are heightened not only because they are more frequent and more complex than in childhood, but because the parent responds differently to criticism from the adolescent. The same words, the same level of shouting, the same amount of protest, criticism or recalcitrance will be perceived differently if they come from an adolescent than if they come from a child. The adolescent too can be hurt in ways different from the ways in which a child can be hurt. This physically stronger and more mature being actually has built into her psychology a new vulnerability, which is linked to her intellectual development. She is now better able to put together a self-concept. She has some grasp on what responses support her self-esteem and what responses humiliate her. There is a new force to protect her self-image and to fight for self-esteem. She steps out of that poignant sphere of childhood in which adults' responses to her and behaviour towards her seem justified. Previously, they had been right because they were normal. What is "normal" is what usually happens within her home. Even the most awful domestic behaviour, including verbal, physical and sexual abuse, can in this sense seem normal to the child.

An adolescent, however, can deal with judgements based on ideas she does not directly experience. In her new ability to handle hypothetical notions, she can formulate some ideal manner of treatment, and gauge her parent's behaviour according to an imagined standard. But just as she has a greater vulnerability to the parent, because the parent can so easily hurt and humiliate her, the parent actually develops a new vulnerability in regard to her daughter.

The mother sees that the daughter has a greater sense of self, and a greater concern for self-esteem. The battle for self-esteem is highly contagious. If one person feels that another is using the conversation or the interaction to bolster his self-esteem, then the interaction tends to become competitive, as each person tries to play king of the castle. Many fights between adolescents and parents arise when the daughter just seems "too sure of herself," or too confidently denies what the parent has said, so that each becomes wedded to certain beliefs and the argument about beliefs or ideas becomes an argument of who is worth more. The battles for self-esteem infect the household. Usually calm and generous parents can find themselves holding on to a point of view, or in some other way desperately "holding their end up" because the point of the argument is not the issue on the floor, but the issue behind the argument—the issue of who wins, and who can be seen to know more. Whereas a child's cleverness and knowledge reinforces the parent's own sense of self-worth, the adolescent's cleverness can seem a "know it all" attitude, depleting, not nourishing, the parent's own sense of worth. The adolescent's often crude battles for self-recognition can reactivate the parent's uncertainty, and each uses the other to make points about herself.

In addition to the sometimes destructive empathy the parent has with the child's battles for self-esteem, is the new meaning the child's rejection and insults take on. Insults from an adolescent daughter are more painful, because they are seen as coming not from a child who lashes out impulsively, who has moments of intense anger and of negative feelings which are not integrated into that large body of responses, impressions and emotions we call "our feelings for someone," but instead they are coming from someone who is seen to know what she does. "Go away! I hate you!" means something very different to a mother when it comes from a tired, angry 3-year-old trying to use scissors and resisting her help, than it does from a 15-year-old who claims her mother is interfering with her "life." Even more minor rejections have a new depth to them, as the parent sees the child's greater ability to take her perspective, to see her as a person separate from her immediate needs and wishes. The adolescent's increased understanding of the mother does not always make her more forgiving or loving. The mother baulks at seeing how strongly unkindness is intended.

This new depth in the relationship between child and parent, and this new depth in the vision of child and parent is strongest between mother and daughter. Hence the daughter has the greater capacity for inflicting pain upon her mother. One perfect example of the shift from a child's to an adolescent's unkindness is described by Anne Frank:

Friday,

2 April, 1943

Dear Kitty,
    Oh dear: I've got another terrible black mark against my name. I was lying in bed yesterday evening

waiting for Daddy to come and say my prayers with me and wish me goodnight, when Mummy came into my room, sat on my bed, and asked very nicely, "Anne, Daddy can't come yet, shall I say your prayers with you tonight?" "No, Mummy," I answered. Mummy got up, paused by my bed for a moment, and walked slowly towards the door. Suddenly she turned with a distorted look on her face and said, "I don't want to be cross. Love cannot be forced." There were tears in her eyes as she left the room. I lay still in bed, feeling at once that I had been horrible to put her away so rudely. But I knew, too, that I couldn't have answered differently. It simply wouldn't have worked. I felt sorry for Mummy; very, very sorry, because I had seen for the first time that she minds my coldness. Just as I shrink at her hard words, so did her heart when she realised the love between us was gone. She cried half the night and hardly slept at all.

The remarkable thing here is that we see the mother's position very clearly—and we see it through the words of the daughter. We understand the feelings of the mother more than those of the daughter, and sympathise, I think, more with the mother. What is distinctively adolescent about this episode is not really how Anne behaves, but how her mother responds to her.

How often do children, accustomed to a certain routine, decline when the other parent steps in? "I want a story from Daddy," a five-year-old will insist, when her mother offers to read to her instead, since Daddy is unavailable. "I want Mummy to tuck me in," a child will reply when Daddy offers to take over the mother's customary role, because she is ill or busy. "No, I want Daddy/Sister/Mummy!" a hurt child will proclaim seeking comfort from one particular member of her family, for that particular injury. Yet few parents are deeply wounded by such a rejection from a child. The parent understands how the child values the routine, and feels uncomfortable, or suspicious, or put in second place when the routine is disturbed. The child may simply be confused, and therefore want to stir up other people, to make things function as usual. Or the child may feel that the interruption of the routine puts her in second place, and so she will make a fuss, to rearrange the priorities. Or, sometimes, the child feels that only one family member's arms will soothe her present wound. The parents may find this inconvenient. They may find it irritating, and even infuriating, especially if the child is rigid, and refuses to accept any shift in the family's rota. But would a parent cry half the night and hardly sleep at all? Hardly.

The diary of Anne Frank has often been used as a case history of the way in which Oedipal feelings are revived during the daughter's adolescence,[20] wherein the daughter again turns from the mother to the father, seeking the father's love, seeking to make the father disloyal to the mother. The supposition is that it now takes a strong and good father to reject the alliance the daughter proposes, to continue to show loyalty to the mother, and to help direct the daughter outside the family to find a suitable mate. But in the group of adolescents I looked at, and from the studies of other psychologists I found most useful, there is no evidence for the theory that the daughter is primed to turn away from the mother. Adolescent girls, in general, did not look to their fathers as someone they wanted to confide in. Many of them did not enjoy doing things with their fathers. And almost all of them felt very close to their mothers. It was the mother they trusted with confidences—even confidences about their (often negative) feelings for their fathers. It was their mother whom they felt knew them best—even better than a best friend. It was their mother they felt would have the most sympathy for them, and whom they would most trust to take their side when they were having difficulty in school, with friends, or in the neighbourhood.

Anne Frank did turn away from her mother, and towards her father, but her diary tells the story not only of one adolescent girl, but two: that of Anne and her sister Margot, who does remain close to her mother, and whom her mother does seem to understand. Always for Anne the issue is understanding, and since this is of such prime importance to an adolescent

girl, she will turn away from her mother if she feels there is no
chance of her mother understanding her. Anne repeatedly makes
this complaint. Her mother does not understand her. Her
mother does not appreciate her. So angry was she with this
failure that she closed herself off in punishment. Punishing herself in this way, she watched as her mother formed an alliance
with her older sister. She was jealous. She was lonely. Being
jealous, she was determined not to make an effort with her
mother. Instead she turned to a sympathetic father, and then
tried to form an alliance with him, against the mother. He
gently, fastidiously refused, yet offered her adequate support.
Anne Frank did not turn to her father as an enactment of in-
evitable Oedipal drives. She turned to him to do the job her
mother could not do.

Some adolescent girls do move apart from their mothers,
but this is in defence, in self-defence, in defence of that self for
whom they are seeking validation. They would love to receive
validation and confirmation from their mothers, but when this
is impossible, when the mother herself is too limited, or too
biased, too rigid in her notion of what the girl should be and
do, then—and only then—does the daughter turn away. The
mother never perfectly fulfils this need. The daughter turns to
other people. Taking her mother for granted, she often complains about her mother's limitations and ignores her strengths.
She is far more likely to remark upon the help and support she
gets from a father than from a mother. She notices the change
in her relationship with a father. More reflection, more consideration, is necessary for her to notice how her relationship with
her mother is changing. Bitter about her dissatisfaction—bitter
because her expectations and needs are so high—she turns in
defiance to others. When someone other than the mother does
provide understanding, to love her for her "self," her response
is always a bit saucy or sulky: "My mother fails to understand
me; now someone else is doing her job."

One shock a parent faces during her child's adolescence is
that the child now has so much more power to hurt her. One
channel of pain is through the child's new power to do herself
damage. Another is through the greater meaning her rejection

of the parent has. The daughter has more fully developed interpersonal emotions. She can reject the parent in new ways, and will decide to reject the parent if she feels her development or self-esteem threatened. Too often neither the adolescent nor the parent is aware of these dynamics, and so the new potential for sympathy, and the new interpersonal responses, become new hostility and new pain.

"The first time I told my mother I hated her, she didn't talk to me for twenty-four hours. Actually, she said a few words before beginning the silent treatment. She said, 'The feeling is mutual.' I couldn't believe it!" 14-year-old Leis exclaimed. "I mean, we're supposed to get angry, and to hate them sometimes. I can't believe that this was the first time I'd been this mad at her. I wasn't aware how bad the whole thing was until she said that 'The feeling is mutual.' That really shook me. I thought I was allowed to get mad. And she is too, I don't mean that she's supposed to be a sweety pie every minute. But I thought she was supposed to love me every minute."

What Leis did not see was that her mother was so hurt she responded as though an equal had rejected her. Unknown to Leis, she had become a fully developed person attacking another person, and her new power prevented her mother from taking that more resigned or even humorous position she might well have taken if a 4-year-old had uttered those words. Instead Leis's anger struck her mother with a new force. This took Leis by surprise. She knew she was asking for help as well as uttering a rejection. It hurt her that her mother responded only to the rejection. Leis's mother was not aware that she was responding differently to an adolescent's outburst. She saw the outburst as being different. "I never thought to hear that from my daughter," she said. Yet Leis was certain she had said it before. She saw how she had hurt her mother, but she also felt abandoned by her mother's wisdom. Also, having said far more than she meant to say, she expected her mother to save her from her own foolishness. Like any adolescent, she was too proud to apologise, too proud to feel apologetic. We have a painful half-way house wherein the daughter has some sympathy for her mother, some regret for the pain she causes her, combined with the need to assert herself, and to maintain self-esteem and self-identity through consistency.

Most episodes like this are weathered. The anger and pride of both mother and daughter eventually subside. There may be lingering resentment, or there may be a new care taken—or attempted. A few days later Leis admitted, "I now tread more carefully. When I say something nasty, it's because I want to hurt her. I know my aim, now. It was a real shock, seeing her face when I told her I hated her. I used to think [my older sister] was a coward, the way she'd dress up whatever she wanted to say. I could see her get angry or stop to think in order to be tactful. I can't be like [my sister] always, but I don't want to go through with that silent treatment again. And I didn't even mean to hurt her so much. I just was mad, and wasn't thinking."

Indeed, the adolescent daughter's ability to see how she can hurt the mother actually helps her, and mitigates that need to hurt her, for the pain the mother feels from the daughter's behaviour is a kind of validation. The new pain she can inflict upon her mother shows that her mother now sees her in a different way, sees her and takes her seriously. Their feelings for one another and their views of one another are now at eye level. One possible troubled area, nonetheless, is that the mother, so used to being the stronger, may pretend to feel strong. She disguises her pain at her daughter's criticism. "I don't care what you think of me," or the more psychologically sophisticated and positively infuriating denial, "You don't know how you feel. You're just afraid because you're so attached to me," deny the daughter the rightful validation of her anger. Adolescents do get very angry with their parents, and acknowledging this anger is part of acknowledging them. If the anger is not acknowledged then its expression is increased. The parent seems super-strong. The adolescent tries to become the super-attacker.

The daughter is more critical of the mother, and closer to her than to the father. Her greater criticism comes from being closer. She sees her mother more clearly as a separate person—that is, as a person whose perspective she can understand and anticipate. Seeing her mother more clearly, she feels closer to her. As her emerging sense of self and other gains strength, her emotions are focused through this new lens. She wants a relationship through this new cognitive awareness, a relationship which builds on, but which changes the closeness of her childhood.

Adolescents are notoriously confusing in the way they vacillate from being much like adults to being more childish than children, infuriatingly childish as only a near adult can be. The parent feels frustrated by this vacillation. She will find this vacillation tolerable only if she has a sense of its rhythm. Many of us, well into adulthood, enjoy temporary regressions, but the adolescent girl needs confidence that in regressing she will not be trapped, that her regressions are seen as temporary—as a true but not complete story. The less contact she has with a parent, the more likely she is to feel that only one side of her can be expressed—either the adult or the child. She cares more for what her mother thinks about her than for what her father thinks. She hears more of her mother's responses to her confidences, and has more chance of influencing them. But for this reason—because of her dependence and high expectation, because of this greater perspective she has on her mother and greater sympathy with her mother—the mother can insult her as no one else can, and these insults, which may seem so slight, are never forgotten.

When adults, looking back on their adolescence, were asked what they resented most in their parents, they frequently cited some insult; not some general characteristic, not some truly mean inhibition, not some grand event or crisis, but a humiliation a parent inflicted upon them. Sometimes the crime was that the parent had taken advantage of the daughter's child status and too easily gained points against her. The daughter then felt she was being unfairly used to enhance the parent's self-esteem. A woman looking back upon her own adolescent sufferings, recalled the way the father smiled smugly when he argued. "What I remember most clearly, and what still makes me feel as though I hate him when I think about it, is the satisfaction he had in proving me wrong." Another woman still got angry when she remembered how her mother shrugged off a complaint or criticism, "like water off a duck's back. It was like 'Humph. What do you know?' " Some women spoke of how a parent had showed preferential treatment to a sibling, thereby making them "a second class citizen" or someone who "always had to take second place." When a parent had gone against the daughter's wishes, by refusing to allow her some after school activity, or by "forcing her to break off a friendship," the underlying complaint was that the mother had failed to see and to respect the daughter's point of view. Such were the remembered wounds, for these were failures in understanding and sympathy. Looking back, the adult can understand and forgive her parents' anger. She can understand how difficult she was for them. What she cannot forgive is humiliation.

If we view adolescence as a time when the child separates from her parents in order to establish an adult identity, then we pack too much into this phase. Few girls in their late adolescence had a sense of an adult identity. At best, they felt prepared to form it. Moreover, however hard they fought for recognition of their individuality, they continued to be well aware of their dependence on their parents in a very basic, bonded way. The greatest fear many of these adolescent girls had was the fear of being abandoned. They spoke of this, mostly through the dreams they had:

> I came home from school and the door to our house was locked. Maybe I had the key—I don't remember—but I still couldn't get in. Every time I tried the door, something was different about it. I looked around, to see if my mother was just behind me, but everything around our house had changed, and was suddenly barren. There were just dust and dirt, and the kind of ridges you get when there has been heavy machinery moving in mud, and then the mud had hardened. I suddenly realised my mother and father were nowhere around, and I was terrified. Then I woke up. (Beth, age 15)

> Sometimes I have trouble falling asleep—not that I can't sleep—I don't have insomnia, in fact it's sometimes too

easy for me to sleep, but when I'm lying in bed, before
I fall asleep, I listen to my parents downstairs. Either
the TV is on, or they're talking, or just sometimes, if I
don't hear anything, I strain to catch the sound of them
moving around, and I worry that I'm drifting off to
some different place, and when I get there—as though
I go someplace else when I sleep—they won't be able
to help me. I dream of calling to them, and they're just
sitting downstairs. They can't hear me. And I'm so
afraid of that dream, that I'm afraid to sleep. (Jenny,
age 16)

It's not dreams that bother me. I feel pretty safe when
I'm asleep. But sometimes, when I'm walking home
from school, or when I'm in a room and my Mum is
somewhere else, I'll suddenly feel afraid. I'm not afraid
about anything. It's really like a physical attack. My
heart will start pounding, and I'll feel almost dizzy. I
used to think that it was physical, that I was sickening
for something. But what I'll do is go to the kitchen, or
into the garden, where I'll find my Mum. I'll make
some excuse. I won't tell her why I'm there. But I'll
just need to watch her for a few minutes, and sometimes I'll need to talk to her. Not about anything in
particular. Just to talk to her and watch her—maybe
she'll get up from gardening and look at her work and
sigh and say "Well, that's done," and everything becomes normal and safe again. I don't want her to know
about this. Not because I'm ashamed exactly—but it
would really give her the wrong idea—about how I
feel in general. Because in general I'm fine. I'm independent. I'm capable, and responsible, and I can take
responsibility for myself. It's hard enough to make her
see all that, without messing things up by showing her
that I need her, too. (Pat, age 16)

The very difficult balance is clear: there are the highly exacting
needs of the adolescent, who wants the mother to watch and

appreciate, but not misunderstand, to watch and see and understand, but not to intrude, to allow individuality, to be enthusiastic and confident about growth and maturity, yet not to let go, not to forget, and above all not to abandon.

NOTES

1. Erikson, 1956.
2. Erikson, 1956.
3. For an extended discussion of this see Gilligan, 1982.
4. Loevinger, 1976.
5. Powers and Hauser, 1983.
6. According to the Bell and Bell study, supportive behaviour from the mother seems to help a great deal, but supportive behaviour from the father actually inhibits ego development, undermines the daughter's independence and self-esteem. There is no explanation for why this is so, but the current hypothesis is that the father becomes particularly supportive when the mother cannot be; and it is the lack of strength in the mother, for which he fails to compensate, rather than his support, which limits the daughter's development. There seems to be no doubt that alongside the fact that girls seem closer to their mothers, girls seem to be more affected by the behaviour of their mothers—that is, the mother's behaviour tends to have a greater effect on the daughter than it does on the son, and a greater effect on the daughter than does the father's behaviour on either the son or the daughter. What is even more startling is the finding by several psychologists who have been working with this very new model of adolescent development that supportive behaviour from the mother helps to validate and strengthen the ego development of the daughter, whereas the supportive behaviour from the father actually inhibits the girl's ego development. (Grotevant and Cooper, 1983.) In fact, it seems that the father's support has a negative effect both on the daughter's ego development and her positive self-regard. The reason behind this must be that the father's support has to be viewed very much in context: is it genuine support, or is it an attempt at coalition, perhaps a coalition against the mother—for there is nothing so unhealthy in a family as a coalition, of two people against another, and they come in all forms: father and daughter against mother, mother and daughter against father, mother and child against another sibling. They are all unhealthy not only because they are cruel to the person against whom they are formed, but because they constitute a spurious alliance, not a meeting of minds or hearts, but a defence against their own feelings, a support for their own defensive anger, a way of

avoiding the problems within their feelings. From these most recent studies, it does seem, contrary to the weight of the theory about daughters and mothers, and about daughters and fathers, that the spurious support more often comes from the father than the mother. This does not mean that all supportive fathers must be viewed suspiciously—rather, I suggest that this takes the pressure of suspicion, which has been so strong, off the mother.

7. The ill-effects of stress from parental arguments do not actually affect the child directly. What does distress the child is the stress or unhappiness these arguments cause the parents. Marital unhappiness itself does not affect the child, but the effect of that unhappiness on the parent affects her behaviour with her child, and this affects the child. It is this model of indirect effect that has been seen in separate studies by Phil Cowan and Carolyn Pope Cowan, and by Jan Jonston in the Human Development Institute at the University of California, Berkeley.

8. Kohut, 1971, pp. 123–4

9. Frank, 1953, p. 40, age 13 years, 6 months.

10. White, 1975.

11. Bell and Bell, 1983, ch. 5.

12. Rosenberg, 1976.

13. Youniss and Smollar, 1985.

14. Silverberg and Steinberg, 1987.

15. Jacob, 1974.

16. Deutsch, 1944.

17. Ehrensaft, 1987.

18. One relevant and recent research finding, reported by Professor Guy Swanson, Family Dynamics Seminar, Human Development Institute, Berkeley, University of California, is that women in their fifties who are disappointed in their children tend to be depressed, and to focus their depressed thoughts on this disappointment, whereas men are far more sanguine. They may be disappointed in their children as frequently as is the mother. They may express anger about the disappointment, but they are not depressed by it.

19. Silverberg and Steinberg, 1987.

20. Dalsimer, 1986.

Chapter 4

SEX, ENVY AND
SUCCESS

It has been said that however well aware we are that our children will grow up, their sexual maturity is like a bomb thrown in the midst of the family. There is surprise, even outrage as a child's innocent deference to the adult world is transformed. Now she has her own sexual power to wield, a new kind of independence, a new kind of will, and a new ability to unlock a Pandora's box of ill-feeling within the parent. The mother may grow envious of the daughter, whose youthful sexuality challenges hers. The father may find himself newly attracted to his daughter. Confounded by these feelings, he may keep his distance from her. Thus the daughter is forced to deal not only with her own confusing sexuality, but also with a gothic domesticity in which people abandon her because they admire her too much and are ashamed of their attraction to her, in which the people who once soothed her now try to instill fear in her because they fear her power, in which people upon whose consistency she depends alternately show tenderness, as their guilt pricks them, and bitterness as envy gnaws them.

But how frequently in fact do these Freudian ghosts appear? Is adolescence that stage which combines, in our society, physical maturity with emotional and financial dependence, really an anomaly, something that goes against natural trends and currents in family feeling?

No one could possibly deny that adolescence poses potential problems for the family, as do all transitional periods in which former expectations are frustrated and new expectations are not yet fed into the system of interaction and response. "Some mornings she'll come downstairs and just by that swagger of hers I know she has something up her sleeve. I know even before it happens that she's going to blow my cool," explained Leis's mother. "I don't know what direction it'll come

149

from, but you bet your boots it's coming. She'll say, real ca-
sually, 'I'll be a bit late this evening, Mom. I'm meeting up
with some people after school,' and I'll say, 'Hold on a minute.
It's Thursday. You have homework,' or I'll remind her that
we're doing this or that, and she's included. And outside I'll
show that I'm angry, but inside I'm in a real flap because I don't
know how to catch her reason. It used to be good enough to
explain that we as family were doing something, or that our
family believed in certain things. But now it's as though I'm
talking to someone who might say anything, just throw away
everything we've built up. There she is, sitting beside me at
the table, pouring the cereal into her bowl, and I'll be trying
to figure her out. Sometimes its like a bomb sitting calmly beside me. I can't find the reason that'll twig with her. That
swagger—I'll tell you—she's trying to get some message across,
and I'm trying to hear it without panicking, but she just keeps
it up." And here Leis's mother put her hands on her hips and
rotated her shoulders in an angry mimic of her daughter's
"swagger."

The family is constantly changing, as each member changes.
Some changes we recognise as developments, and the pleasure
they bring usually makes us more adaptable. Some changes
threaten, or disappoint other members, who may try to resist
the change, or punish someone for changing. The outraged cries
"What is this?" "How dare you?" "Where did you learn that?"
issue from the belief that the norms of family life have been
abandoned, and that the familiar and safe have been usurped by
unwelcome foreign elements. There is no doubt that an adolescent can pose as an unruly stranger lodged within the once
well-controlled family. Moreover, the relationship between
mother and daughter, at the daughter's puberty, is particularly
difficult. Statistically, one can predict that during the daughter's
puberty there will be conflict with her mother, whereas one
cannot, with the same statistical backing, predict conflict at puberty between mother and son or father and daughter.[1]

THE NEW POPULARITY OF UNACCEPTABLE FEELINGS

There is a current psychological trend which involves giving the greatest weight to unacceptable feelings, to desires which seem to be repressed because they are unholy. At one time, in particular when Freud was doing his vastly original and valuable work in psychoanalytic theory, this emphasis was justified. It was justified because a large number of his patients did suffer symptoms that arose from repressed feelings and desires and thoughts. Repression occurred because this psychological material was unacceptable to the ego. The patient, unwilling or unable to admit that he, a decent human being, had incestuous desires or murderous wishes, developed such strong defences against his own wishes that the defences became an illness. There is no doubt that similar phenomena occur today, and that Freud's theories of repression and defence are enormously helpful. Psychological emphasis, however, must change as we change. Given the current bias towards uncovering inadmissible feelings, we often look for something negative whenever we are confused by interpersonal dynamics. We are inclined to see the unacceptable as gravitating towards truth. It is time to correct this bias.

As parents facing our children, or as children facing our parents, we are just as likely to ignore positive and appropriate feelings under the pressure of irritation, or the stress of confusion, or the urge to simplify. Among friends, adolescents find it easier to complain about their parents than to explain how they love them. Among friends, parents find it easier to criticise their adolescent children, to describe difficulties with them, to complain relentlessly, than to express that deep pride of connection many of them continue to feel. Whereas parents boast about infants and toddlers, whereas they laugh over younger children, swapping with other parents stories of the child's inadvertent humour, parents, following unspoken rules governing discussion of children, complain about teenagers.

"I hear how awful other teenagers are," Chris's mother said, "and when I hear that I think I should just shut my mouth and count my blessings." "I wouldn't trade this stage in my daughter's life for anything," boasted Amy's mother. "I know that's not the right thing to say, and maybe next year I'll bite my tongue. But right now I find her a whole bunch of fun." Thus the practice of many parents controls what other parents say: they fear that the family skies will darken, or they fear that they will make the parents who have "difficult" teenagers feel bad. But even the ones who voice their complaints, voice them more loudly than their praises. "When I'm angry—and she can make me angry! Believe me—I want to spill over with complaints. I feel myself go all hard inside and that's what comes out when I talk about her," admitted Marian's mother. "She gets me good and riled when she puts on those airs—she knows it all and I'm a fool—and it feels good to talk to my friends whose children behave the same way towards them. And while I'm saying how awful she is, and hearing about how awful their children are, there's a kind of crust coming over the anger and inside I feel more and more how proud I am of her, and how close we are—or were, and I'm sure will be again. We're all sitting there, ticking off our children's faults, and what I'm really thinking about is what a fine person she is—or will be, once she gets over this highness act. And that's minor. That's nothing. I'm lucky as hell that that's her worst fault."

The rationale of these social phenomena is that we like to bring to the surface a strange combination of what is easy and what is troublesome. We take something that bothers us, but we magnify the more simple aspects of it. Thus it is easier both to share and to dismiss. Parents' irritation, confusion and fear about their children's sexuality, mingle with sympathy for the child. Yet we maintain silence about this sympathy and this continued need to love the child. We distance ourselves through complaints. We may even spot the cruder forms of emotion, concluding that we are "jealous," "angry," or "ready to give up" when our feelings are so complex that we cannot name them.

Mothers do respond quite differently to the developing sexuality of their daughters and their sons. The girls themselves respond to their own sexual maturity more tentatively, more critically, with more anxiety, thus contributing to the web of ambivalence between mother and daughter. As concerned as the girl is with the physical aspects of maturity—with her developing breasts and her body weight, and the shape of her legs and the size of her hips—she is more concerned with the social, or relational, implications of maturity.[2]

Whereas boys tend to concentrate more on the biological aspects of their development, and to see maturity in terms of what they are now capable of doing and of what acts they are now capable of performing, girls view their sexual maturity in terms of "womanhood" or feminity. They look upon their physical development as a sign of their social and emotional role. Sexual maturity marks their capacity—or the approach of their capacity—to assume the role of lover, wife or mother. Whereas a boy focuses on his capacity to make love, the girl focuses on the meaning of being a lover. The sex act itself tends to have much wider meaning for the girl, and she engages in sex for a broader number of reasons. It is not that the boy has no emotional needs or ideals which he seeks to fulfill through sex, or with the help of sex, but the driving need for sexual release, which is often far stronger in him than in a girl, helps to simplify his motivation. Whereas the adolescent boy wants sex, largely, for the pleasure of it, or because he is curious, or because he wants to prove himself, a girl will sometimes engage in sex as a trade off for the physical closeness she seeks, a closeness more akin to cuddling than to ecstasy.

"It's this closeness—that's what to me is the most powerful thing about it. I suppose 'being intimate' is supposed to be a euphemism, but it's not to me," explained 18-year-old Jemma. "And it's always been like that, even when I first 'discovered' sex. It comes as a surprise, you know, that being close to a guy can be so exciting. But what really got to me was how you slipped into a new level of communication." She may have sex because she wants to give pleasure to her boyfriend. "It made me think—'I could do that for him'—and that made me feel important, that someone should get from me that kind of pleasure. I didn't think he could ever forget it—that I had done that for him. I felt, whatever happens, I'll have this special place in his life," a 16-year-old girl reflected hopefully. She may agree to have sex, either because she fears that, if she refuses, she will lose him, or because she hopes sex will establish a sense of belonging. "He said that if we made love we would be theoretically married, and that idea really appealed to me," explained a 15-year-old girl who still clung to the belief that some intimacy had been established, even though the affair had been short-lived and the "theoretical marriage" had abruptly evaporated.

The mother, having experienced adolescence herself, having experienced the ambivalence of female sexuality, anticipates her daughter's difficulties. She tries to protect her daughter, to offer her armour against the awful new vulnerability sexuality thrusts upon the girl. The mother's own adolescence, in retrospect, becomes hedged round with dangers and sufferings. She takes a new look at her own past and imbues it with a new fearful understanding. "My God, when I think what I did with my boyfriend at sixteen, I go hot and cold all over," admitted the mother of a 16-year-old who was just beginning to date. "How can I be complacent about what she'll do? I wasn't even particularly irresponsible. I was just young." "When I think of the risks I took," confided another woman, "I can't see how I got through it. I mean, I would meet someone, and go out with him, go to his flat—anywhere. I had no reason to believe I would not be raped. I had no knowledge of his previous sexual history. I mean—is my daughter going to behave like that? Even now, with AIDS about?"

"I remember sleeping with boys I couldn't stand, just because it somehow wasn't right to say 'No.' I hope that's gone now, and my daughter seems to have more sense. She can say 'no' to me well enough! But I want her to have that inner strength to know what she feels, and not to do anything unless she feels like doing it." "My daughter has just developed this marvellous confidence because of her talent in gymnastics. She was very inward-looking, really shy, until she was 10, and now there's this light glowing inside her—all because of what she can do on the parallel bars. But I don't think that will continue if she gets hurt. Really hurt, the way girls do get hurt because of boyfriends and because of sex. There's still something very delicate about her, and I don't know how she'll manage—I don't know how I'll manage!—if it gets smashed." "I never felt the burden of being a woman as much as I feel it now, when I look at my daughter. She seems so bright, and cheerful, and has a wonderful confidence. But I wonder when I look at her 'What's ahead?' And I want to weep with tenderness for her."

In trying to simplify and protect, the mother may work to limit the daughter's experiments or deny the validity of her daughter's feelings. She may, for example, enforce strict curfews or rules, severely limit activities outside the school and the home. She may become intrusive, asking questions which show suspicion and which have an aggressive effect. "Where did you go?" "What did you do?" "Who did you see?" "Why is your make-up smeared?" "How did you get those wrinkles in your skirt?" Often when a daughter returns home from a date, the mother's expectations of confidence-sharing are high. If these expectations are disappointed, then the disappointment can be felt as suspicion, and the questions become aggressive. "Where have you been, miss? When I tell you to be in by 11:00 you're in by 11:00, and not a minute later. Here you come in with your make-up smeared, and I'm not supposed to know what to think?"

"Mother—."

"Don't 'Mother' me. You think I don't know what it's like to be your age?"

Feeling threatened by her lack of knowledge, she thinks that by knowing what is "going on," that is, by tracking her daughter's sexual experiences she can control them. Or, she may try to control her daughter's sexuality by presenting it in an ugly light, by making her suspicious of a boyfriend's motives and making dire predictions. "He's just saying that to get you to pull your panties down," one black mother repeatedly told her daughter, terrified by the early pregnancies so common among her daughter's friends. Most mothers remember being told as adolescents "He'll never respect you after you sleep with him." "He'll say anything to get you in bed." They remember how their mothers tried to manipulate them, to keep them safe, through shame, fear and guilt. Yet they repeat the process, no longer so convinced that their mothers were wrong. Instead of words like "sin" however, which she heard from her mother, she will tell her daughter that her love for a boyfriend is "mere infatuation," demanding "What can you know about love at your age?" or "You're acting like there's already a cure for AIDS."

The daughter often responds violently, with words like "You're killing me!" or "Stop trying to get inside me!" One girl said that she could almost feel her mother's hands on her viscera, "like they're trying to mould my insides." And for the most part, these cruel manipulations are done not merely in the name of love, but for love itself.

There is no complaint more commonly heard about mothers from adolescent daughters than that they are "intrusive." "My mother just looks at me, and I feel as though she's boring a hole inside me," said Donna. "It makes me sick sometimes, and I think of little things—nerves and thoughts and whatnot— scuttling away inside my dark self to find some place to hide." Chris, who at 13 had a much calmer, more careful relationship with her mother, nonetheless said, "I'll bring a problem to her—something about my friends and school or what someone said or who I want to make friends with—and she'll tell me what I should do, and even though I've asked for her help I think, 'Why is she telling me these things?' It's as though she's standing in front of me and picking up things and arranging them to suit her. How I should be, what I should say, what I should care about. She's talking and I've asked her advice but I think, 'How can this woman tell me how to run my life?' I sort of imagine myself doing what she says, and then my mind goes blank, because I imagine her doing those things and I start squirming, thinking she's trying to make me out to be her."

Because of the special closeness—a closeness of identification which goes beyond intimacy—the daughter feels almost any comment, any glance, any advice, as an intrusion. The mother's remarks, the mother's thoughts home into the girl's deepest self, where she does not always want her mother to be found. The daughter pesters her mother to acknowledge her maturing self, but her sexuality, in its early maturing phase, is so tentative, so unformed, that she does not know what response she wants. She needs support. She needs appreciation. But she also needs privacy—partly because sex is a feature of our lives for which we all require a great degree of privacy, but also because her present vague feelings are especially vulnerable to distortion. She needs to bide her time, to test herself. She needs to make mistakes, and to be hurt. She both needs her mother, then, as someone to help her when she has made a mistake and when she is hurt, and simultaneously needs to reject her protection.

The adolescent's complaint that her mother does not understand her, carries not merely anger, but also self-congratulation. The expectations for sharing information with her mother are very high, and to disappoint those expectations, or to prove that she is able to withhold information, to keep something secret, may give her a delicious sense of power, control, ownership of the self. A 17-year-old described how "smug" she felt as she entered her house after her first sexual experience. "I still felt sore, and still felt the pleasure, and I had changed, but they didn't know. There was the same 'Hello, sweetie. How are you?' which proved they hadn't got a clue." In a more subtle and complex vein, Meg said, "Sex, for my mother, is always linked with power, with giving in, or giving him what he wants and not thinking about your own needs. She destroys the beauty of it, and I know, if I tell her how I feel, or what I've done, she somehow takes it away from me and turns it into something else. What I feel, and what it is to me, just has no place in her scheme of things. There's no point in trying to explain it to her."

The adolescent's romanticism about the self—that it is unique, unknown, misunderstood, that its truth can be revealed only through secret rites of diary writing or solitary confidences among friends—conflicts with her need for her mother to know, to acknowledge, to validate. But in the area of sex she takes special care, knowing that knowledge, understanding, validation here will not confirm but impede her individuality.

The girl's sense that there is a split between herself, as she

is in relation to her parents, and her self as a sexual being, is
clear as crystal from her remarks about what her parents would
say "if they found out": that is, what her parents would say if
they knew about her sex-life, not only if they knew she had
intercourse, but if they knew she petted, either "heavy" or
"light." Kissing was all right, but anything above or below the
waist, any tactile experiences, were not considered something
a parent could know about. The girls tended to anticipate parental knowledge of this as cataclysmic. Their mother would
"hit the roof," "scream her head off," "have a fit," or simply
"die."

These were girls who actually were capable of thinking
seriously about love and sex, and capable of discussing it. Yet
when they imagined a parent looking on, or knowing about
their sexual behaviour, they became downright silly. Their expectations were most extreme in relation to the father, whom
many girls claimed would "have a heart attack" or "drop down
dead" or "strangle me" if he knew what they were doing. They
did not relish going to their mother with any problems, or
anything that would reveal precise details of their sex-life. But
they all said that if they had to go to a parent, they would go
to the mother. She would "raise hell" but she would also "help
me if I needed it."

The great anxiety about bringing their sexuality into the
sphere of their parents' knowledge was also clear from the
number of contradictions in their thinking about parents and
sex. For while they insisted that their mother was intrusive in
regard to their sex-life, they also frequently claimed they did
not know how their mother would feel about them actually
sleeping with someone, or how their mother would feel about
them petting, either heavily or lightly. They both expected the
parent to be distressed, and at the same time, they were not
sure how the parent "really felt."

Many parents eventually did find out—almost always by
the daughter's telling them—that the girl had, or was currently
involved in an active sexual relationship. A girl would tell her
mother that she had intercourse if she needed her help—for
example with a pregnancy or with a health matter. But also a
girl would tell her mother if she was quite disturbed about it,

as she would tend to be if she had intercourse very young. There was no natural progression from early sex to "promiscuity," that is, sexual contact devoid of the belief that her partner played, or would play, a significant role in her life. Nor did sex with one boyfriend mean that she was more likely to have sex with another, or subsequent boyfriend. Early sex did not clearly begin a pattern of sexual activity, yet girls who had their first sexual experience early (before 16) tended to be disturbed about it. A 13-year-old girl who had intercourse with an older foster brother, told her mother because "it kept preying on my mind. I said something to her, told her I'd done it, and she said 'I thought something like that might have happened.' So she made sure the boy moved away. We still see him. He still comes to visit. But I feel safer, her knowing. I keep thinking I'll regret telling her. Maybe I will someday. But now it's all right."

Within less than a year of many girls saying how their parents would die, or that they would rather kill themselves than let their parents know, they were having boyfriends as overnight guests in their homes. The huge block between them was often nothing more than their getting used to it themselves. They need a kind of isolation, a privacy to allow them to see themselves as sexual beings. It was not the parents who could not see it, but the girls looking at themselves in relation to their parents as children, and in relation to a boyfriend as sexually mature. It was the girl's self-definition, and the way in which that self-concept was highlighted differently with different people, that made her think her parents could not take it. Most parents hoped their children would curtail their sex-life, or would not become sexually active very young, but they were also resigned that their children would do as they wished, not tell them what they were doing, and no parent I spoke to expressed the wish that a child would remain a virgin until marriage—as some of their mothers and fathers had wished for them. "Fat lot of good it will do, though," sighed a mother after giving a lengthy description of how she hoped her daughter would approach sex. "For all I know, she's having sex already. Well, I think she hasn't, but then if she had she's not about to tell me, is she? Not unless she has to!"

SEXUAL MESSAGES

Mothers generally claim that they honour their daughters' need for privacy, but such self-descriptions are seldom acknowledged by their daughters. The mother who described herself as "letting her [daughter] find her own level with her boyfriends" was described by her daughter as "always prying. She never leaves me alone about how much time I spend with him, and that sort of thing." "My mother says, 'Well, my marriage was no great shakes and you've got to use your own judgement about men,'" Marian said, "but when it comes to the nitty-gritty—when there's a real live boyfriend on the scene, I see her eyeing him up and wondering whether he'll marry me—she's always thinking about that, whether someone will actually want to marry me! And the keener she is, the more left out of the whole thing I feel. She's excited—and I'm left on the sidelines. I feel she's trying to whip up my enthusiasm, and so I withdraw, deliberately play—and keep—the thing low key." "It's not that I get the third degree after a date or anything," Leis explained, "but when I come in my mother says, 'Well, how was it?' like she wants me to sit down and tell her everything. She looks all excited and dreamy and she wants to 'ooh' and 'ah' or 'oh no' over everything. Then I'll start telling her something, and she'll say, 'Well, it seems to me that this is going on . . .' Her interpretations are so off. I'll start believing them and then she'll just leave me far behind, because I know she's not right, even though I can't prove it."

The peculiar interlocking of emotions, and the mismeasurement of responses, may have something to do with the odd effects of a mother's positive sexual messages on her daughter. For however positive and straightforward the mother tries to be, the effects of her messages are not straightforward. Whereas the impact of parental sexual messages on the sexuality of boys is relatively straightforward, it is quite complex for girls. In the case of boys, it did not matter whether parents spoke of sex well or badly, whether they advised against it or permitted it—any mention of sex whatsoever seemed to push them towards sexual involvement. Moreover, the boy's sexual involvement was directly related to his sexual satisfaction. He liked what he got when he got it.

The far greater complexity and ambiguity of female sexual development is apparent in the very different and more obscure responses of girls. Negative sexual messages from the parent to the daughter do not affect her sexual satisfaction, but positive sexual messages seem to impede it. It appears that if girls receive those now decried messages—"sex is dangerous," "you shouldn't do it," "you have to be very careful about it"— they are not clearly harmed by it. They often grow up to resent it, but their sexuality does not seem to be thwarted. They are not less likely to enjoy sex than if they are told that sex is good and should be enjoyed. These positive messages actually seem to impede her enjoyment. The reason for this is of course highly puzzling. Girls were thought to find sex problematic because they were raised to think it was forbidden or shameful or demeaning. That they remain ambivalent when their parents present it in a positive light may be due to disappointment. Expecting more, they may more often be dissatisfied. It may be, too, that a young woman is likely, whatever her training, to feel ambivalent about sex and about her sexuality. Hence, if her parents have presented primarily the positive aspect of sex, she may be ill-prepared for the ambivalence she does feel.[3]

The mother does not wilfully or gratuitously thwart her daughter's sexuality. The bad press she has got has been through her efforts to protect her daughter from those complex consequences of sex—from pregnancy that would make her an outcast, from abandonment and shame, from disease and degradation. Sexual activity, for women, has a history of vulnerability, in a way it simply does not have for men. The mother has to teach this hidden text to her daughter. The mother's warnings, her attempts to halt sexual development in her daughter, are not so much signs of disapproval or envy, but of fear. She uses disapproval to try to control her daughter, because she knows that her daughter is not fearful. When the mother, in the spirit of enlightenment, avoids this task, believing that the negative teaching is the cause of negative responses, her daughter actually suffers the same amount of confusion.

There seems to be little the mother can do right in this case, because her job is so very difficult. Neither her daughter nor her society is likely to help her. Since the very beginning of modern psychology, it has been supposed the daughter blames the mother for her female "condition," and that from this blame is bred an unholy alliance of dependence and resentment. The girl, initially repelled by the gaping "wound" of her mother's vagina, despises her mother's "castrated" condition, and resents her for passing it on to her.[4] The mother, feeling herself a victim of her sex, is watchful over her daughter, reluctant to let her experience more enjoyment than she, yet eager for vicarious pleasure and excitement. Hence the mother confronts her daughter's sexuality with a persistent ambivalence: she wants to thwart it, and she wants to possess it.[5]

Some mothers are envious of a daughter's greater freedom, and greater sexual potential. Some daughters do form an alliance with the father against the mother—but these cases which have been presented as the rule, are actually exceptions. Missing from these standard psychoanalytic interpretations is the simple and strong love and appreciation the mother has for her daughter. Much of the mother's well-publicised intrusiveness comes from a knowledge that her daughter's sexuality opens her to a new kind of vulnerability, a vulnerability of which the daughter herself is probably as yet unaware. The mother sees her daughter as being launched into a world of many contradictions. "She doesn't know what it's like out there. She thinks being pretty is all good. She doesn't know what it's like to be used," said one mother who admitted that she herself had been highly confident at 14 but had suffered a string of unfortunate "love-affairs" and had an indifferent marriage. "She's so trusting now," explained a mother of a 13-year-old girl who would soon be entering a large and diverse high school, which for the mother represented a new loss of control, and a new set of threats. "She's not exactly innocent, but I don't think she knows that some people would use her, without caring about her. I hate to think what's ahead of her, how she'll have to develop a different kind of strength." The mother had not herself felt that her adolescence had been particularly sad, and had only viewed her own romantic tragedies as part of growing up, but when she thought of her daughter enduring that intense sadness and sense of loss, which is really part of adolescent romance, she felt a powerful regret. Knowing she could not prevent her daughter from ever being hurt through her sexuality, she still regretted her impotence.

Missing, too, from the presumption of a mother's jealousy, is the clear-eyed criticism of the daughter's appearance which I found to be as common as appreciation. Many mothers felt that their adolescent daughters were particularly awkward, that budding sexuality was not attractive but ungainly. Many mothers missed their daughters' childish bodies. They regretted the physical changes not because they were threatened or envious but because they found the adolescent body less appealing than the child's body. Some mothers regretted the loss of the physical closeness they once had with the daughter. Cuddling was no longer appropriate, and the mother herself no longer desired it. She no longer desired it because her daughter had lost, not gained, her charms.

"She was such a pretty child. I suppose I'd thought she'd glide into womanhood as a great beauty. I have to get used to her just being average." "She's going through an unattractive phase at the moment," said a mother of a 16-year-old, "and she's envious of everyone—of her older sister, her younger sister, me." "I can't get used to how big she is," one mother of a 15-year-old admitted. Girls in mid-adolescence were the most likely group to be criticised by their mothers. At the earlier stage of puberty, mothers still saw their daughters as children, however physically mature they appeared. Though the girls themselves saw their physical and biological development as a milestone, and though the father tended to be surprised or impressed by the news of his daughter's menstrual period ("So young?" was a very common response) such developmental signs had less impact on the mother, who usually was less surprised by them, less impressed—since she knew how little such developments meant in terms of actual maturity.

POISON APPLES: THE FAIRY TALE OF THE MOTHER'S ENVY

What we have been persuaded to see, through much of the feminist literature of the last fifteen years, is an image of the mother who thwarts her daughter's development.[6] This destructive tension between mother and daughter is thought to reach its peak in adolescence, where its final thrust is delivered. The initial impact of this self-imposed limitation and anxiety is thought to come in the very early stages of life. With the mother as primary (often sole) caretaker, the baby is helpless, and feels the mother's power over her. When the daughter first feels the stirring of passion for the father she baulks at her own disloyalty. She has a terrible fear of setting herself against the mother, whom she believes to have complete power. Not yet understanding the difference between wish and action, she believes her desire will either destroy her mother or bring her mother's destructive anger upon her. During adolescence, it is supposed, the daughter experiences her mother's envy towards her. This envy reactivates the early rivalry the daughter felt with her mother. Once again she fears catastrophic effects of outdistancing her. She also fears the sexuality which gives rise to the mother's envy.[7] If a mother envies her daughter, and if this becomes part of what the girl learns both to fear and to see as a normal part of life, she will try to protect herself against not only her mother's envy, but the envy of others which, through her mother, she has learned to expect. She will see not only good sex, but any achievement and any success as a threat to intimacy with other women. She will believe that all women will refuse her friendship and deny her acceptance if she surpasses them, in any respect.

The mother's envy is cited as the cause of the many problems women have in general with competition, self-confidence, self-assertion, the urge to succeed, the desire to win. When women's motivation and capacity for business success first came under scrutiny,[8] it was found that women who had achieved success—attained a managerial position in the business world—had been closer to their fathers than to their mothers as children. All of the women in this early study had come from families without sons. The father could give the daughter what he would otherwise have given to a son. This identification with the father usually was accompanied by a dislike, a disrespect, a "lack of use" for the mother, with her traditional woman's role. The managerial women in this study, who were born in the 1930s, chose a masculine professional pattern and avoided a feminine domestic pattern. Those who married at all, married late—usually in their middle or late thirties. Those who had children had step-children from a husband's previous marriage, not their own biological children. Women, it seemed, did not learn from their mothers how to succeed, nor did they learn from their fathers how to be wives and mothers. There was a split between work role and sex role.

Nothing has changed more than this divided image. Women are seen as capable of having everything—children, husband, success in work—and though the image is more prominent than its reality, the image does mean that there is less division in a younger girl's mind between feminine roles and achieving roles and tactics. Young girls today do seem to have a broader sense of possibilities, a more integrated sense of self, so that sexual roles do not isolate them from the desire and will to achieve or compete.[9]

Today, with their potential professionalism more widely recognised, girls who are keen on professional success are not so threatened by traditional female roles. However atypically ambitious a girl is, and however traditionally domestic her mother, she tends to appreciate her mother and to feel that she has gained from her mother's traditional position in the family.[10] Girls, and professional women looking back upon their childhood, value the time and care their mothers have bestowed upon them. They see themselves as benefiting from the traditional style of mothering. As a result, most adolescent girls are aware that they will, in future, face some conflict between maternal and achieving goals. Few are convinced by the current popular image of a woman having it all. Girls who themselves are planning to pursue a profession believe that a professional life from a man's point of view is easier. Girls whose mothers are dedicated to a profession or a career or simply to a demanding job, see their mothers as over-extended, over-tired, torn between her family and her career.[11]

It was once thought that what a girl needs to pursue a career with confidence and determination is a role model.[12] Girls, it was once thought, did not choose demanding and rewarding careers because they did not have the proper examples which would help them envisage their own success. There are far more examples today of ambitious, dedicated and successful women, but these examples are a mixed bag. Girls now know that women can pursue a career with great success. They also believe that such a dedication has great costs. If a girl's mother works she is more likely to receive some negative messages about women and careers. She sees that successful women still suffer conflict between professional and family demands. Most adolescent girls value the role of mother and believe that they will become mothers. Most adolescent girls believe that the demands of mothering will come into conflict with a career. Remarkably, only black adolescent girls (as a rule) have the confidence that they can both have children and work, that they will manage somehow, without elaborate stops and starts. They have better family back-up systems, and a clearer, more determined appreciation of the rewards of working. They, too, look upon a working mother's lot as difficult. But, if the mother of a black adolescent girl has a career, the advantages stand out clearly. She knows her mother's professional skills give them both a better life and better security. While the same may be true in a white family, the benefits are differently perceived. The white adolescent girl whose mother is stretched and fatigued by her work will often try to seek comfort in her mother's job satisfaction. "She really likes her job, even though she complains about everything at the end of the day." "She says she feels more self-confident because she has this job. And though it's often a pain right now, it will make my going away easier." "I'd like her to be home when I come home from school. But I know that's selfish. What would she do when I'm out all day?"

The mothers of adolescent girls feel a deep responsibility

for their daughter's outlook towards her future, and towards her goals. This is a special concern, since many mothers feel they have to fight a mental laziness or vagueness of ambition, an over-feminised look at the daughter's future. The way a woman looks at herself has enormous impact on her development, her confidence, her sense of what she can achieve, and what she is permitted to achieve. This way of looking at herself, this emergence of self-esteem, is one of the crucial developments in ádolescence, and also one of the main concerns of mothers. "I want her to like herself," I heard over and over again. "I want her to think well of herself." "I want her to have self-confidence." "I want her to feel good about herself." "I want her to respect herself." Whereas fathers, when asked about what they wanted for their daughters, speak of happiness and fulfilling potential, the mothers look to the first stepping stone in the attainment of happiness and the fulfilment of potential—that of self-esteem.

Self-esteem is not a simple concept, nor can it be seen as a simple result from a series of clearly outlined causes. Having self-esteem does not necessarily mean that a girl thinks she is better than someone else, but rather that she will think in a certain range of ways, about what she does. Self-esteem is one element in the self-concept, which gives her the belief that she is good enough. It homes in on self-confidence, on the estimate of what her chances of success will be—in any task she attempts, in any goal she embraces, in any personal exchange. It is that which measures her expectations of how others will respond to what she says, how she looks, what she produces. Self-esteem is really her own assessment of the ego, which is a set of expectations about how she will interact with others, either with other people very close to her ("significant others") or how she will function in social conditions and under certain pressures; in particular, how she will meet others' expectations, or how she will cope if she does not meet them. It is a large part of what the daughter receives from her mother, not only during infancy and childhood, but also during adolescence, when the mother is responding to the person the child is becoming. The mother imparts and regulates her daughter's self-esteem level not by doing a specific set of right or wrong things, but through a cluster of mother/daughter interactions.

Yet often it seems to the mother that she is dealing with something beyond regulation, when she looks at her daughter's self-image. Mothers feel both responsible and helpless, both empathic and bewildered, in the face of their daughter's moods. "What can I do with her?" asked Amy's mother. "She's smart. She has a lot of energy, and to me she's beautiful. When I see her moping around the house I want to shake the living daylights out of her. Is she just trying to tease me when she does herself down? Who is she trying to impress with all these bad marks she's giving herself? So I work on her, really go to town on her good points. And I can just see that light coming behind her face."

"What kills me is the way she's endangering her whole future," Meg's mother explained. "What must she think of herself, to let boys treat her like that? He says he'll meet her at five, and then rings with some excuse at seven. He comes to dinner and talks about his other girlfriends. I mean—what must she think of herself if she accepts that kind of behaviour?"

"Sometimes she's so excited she thinks she can do everything," Marian's mother said. "She thinks she can handle everything. She thinks she knows it all. She will not pace herself, and then suddenly she's out of her depth, she can't get her term paper in on time. She wonders why no one thinks she's done a good job. She thinks anyone who criticises her work is awful. What kind of future does someone like that have? I see people like that in my office. They're nobodies. They think they can do everything, and they botch every job."

Adolescents swing from euphoric self-confidence and a kind of narcissistic strength in which they feel invulnerable and even immortal, to despair, self-emptiness, self-deprecation. At the same time they seem to see an emerging self that is unique and wonderful, they suffer an intense envy which tears narcissism into shreds, and makes other people's qualities hit them like an attack of lasers. But self-esteem does not necessarily involve continuous good feeling about oneself, or unruffled self-satisfaction. Instead, it involves a sense that one's life has meaning, and that one can act meaningfully. Self-worth involves self-direction and self-power, both power over one's own impulses and in one's interactions with others.[13]

SELF-REALISATION AND SELF-SABOTAGE

The push towards self-realisation, especially in young women, shows some special resistance in seeing itself through. In the initial stages of the women's movement the answer to this problem seemed simple: women did not succeed because they lacked opportunities and encouragement and direction. The problem was social: it stemmed from prejudice against women, and once society's vision cleared, women's position would be equal to men's. Matina Horner threw a wrench into this perspective as early as 1969 by writing about a phenomenon called "fear of success" whereby women seem willing to sabotage their own chances for success in school or in a profession because they fear the consequences of success.[14] They fear that if they compete successfully they will lose friends. Indeed, according to Horner's study, women seem to fear not only the loss but also the vicious attack of their friends. In success they do not, as do men, see rewards of power, money and love; they see punishment, loss, abandonment. This bombshell study seemed to indicate then, that it was not society, or men who were to blame for women's low appearance in the professions and women's failure to reap the rewards certain professions and careers offered, but women themselves, for women were their own worst enemy. And from whom did women receive this burden of envy-ridden fear? Why from their mothers, of course.

It is through an adolescent's interaction with her parents, and in particular with her mother, that she derives a sense of self-power, of self-worth, of direction and meaning. As the mother offers her validation she confirms not necessarily the truth of what the daughter says but the reality of the feelings behind what she says. The mother who responds well enough, often enough, confirms the legitimacy of her daughter's thoughts and feelings. She does not necessarily agree with her daughter, but she acknowledges the personal meaning of her daughter's thoughts and feelings. Through her mother the daughter sees herself as an agent who is able to communicate her views. It is not the mother's own self-image, or self-esteem, that is passed down to her daughter, but the support she offers, or fails to offer to her daughter, to build her self-esteem. But if this process of validation is riddled with the mother's envy, then the daughter's sense of self, and of self-worth, will be askew. The daughter will be unsure of the meaning of her hopes and feelings. Envy tends to give rise to bizarre responses. The envious mother may have sudden fits of anger, for reasons the daughter cannot fathom. She is simply afraid and doubtful, knowing that something about her and her hopes sparks her mother's disapproval.

There seems to be no direct link between a mother's self-image and the daughter's self-image or self-esteem, but there are many indirect links. Adolescent daughters are able to relate many cautionary tales learned at their mother's side. "Don't be like me." "Don't make the same decisions I did." "Learn to be more realistic in your expectations." "Learn to be more adventurous." "Learn to be more cautious, more fully prepared, more independent." "Be prepared to make sacrifices for something you really want." "Don't try to be a super-mom." "Don't think you can have everything." Adolescent girls also develop their own cautionary principles through criticism of their mothers. Feeling that push of identification—as though they will be like their mother if they don't make a special effort not to be—she has a ready made list of things to avoid. "I don't want my husband to treat me like my Dad treats my mother. I don't want to be a servant." "I want to be able to spend more time with my kids. I don't want to be tired the whole time." "I want to have more friends. I don't want to be so isolated." "I want to accept my fair share of the housework. I don't want to be shouting at my husband every minute to make him do his share."

The mother is always in the daughter's mind when she thinks about her future. Either the mother presents a model to avoid, or she provides an example of what she hopes to become. Adolescent girls do tend to have longer avoidance lists than exemplary lists. However much they admire their mother, they do put an extra effort into not being too much like her. Girls in late adolescence often feel themselves to be paralysed by the patterns of their mother's lives, or blueprints of her characteristics. They "had nightmares" about being like her, in the ways they did not want to be. They fear they will just slip into a lifestyle like hers if they are not on their guard. "I want to spend more time with my children, but I can see how I'm driven to do well, just like my Mum, and will put that first. I can't imagine working at something and then thinking, 'Oh, well, I'll just put it aside to talk to my husband' or anything like that. So I don't know, but I guess I'll have to keep an eye on things." "I don't want to seem so sure of everything, like my mother is, without even stopping to consider the other side. I don't want to be afraid of going into things. But all my friends tell me what an aggressive arguer I am, like I have to punch them into seeing things my way. But what I can try to be, is articulate, so at least I have good reasons, and then I'm not just avoiding things. Like my mother does." What their mother did or was set them on a certain course; they had to summon up determination, and sometimes anger, to resist it, to go a different direction. And yet from what I could see, they were very different from their mothers.

The trouble is that, given the vast complexity of human nature and the many ways in which it can be described, any behaviour can be like another in certain respects, and two clusters of qualities and series of actions can have similar patterns superimposed upon them. That is one of the challenges and thrills of looking into human behaviour—we can see different things in it, and be offered new ways of seeing it. But at the same time, this means that similarities can be spotted between almost any two people, similarities which may not in fact be particularly relevant. Daughters see similarities between themselves and their mothers, when it is not at all clear that any exist. They see similarities between themselves and their mothers as a kind of explanation as to why they are as they are. They stress many "similarities" as causes for concern. They wish to avoid the pitfalls of these "similarities." The adolescent girl feels that a ready-made model for her future can be seen in her mother, but she also feels that this is a model she can either accept or resist. Throughout adolescence a girl is learning to see people not only in terms of their relationship with her, but in a wider context of their roles. In learning this, she is also learning a great deal about gender. Children perceive their parents as figures who have knowledge or power to get things done, especially things children need or want. This way of looking at parents is an outcome of the parent's authority, the child's dependence, the child's wishes, needs and idealisation of the parent. But adolescents are able to take others' perspectives, and to see others more fully. In late adolescence, the daughter tends to be highly interested in her mother's gender strategies—that is, in how the mother treats the father, how their domestic roles are divided, how this division is negotiated, and what compromises were made from these negotiations. Also, the adolescent girl looks in particular at her mother to weigh her career choices and compromises, to assess her independence. Much of the barrage of criticism levelled at the mother by the daughter is an inner dialogue assessing the model she believes her mother presents her.[15] She may view all members of her family in this way, and deal with them accordingly. For other family members too, especially older brothers and sisters, or a younger sister who is close to her in age, present an adolescent with this kind of model—which is not deterministic, but something that figures in her thoughts of her future.

Siblings can play a very important part in a girl's self-development and self-realisation. Sometimes they mitigate the power of the mother's model. "I watch my younger sister with my mother," explained Mary, who at 18 continued to value her mother's views on her career, her boyfriends, her clothes, "and my mouth just drops open. Here I've been guided by my mother right down to the last button on my blouse, and my little sister shrugs off everything she says and has her own ideas about everything and I guess I'm impressed that she can get away with it. I'm impressed she's not afraid—and that my mother's not afraid. They fight—they fight more than I would ever dare to fight with my mother, but my sister sticks to her guns. I'm really impressed. I mean those fights don't terrify me, and it makes me more willing to stand against my mother, if I need to."

Mary certainly seemed to be over-estimating her "under mother's thumb" position. She was studying chemistry ("If it's good enough for Margaret Thatcher . . ." Mary joked), but she felt she had been directed by her mother, who was also a scientist. It was not that she had no belief in her own choice, but that she brought choices to her mother unformed, and let her mother guide her, whereas her sister (from her point of view) seemed to churn up choices and make decisions by herself. In speaking to her sister, Amy, however, it emerged that she guarded against her envy of the closeness between her older sister and her mother. Sensing that she could not follow the same smooth path, she chose very different areas of study, and very different styles of dress, adopting a casual punk attire in contrast to her sister's "preppie" look. Her identity work was done, as it often is with younger sisters, not with the focus primarily on the mother, but with a focus on the relationship between mother and elder sister. The mother and sister seemed to form a unit against which she had to individuate herself.

However strongly one sister influences another, the influence is not simply from sister to sister but from mother/sister to mother/sister/sister. The girl is influenced not simply by what the sister is or does, but also how the mother responds to her sister's behaviour, and how she contrasts this response to her mother's responses to her. Older sisters are often very proud of a younger sister. The older sister, having had the first "go" at her mother's attention, is often surprised and pleased by a younger sister's development. The skills of the younger sister often take her by surprise. "My little sister has suddenly got so smart." "My [younger] sister is suddenly blooming. She has a real talent for art—just like our grandmother." "She [my younger sister] is quicker than anyone else in her class. She's developing in leaps and bounds." A younger sister myself, I was sensitive to the patronage of these older sisters. However genuine her admiration, the older sister was also surprised by her sibling's talents. Accustomed to looking "down" at her, however lovingly, the younger sister's development remained non-threatening. The younger sister herself, however, was far more likely to see the standards set by older siblings and the older sibling's relationship to the parent (especially the mother) as a challenge, and often a challenge against which she would defend herself. She never expresses surprise at her elder sister's achievements.

During adolescence, as the older sister renegotiated her relationship with the mother, the younger sister was frequently tormented by a new jealousy. She might become extra-childish, in order to turn the mother's attention back to her, or she might become hostile, pretending that she did not care. One younger sister, however, described how she would sit at the kitchen table, and watch her older sister and her mother talk, while she would figure out the exact number of days before her sister went off to college. Then she would have her mother to herself.

"I love it when my sister comes home," said Gail's 15-year-old sister, "I really do. But even beforehand, even days before she steps foot into this house, the atmosphere's all different. Mom's real excited, and Dad's pleased, but laughs at Mom, and I'm supposed to make sure her room's ready. You know, seeing my mom like that is almost seeing her in love. I'm happy for her, but there's also this icy thing in me, because I know we're never going to be that close. She loves me as much. I wouldn't be surprised if she loved me more. But I see them being so close, and it makes me lonely, but at the same time it makes me feel that I have to work harder, to be that much stronger. My mother understands Gail more easily than she understands me. They talk more, and I'm a real good listener, so I get to know the two of them more than they ever get to know me. I hear my sister ask for Mom's advice, and I think 'I know how to deal with that!' Sometimes I say something, and they can get a kick out of what I say. They're talking, and I'll say something, and you can see them stop and think 'Wow. She's making sense. She knows something.' Even when I keep quiet, I listen to them, and I think about how much I know."

INDEPENDENCE AND INTIMACY

In their fight for the healthy development of women, the early feminists recommended masculine models of development which present independence and separateness as keys to growth. Many women have faced this task with a special determination, believing that the traditional female pattern of linking the meaning of her life to concern for and attachment to others is self-defeating. A woman must learn to become independent, and the independence envisaged was based on a masculine model.

This pioneering determination is now understood to deny the special, natural skills of women and to thrust upon them principles and values which differ from those that girls most easily embrace. Girls do tend to see themselves in relation to others, even to see their needs in terms of others' needs. They lack the distinct self-direction and self-containment typical in many men.[16] And because they tend to see themselves in relation to others—and to value seeing themselves in this way—independence in girls is difficult to gauge. It is more complex and ambiguous. Adolescent girls are never free of their mother, never free of thoughts about her. Acting independently they still act with some reference to her—to be like or not to be like her. Their independence is achieved through her, and remains linked to her.

Closeness between mother and daughter, therefore, is not in itself an indication either for or against the daughter's independence. What does indicate whether the girl will show independence or not, what does act as a sign that she has a certain maturity, a certain firmness of identity that we call individuation, is how the mother treats her—and particularly important is the way in which her ideas are handled, and how they are shared.

When the mother and daughter are close—that is, when they engage in extensive discussions about themselves, the daughter's future, the daughter's friends, the daughter's school work, there are various ways of sifting out and stimulating the girl's sense of herself, of her identity. The path to self-

confirmation in these conversations is "focusing." These are
responses which draw attention to differences and similarities
in family members' perspectives and which check for clear understanding of one another's viewpoint. In this way, the re-
spective viewpoints are validated, simply because they are not
ignored. In the ideal form of focusing, others' views are taken
up, measured and defined, without anxiety and without judgement. There is a straightforward desire to see what the other
person is, or what the other person feels. Focusing, however,
to be effective does not need to be perfect. There is clear possibility in this category of conversation for the development of
personality myths, so common in the family, myths of self-
definition which we both offer and accept from other family
members. Also, focusing is used, usually by the mother, to explain various points of view to her daughter, and to persuade
her daughter to change her behaviour through this wider understanding. "Your Dad is afraid that all this back-talk will
make you go against everything he believes in. Try to do as he
says—try not to ignore him when he's telling you what to do.
I know it's not important. But he thinks it is, so when he tells
you to come to dinner, you should come straight away." So
there was the implication "don't make father angry," but also
an explanation of why he was angry ("he's afraid for you") and
direction of how she might make him see that his fear is mis-
placed.

When different viewpoints in the family are presented, they
may present a challenge, or a point of competition. Perhaps one
family member's view has more weight, or a family member
believes hers should have more weight, and may be threatened
not simply by the presentation of a different view, but by the
support that different opinion receives from other family members. A mother may be offended if the daughter's view is validated in any way by the father, whereas she may be less
offended, more willing to accept differences if she hears the
daughter's views in private, or if other members of the family
do not support the daughter's views. There may be many shifts
in her range of responses: she may protect the daughter from a
father's attack, or an older sibling's attack, yet she may in turn

reject her daughter's views if they are supported by other family members. In competitive challenging, different views become "crimes" incurring wide-ranging punishment, from outrage ("How can you say such a thing!" or "How dare you say such a thing!"), to verbal attacks ("That shows what kind of person you really are. No wonder you dress the way you do—your thoughts are as messed up as you"), to threats ("If that's what you think, you can walk out of this house this minute"). The vanity that comes into play with competitive challenging may crowd out all room for growth. The parent's ego seems to take up all the space, to have the loudest voice ("the most say").

In kinder and less drastic ways, too, a family may feel threatened by the adolescent's new growth of ideas and feelings. Even without direct challenge, there may be a pervading sense that the family is some kind of unit of thought and opinion, and any variations threaten the unit. To control differences, then, the mother may avoid, rather than attack, her daughter's feelings and ideas. She can fail to hear, or change the subject, or register her daughter's remarks absent-mindedly, with an "Mm-hmm," or "Oh, really?" which feigns acknowledgement and renders the remark meaningless. Many adolescents try to treat their parents in this way, try to ignore what they do not want to hear, but they seldom are able to do this with any success. For the adolescent, the bland responsiveness which soaks up the sting in any remark as though it were accidentally spilt milk, is a form of deliberate rudeness. For a parent it can be a successful avoidance technique.

A more sophisticated form of rejection is distortion, wherein what the adolescent says is exaggerated, and then, having made the view ridiculous, is easily put down. Sandra complained that her mother was too easily reassuring; when she expressed her fears about her popularity in college, her mother said, "I'm sure you'll be all right." When Sandra complained "How do you know that? How can you say that when you don't know what things will be like?" her father demanded, "Well what should she say? 'Of course you'll have trouble'?" The father makes the daughter's complaint about her mother's response ridiculous. He denies that she is asking for a better response, but instead interprets her frustration as mere wilful criticism. Not only does Sandra lose in her attempt to have her mother focus on her, she is placed in the position of someone just prone to criticise, with no valid point to make. Many examples like this one make it clear why girls were so keen to talk to their mothers alone, or, if not alone, then only with a sister or brother present. They need their mother's attention, and they need to direct her attention. Her responses are often deflected in the presence of another family member— in particular the father. Only when a girl wanted her mother's response to be modified or deflected in some way, did she actually want her father to be present, too.

Distortion is a very common technique used by parents to get the better of their children in an argument, and they begin to use this when their children are in their early teenage years. Many adolescent girls speak of their determination to improve their arguing methods in order to overcome the disadvantage at which their parents put them. Many mothers and daughters complain that in discussion or argument the mother or daughter "twists her words" and makes out that "I said something I didn't mean at all." Adolescents themselves are adept at another form of distortion—exaggeration. "You never like any of my friends." "You're always criticising me." "You hit the roof whenever I try to explain something." "You never let me do anything I want to do." Parents, of course, respond in kind. "You never listen to a word I say." "You never do what I tell you." "You always assume I'm wrong."

Family discussions are games in which the participants are constantly trying to discover who has the loaded dice. As one 17-year-old girl put it, "It's a shame to waste good logic on my stupid family. You can make a point as clear as crystal, and they just won't see it." But the clarity or obscurity of an adolescent's point is not always to the point. What an adolescent is seeking is a better focusing from her parents, and the parents may be caught off guard, pursuing their own logic or illogic to "keep their end up," "stand by their authority," or prevent them from suffering the humiliation they are so willing to inflict upon their child.

Teenagers learn to hide their feelings and to lie when they are getting responses which demean or in other ways attack them. Some interchanges are not only rejecting, but markedly hostile, closing off any opportunity for explanation, for focusing. They block participation and convey threats. "You have no say," "This is none of your business," "Leave me alone," "Don't mess with me." And so the parent and the teenager lock one another out, and threaten one another for approaching, suspicious of every interchange.

All families exhibit these dreadful behaviours to some extent, and we all have some tolerance for them. We can take as we can give. But when the parents' responses (and in particular the mother's, because she is the one who influences her daughter most) generally distort, deny or exaggerate, the daughter's ego development is impeded. One reason the effect is so strong is that poor behaviours go together. The challenging mother, the mother who sees a daughter's differences in views and feelings as a threat to her self-esteem or to her power, is often also non-supporting. If the mother is challenging, she will not be open to her daughter's views, nor will her daughter get a validating response. Every exchange becomes a challenge. Such a mother is often highly controlling too, believing that her daughter should conform to very rigid expectations. Yet these highly controlling mothers also lack self-control. They display great aggression through angry outbursts—throwing tantrums which involve hurling of abuse, distortion, and extensive blaming, so that everyone in ear-shot, everyone within the family, becomes a target for blame—a technique one 19-year-old described as "guilt throwing." On the other, happier hand, when a family displays a large degree of non-competitive sharing, this tends to be in a context of little avoidance and distortion, and the smallest amount of rejection or affective conflict.[17]

Focusing and non-competitive sharing enhance a girl's ego development; avoidance, rejection, competitive sharing, distortion and affective conflict impede it. The adolescent daughter is trying to grow through her mother, and these techniques will help her. A girl who has a close and sharing relationship with her mother describes herself differently from a girl having a poor relationship with her mother. She will see herself as warmer, more open, more trusting, than a girl who cannot share her thoughts with her mother. What she can be with her mother becomes a definition of what she is. When a teenage girl decides to avoid her mother by leaving home prematurely, the running away kind of leaving home, it is to avoid feeling what she feels herself to be in her mother's presence.

Humiliation is a very strong issue between adolescent and parent. The adolescent may fight this out, in the competitive spirit in which she was raised, or she may decide to withdraw from the scene of fire, and to keep her ideas and plans to herself as much as she can, or she may cut back her own ideas, prune them to the family configuration. As most parents of adolescents know, the last is the rarer decision. But it is not at all unusual for an adolescent to decide that sharing her feelings is not worth the trouble, not worth the anxiety, not worth the fights, not worth the dreadful anger which accompany humiliation. For many adolescents this is a conscious decision. "I just don't tell her anymore how I feel." "I keep quiet about him [her boyfriend] now. I just say I'm going out with friends," said a girl whose parents disapproved of her boyfriend. "I just sort of say 'Yeah, sure' when they tell me I have to work harder. I'm not going to have that university thing out with them again."

Most adolescent girls, however, were exceedingly willing to "have things out" with their mother. This could be seen in one of the many variations of the "ping-pong" effect I mentioned earlier, with swift exchanges of feelings and ideas between mother and daughter. These would begin with a few exchanges or queries and answers, then rise to a pitch of accusation and counter-accusation, when the daughter felt that the mother was intrusive, or unfairly interpreting her words, or, at the other extreme, was not putting enough weight on her words. The daughter would respond with lively exaggeration: "You always try to take the words out of my mouth," "You're making a mountain out of a mole hill," "You always suspect the worst," or, to prod her mother into a response, she will insist, "Don't you hear what I'm saying?" "Look at me, Mum. Listen to what I'm saying. It's not all right." These girls were like an eager athlete waiting to enter the boxing ring. They wanted to take and receive punches. They wanted to feel the rise and fall of the mother's response. These were not quarrels of people trying to separate but of people, sometimes very awkwardly, trying to get closer. The daughter fought to get closer to her mother, to achieve a greater intimacy with her in terms of forcing her to acknowledge her individuality.

I remember watching, from the younger sister's protective vantage point, my sister and my mother sit down after dinner each day for what I privately called "fighting time." I could never understand how my older sister sat down after dinner with such equanimity, with such equability, as though oblivious of the battles to come. My father would go upstairs to his study, my mother would recline on the couch, and my sister would take his chair, while I would perch either on the ottoman beside my sister, or on the floor beside the couch, seeking a low profile, and the possibility of an early get-away. Then, after a little small talk, the real stuff would begin. A chance comment my sister made about what she did in school, what she said to a boy, would make my mother's chin raise, an animal on the scent for danger. Then she would take my sister's words and wave them like a flag while she ridiculed them. It gave me the absurd image of her taking my sister's underwear and shouting at everyone to look, and I could not understand why, every night, my sister would subject herself to this. But later, I was to understand that same push and pull towards self-revelation and self-justification. Later I was to learn the wonder of having the tiny details of my day turned into grand drama, whereby sometimes, just often enough to keep me going, there was a new sympathetic description offered me, a sense of how deeply right, after all, I was to have such emotions and ideas. Later I was to learn the thrilling victory of stopping the flight of my mother's indignation, watching her reconsider, and come over to my view.

The adolescent girl's need to make her mother hear, and make her mother see, is like a compulsion. She wants both to confess everything and to guard the treasure of her individuality. Spurred by her hope for understanding and acknowledgement, she braves many emotional dangers. She risks humiliation. She risks disapproval. She risks further confusion and further self-doubt. She puts herself at risk because she hopes that, in self-exposure, she will receive self-confirmation. Her hope registers such a strong need that only persistent and very cruel disappointment will extinguish it.

FIGHTING TIMES

Mothers and daughters face a rhythm of rising and falling tension in the course of the day. Each family has a special time for these fighting periods. The most common time for them, the time that seems to present a challenge to both the mother and the daughter is when they meet, at home, after having spent several hours in the company of people outside the family. This then would either be when the daughter came home from school and the mother was home, or when the mother came home from work and the daughter was home, or when the daughter came home from a date, or after spending time with friends. There seems to be, at these meetings between mother and daughter on domestic territory, an attempt on the mother's part to re-establish control, which she does through questioning and challenging. The daughter often begins by being pliant—answering her mother's questions, and trying, through her tone of voice, to placate the mother, but if the questioning becomes too insistent, then the daughter becomes defensive, frustrated at her inability to persuade her mother that she is all right, and has done nothing stupid or wrong. One of the most upsetting things for a daughter is to feel that she is under suspicion.

Homecoming itself can be ripe with challenge. When 16-year-old Anne came home from an after-school activity, she raced into her bedroom and slammed the door. Her mother was particularly sensitive to loud noise. Anne must have known this, for her mother said, "Ever since my children were babies I noticed how loud noises made me scream. I can't think. I'll be in control, and then something crashes down, and I start shouting. I feel that all the patience I'm building up just tumbles down." After slamming the door, Anne turned on her music system very loud, which also was bound to annoy her mother. Riled, her mother came to the bottom of the steps and shouted, "Turn that thing off. This minute." Anne waited until her mother came up the stairs, banged on the door and then opened it without receiving an answer. Mother and daughter glared at one another, each feeling slighted by the other. "There are other people in the world, too, you know," her mother reminded her. "Anne, I want you to turn that thing off and I want you to go downstairs and clear up your breakfast things, which I've told you over and over again to take to the sink and let soak. I do not want to come home from work to have to do everything. Now get downstairs THIS MINUTE and do as I say." Anne grunted. They were both so angry they were shaking, and close to tears.

"Clean up the kitchen. Come on! Now! Come on!" The mother's voice was subdued, and Anne responded to the low-key persistence. She dragged herself to her feet and they went downstairs together.

Later Anne's mother explained, "I come home from work and everything seems out of control. No one has bothered to do any housework, which means I'll have to do it all. Then Anne comes home, and the way she moves—you saw her!—it's like lighting a fuse, just ripping my last bit of composure to shreds. Then I looked at her. She was so angry, a real sour puss. But even when I'm angry things can suddenly change. It's as though a door opens and—whoosh—I'm right in there with her. All those awful feelings, that I know I hate too. But I can't give in. She has to clean that kitchen—or, I don't know, maybe I did most of it. But I wanted to help her, show her that she wasn't alone. She doesn't always storm into the house like that. Something must have upset her."

Anne's door slamming and music drowning communicated her anger or unhappiness, but she was clearly communicating in such a way that her mother would not respond sympathetically. Anne had "proof"—in her mother's glowering—that her mother was insensitive, and did not care about her. Adolescents are very good at setting up situations in which a parent will respond poorly. There is some pleasure to be had in being mis-understood.

Often, in meeting the daughter on home territory, the mother wants to regain the control she has lost by the daughter having been out of her jurisdiction. At the same time, the daughter is keen to bring her experiences back to her mother, and can be highly offended if the mother is only challenging and controlling. The daughter can get the mother angry as a way of regulating the mother's preoccupation with power, but many of these girls were very patient, awaiting the right mo-ment for the mother to look things over, to regain a sense of control, and then to go on, showing a sophistication in han-dling the mother that is often over-looked.

When parents are slow (as they usually are) to accept her individuality, the daughter becomes hypercritical of her moth-er's responses. Even a 4-year-old will become perturbed and belligerent when she believes that the smile an adult offers her is somehow inappropriate—that it over-praises her, or makes her out to be cute, when she was trying to be serious, or in some other way fails to register what she thinks she is, or what she thinks she has achieved. For the adolescent, this momentary anger turns to rage, and to a push to correct the response, to justify the self. For this reason, the adolescent is highly willing to fight, to have things out.

At the same time, to avoid misunderstanding, to avoid con-fronting a parent's definition of her, she will try to sustain her privacy. Girls, under the pressure of frustrated quarrels, spoke of attempts "to pretend I'm not myself" when they were home, to "put myself on ice" when in the company of a parent; yet the quality and the passion of their relationship was such that they could not wilfully negate themselves, nor could they find any defence against a parent's pressure of disappointment.

"I can't turn my head without my father reminding me I should be doing better in school." "I can't see my mother without her telling me I should lose weight." "I can't walk into a room without my father criticising me." "Two minutes in the same room with my mother and she's calling me a whore." It is adolescents like these who leave home, because home has become a place of humiliation and attack. The parent, usually, is fighting on behalf of the adolescent's welfare, but the effect of this battle is to attack the self which the adolescent is learning to value so highly. Yet this self, as yet unformed, is vulnerable and, like a child's developing sense of self, requires for its well-being an enthusiastic response, a response not exactly irrational, but not regulated solely by "objective" value. The adolescent still needs from her parents a loaded enthusiasm, a rosy view, to keep alive her own faith in herself.

Adolescents who leave home, who run away, do so because they simply cannot get the response they need, and feel they have no facility for growth. "I couldn't breathe in that house," said one 15-year-old who had impulsively left home after an argument about what school she would attend in the autumn. "My mother was always at me. Always. Every minute I was in the house, I was being told what was wrong with me." Repeatedly, children who had left home suddenly, determinedly angry, described a domestic atmosphere in which they felt they could not grow. There was a physical sense of "being strangled" or "not being able to breathe" or "having eyes that are directing me every minute, like strings on every nerve, so that every time I move, even just to wash a piece of fruit at the sink, there's this attempt to pull me up, tell me how to do things." Many of these girls were still technically highly dependent—they could not make decisions for themselves, they could not finance their room and board even for a short period, they had no sense of what kind of life they wanted. The family behaviour that had pushed them out of the home was also behaviour that prevented them from being able to survive in any healthy way outside the home. Having had no freedom, no free development of the self within their home, they had little sense of what they wanted to do, and how to go about getting it. They left home not because there was something waiting for them outside, but because inside was intolerable. Thus they developed new dependencies on people who pretended to care for them, initially, or who seemed to accept them, but who had no real concern. Or, they left home with a boyfriend, of whom the parents were highly critical. With this base some of them actually were able to create some kind of healthy life. Susanna left home at 16 to live with her boyfriend, whom she married as soon as she was of age. She had a job, and she had a home, and though she was not fulfilling what her academic parents saw as her potential, she was getting by well enough. Her success was the result of "foreclosure"—settling upon a fairly simple identity too soon, before she had explored and tested other options. From her point of view, however, this was the best option. Living in her parents' home, the criticism had been so intense that she felt "obliterated." "I don't think people in prison are treated the way [my mother and stepfather] treated me. Everything, and I mean everything, I did or thought or felt was wrong. My mother's always said she wants me to think for myself. She feels torn about social acceptance, you know. My father—I mean my real father—was killed in Vietnam. So here he was, someone who did what he was told. He went out to fight a war for his country. But my mother was stuck at home with her student friends who thought my father was the devil and deserved to die. Well, she thinks she's suffered, but let me tell you, that little episode of her life was over pretty quick. She got married and had [my half brother] before I knew my Dad was never coming back. No—that's not quite true. I think I was told my Dad was never coming back when she told me she was going to marry [her stepfather]. So there's this darling brother of mine who's so like his professor father, and then there's me who somehow just isn't right, just doesn't fit in with this family. I know I'm like my mother was when she was my age. She was no intellectual either. But do I get the time of day? Do I get a hearing? All it is is 'do this,' 'do that,' 'why can't you be like someone else?' I saved them the trouble of making me fit in by leaving them to themselves."

Though Susanna's stepfather was shattered by her flight (he seemed to age fifteen years in the course of a few months), Susanna's mother clearly felt ambivalent. "I think she should be home. She was a fool to run away. There's no future with [her boyfriend]. But that's her lookout. I'd do anything to get her back here, but I don't think anything I did would work. I'd open my mouth and you could just see this iron wall come down over her. I'd feel physically ill from our fights. I'd look in the mirror and think 'What's this girl doing to me?' She was tearing our lives apart." As did many mothers of runaway teen-age girls, she said that home was now peaceful, that for the first time in years she no longer felt like a monster. She no longer had to face her reflection in her daughter's anger every day.

Mothers seemed to have a reciprocal identity in their rela-tionship with the daughter. The daughter who had to run away from home in order to preserve her identity often had a mother whose identity had been lost and distorted in quarrels with the daughter. These battles between two changing selves can be terrible dramas, leading to wilful destruction of one an-other, as each identity looks for its reflection in the other and sees nothing but the ugliness of anger, which then leads to resentment, to that awful hatred when we feel dirty in another's presence.

It is not only the adolescents who have to face criticism, and who learn hard lessons of humiliation within the family. Adolescent daughters are critical of the mother's personality, of the choices she has made, of her fears, of her habits. They are also sympathetic. Seeing her more clearly they understand her more. But at the same time they feel threatened by her identity, and try to resist it. The most common way of resisting it is through criticism. Mothers, on the whole, expected this and accepted it. What they found most difficult to accept was the daughter's criticism of her marriage. The setting that in child-hood was simply normal, and beyond question, regardless of whether it made her happy or unhappy, now comes under the daughter's scrutiny. Because she so recently accepted it as right and normal, she now has to work extra hard to expel it with her criticism. It is this criticism of "how Dad feels about her" or "how she could have chosen a man like Dad" or her insis-tence that the marriage is "only lukewarm" or that her parents are "happy for them" that makes the mother deeply angry. She feels betrayed because such an important part of her life is being judged so superficially. The daughter becomes an outsider, and the mother tends to remind her "she knows damn all about it."

Daughters whose mothers are newly divorced tend to be

loyal to them, sympathising with their wounds. Girls whose mothers have been divorced for several years, however, tend to be critical of how her mother "probably acted with [her] father" or how "she went about with men when she was single" or "how she kept hoping someone would come along" or how "she shut herself off from men." The adolescent girl at this time is thinking about her life, and her "gender strategies"—how she will handle the roles of lover, wife and mother. Criticism of her own mother becomes a way of thinking about her own future. There is a triangle with the daughter's new powers of, and urge towards, individuation at one point; her accompanying ability to criticise her mother's life, to make different choices is at another; her need to be confirmed by her mother is a third point, which leads her to present her criticism to her mother, hoping these, too, will be confirmed by her mother. She needs her mother to say "You do not need to be like me. You are different from me." The adolescent also wants more. She wants to say to her mother, "I do not want to be like you because you are wrong to be as you are," and then expects the mother to offer confirmation by saying "Yes I am wrong and you are right."

Mothers become the greater target of criticism partly because in appraising her own future the daughter turns to the mother, but also because the mother will listen more. Having had her vanity bruised gradually throughout the daughter's childhood, with those hundreds of attacks each child offers a care-taking parent, the mother's empathy is likely to be stronger than her self-defence, whereas the father, less schooled in the diminishing returns of parental vanity, either ignores or belittles the daughter's criticism.

The adolescent daughter often does change the mother. Just as she has learned to empathise with her from childhood, just as she has felt her life to be extended by her child's vision, so the mother empathises with her adolescent's growth. The mother too may experience a growth in expectation. She may accept her daughter's criticisms of her life. She may share her daughter's new outlook and excitement. Just as her daughter reconsiders her own beliefs, the mother begins to reconsider hers.

Just as her daughter feels the pressure of choice and decision upon her, so the mother too may realise that she still has choices to make. The sudden uncertainties and self-questioning of adolescence become infectious, from daughter to mother. As the mother sees the daughter coping with challenges of her own life, she may feel stagnant herself, and proclaim with more envy than admiration, "What young people can do these days," or "If only I were young again." But more common than envy is a transfer of energy from adolescent to mother, combined with the released energy no longer needed for a highly dependent child.

NOTES

1. Anthony, 1969; Gagnon and Simon, 1973.
2. Gagnon and Simon, 1973.
3. Darling and Hicks, 1983, p. 245.
4. Freud, 1933.
5. Anthony, 1969.
6. Dinnerstein, 1976; Rubin, 1985; Cohen, 1987; Friday, 1977; 1985.
   By "feminist" I include women writing about women's lives and trying to understand their development within our society, with particular reference to psychological limitations. Strictly speaking, neither Nancy Friday nor Lillian Rubin write as feminists, that is, as campaigners for women's rights.
7. For expansive, bitter views of the mother's envy for the daughter see Cohen, 1987, and Friday, 1977.
8. Henning and Jardim, 1977.
9. Keyes and Coleman, 1983, pp. 443–59. Keyes and Coleman found that high achieving girls show no more sex role conflict than do less ambitious girls.
10. Apter, 1985.
11. Hock and Curry, 1983, pp. 461–70.
12. Friedan, *The Feminine Mystique*, 1963, explained that girls of her generation did not learn to think in terms of a career because there were so few women who acted as role models, and those women who did pursue careers seemed deliberately to deprive themselves of a feminine image.
13. Hence Jessie Bernard, in *The Future of Marriage*, 1972, declared that marriage, which involved a woman's subservience, financial dependence and emotional isolation, which was embedded in a society which sought to deprive women of power, was not good for women;

and hence throughout the women's movement, there has been great concentration on the way in which women's self-esteem, because of her lack of self-power, is undermined from her very first emotional bond with her mother, through an education that begins with fairy tales of helpless maidens, and toys which bind her to domestic and hence powerless roles. Recent studies however indicate that the housewife is not worse off than the working mother in terms of a sense of power, self-respect and confidence. What Jessie Bernard's 1972 assumption did not bargain for was the considerable stress placed upon women who work outside the home, since they continue to do about the same work in it as before.

14. Horner, 1969.
15. Apter, 1985.
16. See Chodorow, 1978, and Gilligan, 1981, for two different but complementary analyses of this relational bias. Chodorow's analysis is theoretical, and largely Freudian, whereas Gilligan's conclusions are based upon empirical research into certain types of problem-solving and moral questioning.
17. Powers and Hauser, 1983.

Chapter 5

MOTHERS ON A SEE-SAW: FRIENDS AND PEERS

Does the mother really play such an important part in her daughter's development? What about the daughter's friends? Do they not become more important to her than the mother? Do they not provide her with a system of values? For many parents the nightmare of adolescence begins when they see their influence and their power at an end. "Peer pressure" is thought to rip the child away from the parents' haven. As children develop strong attachment to friends, the parents' influence and direction diminish. Children's goals go off the rails that were set down by the parents, with such care and at such great expense. The adolescent, it is supposed, no longer shares the parents' hopes, no longer comes under the parents' sway, will no longer "listen" to the parents when making the myriad of small but crucial decisions which go into building her future. Fads or fashions in drug use and time abuse are thought to over take all those meticulous lessons in and examples set of responsibility. The parents become voiceless as the peer group becomes the adolescent's educator and pace setter. These best friends become the parents' greatest enemies.

The view of adolescence as a time when parents lose control to the peers originated with James Coleman's 1961 book *The Adolescent Society* which offered a see-saw dynamic: the stronger the adolescent's attachment to his peers, the less his attachment to his parents; the greater the peers' influence on the child, the lesser the influence of the parents.[1] Nearly thirty years ago, when Coleman's book was written, there seemed to be a good deal of truth in this. A youth movement, or youth culture, seemed determined to reject adult values, goals and expectations. Erikson's presentation of the teenager as turning away from parents and towards a society of peers, of being urged on to a new self definition through them, thereby finding through peer socialisation "irreversible role patterns" and "commitments for life"[2] seemed to confirm the hopes of that youth culture. But even as these ideals were jealously guarded their reality faded.[3] Now the guardians of youth are themselves parents, and many are the parents of adolescents, who on the whole are as traditional, as conforming, as dedicated to common goals, as the parents themselves have become.

Was the earlier social trend really the enactment of a psychodynamic phase? It has been thought, and accepted as fact, that friends play a substitution role in the adolescent's separation from his parents. As the teenager turns away from his parents, and quenches his childhood love for them, he seeks substitute love objects. Friends become the objects of this idealisation and affection. They offer him support, connection and direction, filling the gap caused as he discards his love for his parents. Friends fill the gap without filling it too well, so that with their help he manages a temporary bridge between connection and individuality.[4]

Whatever validity this model has for some young men, however, we simply cannot see a girl's development in terms of her turning away from her mother, shutting off her affection and her identification with her mother, and turning to friends as a half-way station. The strong tie to parents which most girls and many boys carry with them throughout adolescence must be something other than a relic, a residual immaturity. However important a role friends play in the lives of adolescent girls, their mothers dominate them, and the role of friendship should be seen to reflect this domination.

A girl enters adolescence harbouring the assumption that she is like her mother. She learns to resist this assumption. Through the natural push of her individuality, through the abrasion of mismatched responses and expectations, she begins to identify her difference from her mother, all the while directing her mother's gaze, seeking maternal acknowledgement and validation. The mother's role in her identity endeavour is enormous, but the girl, with her self in flux, requires many touchstones, both familiar and new. She needs the stability of her mother's love, and she needs the changing responses and personalities of friends. She needs people who, like her, are unformed yet formative. She fulfils these needs through friends.

FRIENDLY MIRRORS

During adolescence a girl is particularly sensitive to the way in which being with different people brings out different aspects of herself—so much so that she feels herself to be different with different people. We have seen how she describes herself differently in relation to her mother and in relation to her father. Different qualities and characteristics emerge in the different relationship with each parent. Sensitive to this relational identity, an adolescent girl will use friends to balance, to highlight, to flatter herself.

The adolescent girl's search for confirmation and validation is directed towards her mother, and her relationship with her mother comes to be characterised by the strategies of this task. However, there are reasons why, for all her importance, the mother does not find this task easy, and why the daughter seeks help from others, too. The adolescent girl has to work very hard to overcome, and to force her mother to overcome, earlier images of her as a child. She has to overcome pre-established expectations, and, however sensitive and flexible her mother, she has to work against, or feel stuck within, pre-conceptions, sometimes even stereotypes, of her abilities, her character, her potential, her interests. The history which binds them and makes sense of her efforts, also burdens and frustrates her task. While she fights tooth and nail for her mother's acknowledgement of change, development and individuality, she is also eager for a fresh start, a new chance to exercise her emerging self.

The special excitement of adolescent friendship involves a sense of agency. Her childhood loves have been thrust upon her. She can choose her adolescent attachments. She not only uses friends as mirrors, to persuade them to respond to what or who she is, but also chooses mirrors as friends, seeking to understand herself more by looking at girls very similar to her. She not merely looks in the eyes of others to consider her reflection, but also chooses which eyes to use as mirrors. Her self-esteem, self-image and self-ideals direct her choice of friends, which is one reason she stands so loyally by them. Just as her friends may reflect her, they offer proof of her agency, her ability to present herself and form a relationship through that self-presentation.

The switch from old channels of response and reflection to fresh ones, from a parent's view to a friend's, from the self with parent to the self with friend, is frequently described as "relief" or "reprieve" or "a sudden switch of points, where miraculously, you're on the right track." It is in mid-adolescence, when a girl is caught up in her task of correcting the mother's presumption of the girl as child, that the split between friend and parent is greatest.

"It's such a relief, to get out of the house, or just to close the door to my room, and talk to a friend." "My best friend understands me more than my mother." "Sometimes, like after a weekend where I've been home the whole time, just seeing my folks and my brother, I feel like there's a cloud over me, like everything inside me is all grey. I feel I'm so uninteresting that nothing is going to change me. I'm dull, and everything else is dull. And then I go to school on Monday, and I walk through the hall, and I stand by my locker, and my friends will say 'Hi' and at first I'm still sort of stone—well, I still feel like stone, but gradually I'll see that these people I'm talking to really do see me as interesting or different, or just somehow there, and a part of them, and all that dullness washes away, and I'm me again."

Parents "mirror" us as we grow up. They express pleasure or anxiety about what we do. They name our activities as achievements or transgressions. And we develop a sense of our self, as good or bad, as creative or destructive, as strong or weak, with reference to the language of their responses. But as we grow we seek new mirrors, new indicators of self-definition. Especially during adolescence, when we are enamoured of the strangeness, the unexpectedness, the glamour of the self, we seek people outside the family to show us new, unfamiliar ways of seeing ourselves.

The special self-seeking of adolescence is difficult, confusing and often frustrating. Short cuts are tempting, and wherever there is mirroring, there is the possibility of a short cut. Some girls continue a psychological residence with a mother, creating an easy, enclosed friendship between daughter and mother, a stifling "we" in which the daughter fashions herself precisely according to the mother's ideal. Other girls may overuse the mirroring their friends offer. Lacking self-direction and self-definition, suffering from emptiness and aimlessness, a girl may use friendship not to construct her identity, but to beg, borrow or steal a self. Rather than construct an identity, she seeks one ready-made, with those clear boundaries other people often have and we ourselves seem to lack. At other times her social conditions may be such that only a negative or rebellious identity makes any sense. She will give up self-ideals, then, to join a group whose only strength may be its clarity, or its offer of support in a social context which refuses to answer to any of her needs.

These easily recognisable types of adolescent friendships, however, occur only when something has gone badly wrong—when the family or society simply refuses the confirmation and validation the normal adolescent seeks. For the most part adolescent girls describe friendships which link intimacy to self-discovery, to self-definition, and to self-realisation. They seek understanding from a friend, and hence they try to explain themselves, or "how I really feel." They seek the help of friends to allow them to see themselves as others see them, or to gain the confidence that others see them fairly. They use friends to air their hopes for the future, and to test whether these hopes "fit" them in some way, fit their appearance, or fit their personality, or fit their image.

The techniques used to achieve these aims are largely verbal. "What do I do with my friends?" 16-year-old Shelly laughed loudly at my question. "I talk. I mean, we talk about everything. And I mean everything. I tell them how I feel. I tell them what I said to my father, I tell them how cross my mother gets with me, and what I do when she's cross. I tell them why I think my mother's wrong, and how she won't listen to me, or see how I really feel."

"We talk about ourselves," her friend continued. "Shelly and I talk about me a lot. Because I'm so hung up about how I look. And she says to me 'You really look great,' or 'Your skin's not bad!' or she might say, 'Try your hair this way,' or 'Why don't you wear a certain colour?' and I feel like she's putting me together, giving me a spare skin of confidence. I need someone to tell me how I look, otherwise I just feel myself falling to bits. I know it's silly, and we laugh about it, but I'll remember her help all my life." "Sometimes we sit and say how we see each other. Maybe we'll describe what we can imagine each other being when we're grown-up, what kind of life goes with our personality. Sometimes I can see my friends as real high powered, go-getters, you know, even if they don't see themselves like that now. And I'll say, 'Yeah, but I bet you'll change.' And sometimes they say to me 'You'll change when you get married' and they know that makes me mad, but I just concentrate on what I really want, and I'll prove them wrong one day. But my best friend's on my side, and when I tell her how far I want to go—and I mean all the way through law school—she'll just nod and say, 'Sure you will. You can do it,' and together we'll go through all the people we know who have gone to college, and she'll say 'He's not smarter than you,' or something like that, and it'll all seem real close."

Adolescents are well-known for being self-centred. Having lost the innocent selfishness of childhood, they come under criticism for being egotistic, for thinking only of themselves and acting only on their own behalf. But the self-centredness seen in these friendships among adolescent girls, is different from selfishness. The girl uses the friendship to confirm her individuality, and in part to confirm her autonomy—her ability to choose a friend herself, and to establish a friendship herself— and as she develops autonomy she gains a sense of responsibility to other people, in particular to her friends and parents.

DISCIPLINE AND REGULATION OF FRIENDSHIP

Friendship offers support and confirmation, but before it can function in this way, friends have to show themselves capable of interacting effectively. Before these girls can sit down and talk about "everything," and get the responses they need, before they receive confirmation or understanding, they have to be able to make themselves understood. The verbal barrages of female friendship offer practical skills in self-explanation. Finding a friend who understands her involves developing the ability to make herself understood, in ways far more mature than she needs to make her mother, or father or brother or sister, understand her. The parent or sibling knows her by having observed and interacted with her throughout her childhood. She lacks the opportunity to mould their knowledge of her, to select aspects of her newer self and make sure they are seen as more important than her childhood self. Among family, she feels trapped by their clear knowledge of her in many respects, combined with their gross ignorance of the extent to which she has changed and is continuing to change. Among family, she often feels deprived of what she believes to be the most interesting facts about her. Among friends, she will try—and try to learn how—to highlight this more adult self.

Since friendships are usually reciprocal, she will have to learn not only how to present herself so as to get support, but also how to show effective support for her friend. This—even if it is only offering advice—allows her to adopt a more mature role, and once again, to experience her own agency. However close she is to her mother, however much use she puts her mother to as a sounding board for ideas, as a source of support and confidence and understanding, her relationship never has the thrilling reciprocity of friendship.

Even as this new mature agency in friendship, and the support found through friends, bolsters self-confidence, it can also ground the confidence, give it a centre, a realistic gravity. The adolescent has a tendency to self-aggrandizement which, for the girl, presents both a good deal of pleasure and a good deal of revulsion. What emerged from hesitant and not always articulate complaints and comparisons, was that a girl could enjoy a conversation with her mother in which she accepted praise and compliments ("You're prettier than any of your friends," "You're as smart as anyone I know," "You have it in you—

go for it"), but afterwards suffer a surge of anger, declaring
that there was "something yucky" about the hyperbolic expectations and evaluations. "She gets so excited about me, and I
think 'great' and then I think, 'This is rubbish. This is just a
stupid mother talking.' She's looking at me and saying I'm
great, I'm better than my friends, but she doesn't even know
my friends. I'm better than them because I'm her daughter,
that's all." The level of narcissism, it seems, is not regulated
when a girl speaks about herself and her future to her mother.
She seeks from friends not only a complimentary reflection but
also a regulating, realistic one.

All adolescents indulge in daydreams. They are a tonic to
uncertainty, and one of the perks of a transitional phase. Not
knowing what she is or who she will become, she is anxious;
the daydream soothes her anxiety. Not feeling herself to have
definition, she can become anything, and the fantasy allows her
to enjoy possibilities without risk and effort. Daydreaming can
be a support. Sometimes it is a necessary support, putting disappointment and frustration in a perspective which allows the
girl to continue making efforts, and prevents her from seeing
hope as ridiculous. But she fears daydreams too, in particular
because of the way in which they might impede her capacity
to form relationships with others. A similar fear, and a similar
attempt at self-control, will persuade her to keep her mother at
a distance, and be highly critical of her, if she thinks the mother's admiration is too easily won.

Within a family context, a child is either thoroughly
known, thoroughly familiar, "just like" another family member—or she is unique, marvellous, forever amazing. The teenage girl, too, vacillates between finding herself wonderful and
strange on the one hand, and dull, empty or totally unremarkable on the other. Much of the conversation among adolescent
girl friends seems to be an attempt to anchor dreams to a reality, to see the future through her present. Also, the girls are
intent upon testing their sense of their own uniqueness. Struck
in amazement by her new ideas, her new capacity for imagining and thinking, the young girl tries to discover, through
her friends, whether these thoughts are shared, or shareable.

Friends are used to prevent her from coming adrift in her fantasies.

A friend can do this not by keeping her "down on the ground" or "in her proper place" but by sharing even some of her outlandish or extreme hopes. By offering her fantasies some reality, a friend helps forge a link between daydream and her present self. With this link in place she can work towards the realisation of her fantasies. But it is not only a friend's sympathetic response that helps solidify the fantasies; it is the reciprocal process of hope sharing, "I love talking about our future. [My friend] really admires me, and I admire her. So that when I see her as turning out well, doing real well, I guess I can think I might do well to, that things might turn out well for me." This was presented almost as "tit for tat": my friend thinks well of me, so I'll think well of her, and if we pool our admiration, if we suppose we're both right, then if I see her future as favourable, I can see mine as favourable too.

These gifts of exchange are common. Compliments are reciprocated (on average they are reciprocated very quickly, the reciprocating compliment following within three minutes of the original one) as part of the good manners of friendship, just as confidences are reciprocated, but with a different rationale. If one friend knows another's secret, and the friend herself has imparted no secret, then the more confiding one is more at risk of betrayal. Even if a friend who knows her secret does not in fact betray her, a girl feels herself to be at great disadvantage if she is the only one who imparts confidences. "I used to tell [my friend] everything. I knew she was reserved. That was one of the things I liked about her. But when I realised how little she was ever going to let on about herself, I got—well, I got a little uneasy. Then I heard she had broken up with her boyfriend, and started dating someone else. I'd seen her the day before. I'd been talking to her the day before, and she hadn't even whispered a thing about it. I asked her why she hadn't said anything. 'Well, I wasn't sure how it would all work out,' she told me. All right. Fine. She can play her cards close to her chest. That's her right. But this kind of reserve gives me the creeps. There I was, talking about me, and she didn't say a word about her, just because she wasn't sure how things would turn out. I never know how anything's going to turn out! I'm not comfortable talking to a friend like that." Friendship is based upon exchange. Without exchange there is no trust. Exchanging secrets and being "frank" or "open" are apparently more important even than keeping secrets and offering compliments.

THE COURSE OF FRIENDSHIP THROUGH ADOLESCENCE

Since friendship and development are so closely linked in the adolescent years, it is not surprising that the emphasis and characteristics of friendship vary during the different phases of adolescence. In late childhood, just before puberty, girls form touchingly romantic friendships, involving quite diffuse thoughts ("She has such a nice house. I love the pink carpets. She has wallpaper in her room that's like velour." "She's so pretty." "She wears lovely silver ear-rings, and her hair clips always match her dress") and a good deal of physical affection. These girls walk home from school together arm-in-arm, complimenting a friend on her soft skin, her smooth or curly hair, her long eyelashes. They see one another every day for weeks or months, and then the affection stops. It stops quite suddenly, without a quarrel, without a visible cooling off period, without hurt feelings or embarrassment on either side. What was "on" is now "off."

Afterwards there is often a kind of amnesia—not that the 10- or 11-year-old forgets she has had such a close friendship, but that she needs to be reminded. "Where's Cindy?" I asked a 10-year-old girl, who, three weeks before, had regularly been seen walking out of the school gate holding Cindy's hand. The pair had been described by her mother as "inseparable." "What?" she looked at me, then looked around the schoolyard. "Oh. Over there, I guess."

It is not that these girls are incapable of tracking their feelings, or of being hurt by a change in favour. Girls of 9 or 10 can be highly sensitive in their approach to friends, and they justify their friendships in terms which may lack sophistication but which nonetheless make sense: "I like playing with her," or even simply "I play with her a lot." They move away from friendships, or avoid them because "she says things that hurt my feelings," "she never lets me do what I want to," "the games she plays are boring." There is some continuity and stability which give so much meaning to friendship in later development, but these tend to matter less to younger children. By the time a girl is 9 she has moved a long way from the very young child's "I don't like her anymore," "If you don't give me that I won't be your friend," syndromes, but she accepts a fickleness among friends, and hence will see no contradiction in adoring a girl one day and feeling indifferent the next. "I don't like her anymore," seems to require only brief explanations, ranging from "I just don't," "She annoys me," to "She teases me," or "I find her tiring." The girl will carry this incipient sophistication over into early adolescence without much change other than an increased need to talk about herself—in particular to hear her friend's opinion of her. She tends to accept this opinion at face value, and disillusion tends to be reciprocal: if her friend's opinion of her diminishes, then she will lose interest in her friend.

A few years later, in mid-adolescence, girls' friendships change, and girls are proud of this change. Their new capacities for intimacy and sharing are seen as an achievement. Fourteen-year-old girls look back upon previous friendships and see them with diminished importance. "I used to care about being popular, and just worry whether people were liking me." "I used to let my mother arrange all these play times, and when she'd ask me whether I wanted to play with someone I'd just shrug. I mean I really didn't know. It didn't make much difference." "I used just to want a friend to spend some time with. Now I don't need a playmate. I don't worry about being alone in the afternoon. But if I invite someone to my house, it's because I want to talk."

As soon as girls reach mid-adolescence there is a shift of emphasis from a friend as someone to play with to a friend as someone to talk to. During this phase of adolescence there is a very close and clear resemblance between their ideals for friendship and their relationship with their mothers. What they like doing best with their mothers—unstructured activities which allow for talking, some of which is casual and "goes nowhere" but is "just fun" and some of which leads to revelations and discoveries—is what they like doing best with their friends. As this sharing of confidences, and this aim towards reaching an understanding of the self, is central to friendships, trust and loyalty are highly valued. These qualities go hand-in-hand with the reciprocal self-exposures, the sharing of secrets, the bolstering of confidence. What is told to a friend is told in confidence, and is meant only for sympathetic ears. The worst thing a friend can do is betray a secret, or use something she said "to laugh at me behind my back."

Trust involves trust to keep a confidence, trust to be sympathetic or understanding, trust to remain friendly and constant in affection. They need to trust a friend to be accepting, and place great value on her "not being shocked by anything I say." "There's only so much I can tell my Mom," a 15-year-old explained. "I know I could tell her everything if I had to, if I were in trouble or something, but I couldn't just tell her and explain things, say, about sex to her, without everything getting very deep. Or I couldn't tell her about something bad or real stupid I'd done, without making her real upset. With a friend, I can say 'I did this really dumb thing,' like using someone else's homework and getting in dutch [trouble] with the chemistry teacher, or driving someone's car, or even having a fight with a friend, when I know it's my fault because I lied to her, or said something mean. If I tell all this to a friend, she's not going to say 'Philly, how could you?' And it's not going to stay with her, and keep bringing it up. I don't have to worry about her mentioning it every time I get a low grade, or fight with my brother or something. She's just not going to worry about my character, like my Mom does."

These high standards of acceptance and trust in friendship were often met, or met often enough so that many girls did trust and were trusted by their friends. Along with trusting and being trustworthy came a cluster of personal qualities. Among friends a girl was likely to describe herself as outgoing and relaxed. Among friends a girl invariably considered herself trustworthy, and prepared for friendship, and therefore she described herself as open, accepting, honest and trusting.

However high a value each girl placed on trust, and however certain each girl was that she herself and her friend were trustworthy, trust was bound to fail at some time, in some friendship. The most common and most passionate complaint about a friend was that she had "betrayed" her. Betrayal always involved a secret kept from her or a secret revealed. A friend might betray her by "flirting with this boy she knew I liked and getting him to take her out and not telling me anything about it." Or it might be "going behind my back and telling someone else exactly what I told her, and she knew I didn't want anyone else to hear." Or a betrayal could be "planning to run for Class Secretary without saying anything to me, though she told tons of other people." To guard against the failure of friendship through betrayal the girls set up a hierarchy of friendship, with inner circles ("my good friends") and highly select audiences ("That, I'd only tell to my best friend") which are subject to many shifts, and to redefinitions, so that a "best friend" may find herself giving way to a "best best friend" or a friend may be honoured by a confidence "that I wouldn't even tell to my best friend" as the sweep of intimacy gets underway.

Most girls say they have been disappointed by a friend, that they have experienced the let-down of discovering someone is not being sufficiently trustworthy. But few girls broke off the friendship for that reason. Sometimes the friend was demoted from best friend to just "still a friend." Whereas boys tended either to ignore a betrayal or to move on to another friend or group of friends, viewing his choice in terms of ignorance or avoidance, a girl was likely to forgive a friend who betrayed her. Nevertheless, she seldom let the transgression pass without saying anything. Whereas a boy might say "Forget it," and either decide to "act as though it didn't happen," or decide he doesn't care that much, redefining the betrayal as something of little importance, a girl will seldom forget and forgive. She will talk it out.

"I wanted to know why she went to Diane with all that

stuff about me and Rich," explained a 16-year-old girl who was describing a friend's betrayal which involved her telling a mutual friend about an argument (about whether or not to have sex) she was having with her boyfriend. "That was private. I wanted to know what I was supposed to think. Was she just nasty, or was she angry? When she was sitting in my bedroom talking to me, was she planning to tell Diane what I was telling her? Or did it just sort of come out, when she was talking to Diane? I know that can happen. You want to hold something back but it's in your mind and you just can't. So I guess I have to realise she's that kind of person, and I can either keep her as my friend, or never speak to her again, which is silly, I guess, because we've been friends a long time. I just have to try to keep that in mind about her, that she's not too good at keeping a secret. So there will be certain things I'll try not to tell her. And I shouldn't have told her that anyway. It really didn't sound right as it was coming out. I didn't want her tracking my sex-life. What if I do decide to go to bed with him? I don't want to tell her all about that. I was just trying to get some kind of support for my decision. You know, he was on my case, saying I'm uptight, I'm not this, I'm too much of that, and none of my arguments made sense. I could get my mother on my side, but that would be too easy. She'd be more than on my side! She'd start saying I shouldn't be seeing him if he keeps on at me like that. So it was stupid to tell her in the first place. I guess it's all too juicy to keep it to yourself."

Under the pressure of betrayal, and the accompanying threat that she may lose a friend, she views the problem in a variety of ways. Why did the friend betray her? Was it intentional, or was it a slip? If it was a slip then this is understandable. She knows how it can happen. She has felt it happen to her, and decides it doesn't mean that her friend is essentially inconsiderate. The fact that it was the kind of information to slip out means that she should not have given her friend the information in the first place. It was too private, after all, and hence too tempting a piece of gossip. So the friend is forgiven after it has been established that "she didn't mean any harm," that "it just happened," and that "she's sorry and feels bad about it." In talking it over, not only does she see it from her friend's point of view, but also she changes her point of view, so that the betrayal is not so great.

In speaking about friendships girls repeatedly mention trust, which involves not only being able to keep a confidence, but also sympathetic understanding. In addition, there was great importance placed on trusting a friend not to be "shocked by anything I say." This did not mean that her friend would never show surprise at a confidence, but that she would not jump to the conclusion that she was "no good" or "rotten" as a result of the information offered. But when I observed their conversations, the confidence-sharing was overshadowed by a large amount of advice-seeking and advice-offering, and this advice was in the area of emotion management. Teenage girls have a distinctive subculture which involves plotting strategies. What should I do, the query may be, when another girl is being snobbish, off-hand, or seems to be bearing a grudge? Should I confront her, should I give her a "dose of her own medicine," or just leave her alone, and hope for things to get better? If I want a boy to notice me, do I flirt with a friend of his, or flirt with him directly? What is the best strategy with the physics teacher? Is it better to appear highly serious, or is he impressed by girls with a bit of swing? Often girls discuss such strategies with their mothers, but this does not prevent them from going over the same ground with a friend, who often knows the territory and the personalities much better. What is more, they thoroughly enjoy discussions like this, eliciting and offering advice, pooling information about friends, teachers, clothes, make-up and hairstyles. The activity itself is valued, and all information seems interesting, even when it is discounted or rejected. Such conversations brim with excitement, and the girls give the impression of working hard, even hectically, to come to the right answer. They also indulge in gleeful presentations of doing precisely the wrong thing, or describing excruciatingly embarrassing scenarios which they find hilarious.

In a more serious vein is discussion of emotion management within the self.[5] How should I deal with this horrible attraction I have to someone who doesn't like me? How am I going to deal with a friend who has hurt my feelings? All of us, once we are past the age of 2 or so, try to manage our feelings, not only in the sense of controlling their expression, as a necessity of our lives as social beings, but also because we "can't live with" or don't like certain feelings and are more comfortable with others. We try to get out of a depression, or get over a hopeless love affair, or keep a level head within a relationship, or "keep a grip on my priorities even when lots of other exciting things are happening" and a good deal of advice about how to do this is offered and received in mid-adolescent friendships.

Virtually all relationships of this sort are among girls only. There is a far greater homogeneity among girls' attitudes towards friendships than among boys' attitudes. Some boys do discuss personal matters with friends. Some declare "Never!" or "Not bloody likely," when asked if they spoke to friends about their deepest feelings, for example, towards a parent or a girl friend. For the most part boys choose friends as "buddies" or "mates," as a person or a group to go places with or do things with. Many boys speak of themselves as being guarded, critical or even dishonest with friends, whereas for a girl, to feel this way would be to contradict the terms of friendship.

A girl sees no point in having a friend who makes her feel dishonest, or phony, or critical. When a girl realises that she does feel uncomfortable, or "not herself" with a friend, she admits either that the friendship "just isn't there anymore. We see things too differently nowadays," or that "I guess I was never her friend for the right reason. I wanted to go around with someone popular like her. I feel rotten about that, but it was never really a friendship." If a girl does not "feel right" about a friendship, that is, if she is not happy with its sincerity, honesty and authenticity, she feels "wrong" or even guilty, or judges that "it isn't working out."

The techniques used for emotion management within the friendships are also typically female. Sometimes the advice is on the "butch" side, in that it involves suppressing a feeling by ignoring it. "Just forget him," or "Don't think about it," are among these more direct techniques, but unlike a true butch attitude, the advice never stops there. The initial attack on an emotion by neglect is followed by a more positive series of strategies. "He's not worth it," or "She's always had a high opinion of herself. She shouldn't bother you," or "It's embarrassing, but everyone will forget it in a day or two," or "You shouldn't feel you have to do that for her. You don't owe her that much, anyway," are examples of re-descriptions of the person or event or obligation which is proving troublesome. The re-descriptions diminish the importance of her behaviour, or take the sting of regret or anxiety out of it, or try to manage the emotion by defining it as a limited, perishable thing.

A friend's technique in emotion management tends to be different from a mother's, whose "Never mind dear" is not so much a direct attack on the problem but a gesture of comfort. "Don't worry about that," "Well, you're home, safe and sound now," "I'm here, I love you," "Let's do something to cheer you up," all have a compelling effect. But the adolescent girl sometimes resents this as making her feel too "cozy" or as "muffling" her, or as one girl said, "She brings me in, when I want to go out." In this area especially the girl needs a friend as well as a mother, and quite consciously will go to each, knowing that her mother will soothe her, by reminding her that she is loved. The mother may also, however, through her anxiety and her overwhelming sympathy, have no patience with a daughter's depression. She will tell her abruptly to "snap out of it," or "pull yourself together," or, very common among middle-class mothers, "Goodness gracious, just think how much you have to be thankful for." The daughter's unhappiness is too hot for the mother to handle, and so she pushes it away. Even if the mother does offer advice in the same vein as a friend, the advice from the mother will be treated far more critically, because "she doesn't really see how it is at school," or "she doesn't even know the guy. How can she tell me how to handle him?" On the other hand, though the friend's advice is not always followed, it is not rejected in the same way, partly because adolescents have higher standards of etiquette towards friends than towards mothers, but also because they believe that a friend is more likely to know "what she is talking about."

In the intimacy of friendship girls do not only expose their feelings to one another, they seek to change their feelings, and seek help in changing those feelings. The sharing of ideas and sharing of perspective is sometimes used as a means of changing, handling, managing their feelings. To see something in a different way, to have a different perspective on it, may also change the ways one feels about something or someone. Friends deliberate: "Let's look at something in a different way," or "Let's work on re-describing someone, so that he isn't worth the love/she isn't worth the trouble/her insults or affection don't count for much because of what she is."

There is an enormous emphasis in these friendships on helping to make a friend's emotions tolerable to her, or putting her behaviour in a sympathetic and acceptable light. "You did it for the best," or "You have to think of yourself too," or "He'll get over it," are among the frequent remarks cropping up which show the consolatory function of conversations. Adolescent girls suffer enormous anxiety about the effects of their behaviour. The anxiety is often social (Did I say the right thing? Did I make a fool of myself? Will he think I'm stupid now?) though it extends to a moral concern, usually about whether or not she has hurt someone ("I never imagined she'd take what I said that way. I didn't mean it the way she said. She shouldn't have got so upset." "I want to break up with him, but I don't want to hurt him.") This anxiety is aired among friends, when a girl often hears that what she said or did was all right—it was the best that could be done; she was just being honest—after all, she was doing what was best for her, and she had to do that (this was a constant reminder, a push against the anxiety that it was not all right to think about yourself); even if she had hurt someone, the hurt was not permanent, or even long-lasting, and anyway "everyone has to get hurt like that sometimes."

ILLUSION STRATEGY IN FRIENDSHIP

Friends support and mirror a girl. She trusts them, confides in them and believes herself a worthy, and therefore trustworthy, friend. She believes herself, in their company, to be as she is

with her mother—"open" and "honest." She looks with genuine puzzlement upon a boy's sense of himself as "guarded" or
"critical" or "evasive" among friends. Yet at the same time she
herself engages in behaviour which, while not quite dishonest,
is certainly not honest.

Linked to the new adolescent self-consciousness, the
awareness of an emerging self which has value and meaning, is
the sense of a self that is observed. An imaginary audience,
fickle in its assessment, but constantly observant, both pleases
and plagues the adolescent girl. Therefore, when a girl seeks a
friend as a mirror, she does not merely seek a true reflection;
she also tests out possible appearances. Friends can mirror not
only in the context of acknowledgement and confirmation, but
also to register the success of her self-presentation.

Self-disclosure is crucial to adolescent girl friendships. In
conversations with girls about friendships they always say how
much they value "talking about things," or "sharing things
that we're going through together." But in the initial stages of
the development of skills for self-disclosure, she must also learn
to conceal herself in new ways. She is interested in acquiring
information from a friend ("I want to hear all about it," "Tell
me exactly what happened") but she is also interested in con-
cealing information she does not want to "get around" or revealing information which puts her in a good light, or because
she has some impressive news. She may be cheerful in order to
conceal disappointment or depression. She may learn how to
steer the conversation away from certain questions, which she
does not want to answer. A girl may ask a friend how she did
on an exam, in order to be asked the same question in turn, so
that she can reveal that she did very well. She may manipulate
a group of people so that they observe her meeting a boy. She
may steer the conversation to a particular teacher, where a personal success will then be discussed. She will arrange to be
telephoned when visited by another friend, to prove her popularity.

Girls in the early phases of adolescence are masters of these
"strategic interactions."[6] At the very time they are learning the
value of sincerity and the skills of self-expression, of agency

through sympathy and advice, of trust in friendship and appreciative mirroring of one another, they are also learning new ways of showing-off, or presenting themselves as they would wish to be, with some disregard for how they are.

In pre-adolescence, because the concept of the self is vague, self-presentations will be fragmented, and amount to not much more than "showing-off." Between friends, unless there are grounds for defensiveness, this kind of showing-off is inclusive rather than exclusive: they will be playing "being grown-up" together, rather than the "I'm more grown up than you" which will occur when the game falls apart, or between sisters who have a competitive scheme built in to their love and their play. In early adolescence, when the self, and with it the fantasy self, are emerging, friendship may provide an opportunity to test the fantasy self to see if it has any credibility, to see what behaviour comes off. In these early stages lying is not unusual, because it is hard for girls to come to terms with just what they are, in contrast to what they would like to be. They often feel they have to offer more than they actually have, to appear to be other than they actually are, for someone to like them or even to notice them. To these ends they can pretend, and they can downright lie—though most find that lying is not "worth it." Lying is accompanied by a good deal of anxiety, not only because there is the worry about being found out, but because lying excludes them from the very process they are engaging in. For by mid-adolescence—that is, by 15 or 16, these strategies have normally been superseded by the sincere aims of friendship, by trust and loyalty, by the desire to help a friend through trying times, or to sort out mistakes together. Looking back, many girls say, "I used to care about being popular, but now I choose my friends for more personal reasons," or "I used to care what everyone thought, but now I care more about being understood by my friends."

Presentation of a genuine self generally, by mid-adolescence, overtakes presentation as an exercise in pretence—at least for girls. Boys' tendency to present a fantasy self, and to use friends as audience for an imagined or wished-for self, lingers throughout adolescence.[7] It seems, however, that when a boy lies in order to present a false, or imagined self, he does so easily, half-heartedly, without regret, and without much likelihood of being discovered, since the detail of conversation among his friends does not get so much attention. The girl who carries on lying into mid-adolescence, however, has a rougher time. Girls are highly particular about precisely what a friend said about herself, her family, or other friends. Girls remember clearly what someone has said (or believe they do) and find it difficult to forgive someone who has "conned" them. They feel "cheated" when a friend lies to them, though the lie seldom has actually cheated them out of anything. Being so trusting in a friend's company, they feel "foolish" or "astounded" when they discover a friend has lied. They measure themselves against one another. They put emotional energy into a friend's problems. They are deeply offended when they discover that they have been given false information.

The girl who continues to lie throughout middle adolescence cheats herself of opportunities to test the reality of her maturing self. She simply constructs fictions about herself. This sets her apart from other girls who are working hard to develop genuine techniques of self-presentation. The liar is so sure that she is unable to present a strong image, that she is willing to trade off the benefits of a brief success-image for subsequent humiliation. Connie, 15, who also suffered from the eating disorder bulimia, described her compulsion, humiliation, and terror of inner emptiness: "I can't help making up things. Other girls always have something interesting to say, and seem to have so much going for them, and going on around them, so I get ideas from them, and once I start making something up, I keep going and going. Nothing can stop me." When she made a good impression she felt a glow of light, and she would say to herself "They like me now," or "They're impressed right now," and even if they found out later that she was lying, she would still have this scrap of time, in which she had shone. She gobbled up these titbits as her only diet. Her self-doubt was so great that these tiny moments were essential to her self-esteem. She assumed that genuine self-reinforcement was not worth seeking.

What makes it worse for the adolescent girl who lies about herself to friends is that though she presents a false self, she does not develop a false relationship with her friends. She genuinely admires her friends, and has real affection for them. But the friends' discovery of a lie—and since there are so many, it is highly likely one will be discovered—puts not only her self-esteem at grave risk, but also negates any genuine work she has done in establishing the friendship. The lies undermine all her attempts to grow through friendship, and threaten her with isolation and shame. She knows this, yet compulsively seeks that moment of glory which, in her view, is the best she can do.

The liar's friends may also be genuinely fond of her, and however angry, startled, and foolish they feel when they have discovered her, most girls of this age have immediate empathy with silly or stupid behaviour. This empathy, however, may make them harsh judges. "I would never do that. Not now. It's so childish." Having passed into a stage of greater control, and being able now to take responsibility for what they say, the more mature girls are outraged by someone who appears to be at their developmental level, but in fact is far behind.

"Why did she say that?" Connie's friend demanded when she discovered some senseless lie (about what had happened to her during a family holiday) she had told. Connie had said that she had hurt her leg during a riding accident. She described the incident on the telephone, and her friend related it to her mother, who then called Connie's mother to express concern and sympathy. The thing which so puzzled Connie's friend was that the lie was bound to be discovered. Even if her mother had not telephoned Connie's mother, Connie would have had to attend school the following week. How could she then maintain the fiction that she had been badly hurt? "Oh," Connie shrugged when I asked her. "I maybe would have made a good recovery—you know, surprised the doctors and all, but still had some pain." She grinned awkwardly. "I don't know."

The liar's friends feel duped, and are angry because they have been taken in; but girls of this age value compassion, and do not want to hold a grudge. When the shock and anger subside they often take steps towards forgiving—though not for-getting—the liar's transgression. "I wish she hadn't done it. It floors me—why did she do it? What can I believe now? Did she want attention? My Mom says she wanted attention. But what a stupid way to go about it. And my attention! She has that anyway. She only has to pick up the phone. She can talk to me. I'm listening. I guess she has problems I don't under-stand. I still like her, but it changes everything. I don't know where I am with her. And what's real odd is that she's really a very sincere person. She's not sneaky, or anything like that. I don't know. I always feel she's up front—showing me what she really feels. So it's confusing. And I feel bad because I got her into trouble by telling my Mom and my Mom ringing hers."

The adolescent girl who lies to her friends, who "makes up things" is not, as Connie's friend noted, insincere. She is brimful of need for her friends' responses and for her friends' admiration and attention, but has so little confidence in her ability to earn their regard that she takes highly inefficient short-cuts. She does not actually lack self-esteem, but rather she lacks the ability to test and build it. Coming from an ex-tremely high achieving family, Connie had—and had thrust upon her—excessively high expectations of herself combined with a fear that in her present, real world, she would never quite meet those expectations. A parallel between her behav-iour with her friends and with her mother could be seen in the deliberate effort she made to present herself as successful with her mother. As soon as her mother came home from work, she followed her into the kitchen, and while her mother unpacked the shopping she had stopped to do between work and home, Connie began to relate stories about her day in school which showed her to have "shone" in front of the class.

"Mrs. Campbell wanted to know who could think of a way of combining science and maths, and I said you could make mathematical models of biological systems." Connie's mother stopped putting away groceries to beam at her daugh-ter. Thus encouraged, Connie continued to cite tiny incidents of her supremacy: a friend had tried to copy her French exam,

a boy she didn't like was probably going to ask her out but
she fled into the lavatory, a teacher indicated special approval:
"He was talking to the assistant principal and just stopped and
turned and said right in the hall, 'I liked that paper of yours.' "

Whether or not Connie was lying when she was speaking
to her mother, it was clear that there was some similarity of
pattern in her "disclosures" to her friends and to her mother.
Whereas another 16-year-old girl said, "I never feel that
something's really happened until I tell my Mum about it,"
Connie seemed to feel that if she told her Mum something, it
really had happened. Communication for her was a hectic self-
presentation. Success depended upon the momentary response.
Clearly she lacked the belief that her mother would accept her
as she was, would love her for herself. She had given up on
this without giving up her need for her mother's and her
friends' acceptance. Her compromise involved the haphazard
construction of a self-image, not in the usual sense of an image
one has of oneself, but as an image one sells to others. She was
sincere in that lying for her was not a disguise, but a filling or
filling up. She is "sincere" because her responses to her friends
are indeed genuine: she lies because she sees their reality as a
miracle. Thus, her friends are torn between her deception and
her sincerity. They are sufficiently sympathetic and responsive
to shift their notions of betrayal and trust to forgive her. Usually it is the liar who cannot accept forgiveness. Her need to
shine is what got her into trouble in the first place. She cannot
therefore tolerate the humiliation of being unmasked. She is the
one who will turn away from a friendship when her lies are
disclosed, and seek another, more gullible audience—or, gullible herself, she may believe that her friends have forgotten her
transgression, and use the same tactics over and over again to
solicit the response she desires.

SIBLINGS AS FRIENDS

Friends can offer enormous help in mapping out the tricky ter-
rain of one's emotional life. What is it appropriate to feel? What
should I call to mind to make me feel differently? These are

issues passed from friend to friend, like dough at a bread-making session, but a girl can only make use of a friendship in this way if she already is fairly strongly individuated, if different and changing ideas and different viewpoints are acceptable and non-threatening in her family. If she already has some sense of herself as an independent mind, and if she already takes responsibility for her emotions—if she sees them as hers to regulate, to deal with—then she can make further strides towards individuation in friendship. If her mother strongly regulates her thoughts with "feeling rules" and "feeling reminders" and "feeling comforts," showing her that different ways of looking at things are "not allowed," then even if the girl has friends, and speaks openly to friends, the effect of these discussions will be superficial. If, in her home she is told repeatedly, "We don't say things like that," "No daughter of mine behaves like that," she will believe that different views, ideas and behaviour threaten her mother and her attachment to her mother. She may want to protect her mother, or herself, from an intolerable level of anxiety which her mother registers when she says, "You can't mean that," or "You know you'll be sorry you said that one day," or when any expression of individuality is met with not quite suppressed tears or sulking or silent anger. Friendship, or the way in which girls mould and establish friendships, can be of great use, but only if there is already work done between the girl and her mother, granting her the independence to move forward.

When the family is so constricted by a dominant member—usually a parent—there are still possible ways out. The daughter can use her spunk to fight it out with the mother. She can change her mother. She can ignore her mother, and find support or confirmation elsewhere. She may know her mother well enough to spot some "safe areas" wherein she can remain communicative with her. Most adults have developed these "spot skills" with their parents whereby they know there are certain topics of conversation which they must avoid if they are to avoid bad feeling. They know, too, that they can expect support in some areas of their lives, and that in other areas their parents will be thick- or pig-headed. These narrowing methods of communication, which control and preserve our love, are not often practised by adolescents who retain the emotional greed of children, but when necessary they can be developed early. Another very common safety valve to protect against an enclosing or diminishing mother is sibling friendship.

A sibling can help maintain a critical and independent vantage point. A sibling is so much better than a friend because the sibling already knows so much about the family, and shares the list of forbidden and permitted things. Among friends, complaints about mothers are simple. They are complaints which can be easily shared, as though these girls have not quite appreciated the enormous differences within families. "We all have our problems," or "Yeah, I know, my Mum's the same," can actually block a sense of sympathy, when a girl feels she has something highly disturbing (often described by her as "dirty" or "ugly") in her home. With a sibling, however, complaints about a parent can develop an extraordinary sophistication.

Among friends, girls do a fair amount of complaining about their mothers, but the gripes are superficial, and a little bit of an act. Their standards of sauciness and irreverence are often met in this way. It is rare, however, for a girl to approach a friend with problems about her father. She might bring her complaints about him to her mother, but she is usually frustrated by the mother's response. Either the mother tries to explain the father to her ("That's just his way," "He doesn't mean any harm," "He needs you to tell him how you feel"), which indicates that the mother is taking the father's side, and not giving her complaint a proper hearing; or the mother agrees with her, and arouses the irritation a child is likely to feel when one parent complains about another.

In late adolescence, when the girl's powers of description and explanation are more developed, and when the sympathies of her friends are broadened, she has more opportunity to judge her family's control strategies, and to begin to steer clear of them. But in mid-adolescence, when she is still confounded by these techniques, she can get enormous help from a sibling. Many girls look to a sister or a brother as a great reprieve from intensity and constriction with their parents. The capacity girls now have for friendship can be extended to build on the strong (whether positive or negative) relationship already developed with a sibling.

Somehow, at about the age of 5, I had gone from being my sister's adored baby who was allowed to share a chair with her, who could sneeze gobs of mucus with her saying only "poor thing," to a menace who was ritually greeted with a fist pounding the crown of my head, and a response of "stupid" to every query I put to her and to every piece of art work I brought as a gift. Whereas once my drawings and early speech were a delight to her, I found that everything that issued from me was bound to be "dumb." Whereas once she proudly pointed me out to teachers and friends, I was now an embarrassment, and even my presence in the schoolyard was hotly resented since it implicated her in some degrading connection. I was left holding the love she had inspired in me as a baby, but now it knocked hard against her compulsive abuse.

Secretly, however, with the secrecy of deliberation, I grew to feel a kind of superiority, since it was she who in adolescence knocked so clumsily against my mother. I took notes, learned lessons, and steered clear of my mother in certain areas, learned how to keep things private—especially sexual feelings, or feelings of admiration and adoration of others, which my mother was so adept at reducing. But my sister offered different protection, too. In adolescence we were closer to being equal, though perhaps the trick of our new compatibility was that we each felt superior to the other, and kept these feelings secret, protecting one another from our certain judgement. Whatever the reason, the childhood irritation and rejection we had flung upon one another suddenly changed. In retrospect all the physical fighting looked like fun, like horse play, and we re-created our childhood memories so that only the strong affection emerged from the mass of feelings we had hurled at one another.

The role my sister and I played, and continue to play, in one another's bid for sanity, in those life-long attempts to free oneself from inherited but useless patterns of response, evolved during our verbal gymnastics in adolescence, when we worked so hard to define the causes of our anger and frustration. The greatest surprise and pleasure of mid-adolescence was being able to make use of one another in this way. The quarrels we each had, in our very different ways, with our mother took on a smaller, more circumscribed area when we shared our information about her. Our mother's anger, too, which fell on the house like a bank of fog, was thinner, and we had more power within it, because we could turn to one another with our common complaints. Never feeling disloyal, because it remained within the family, we could paint our parents in the most grotesque fashion. So used to this did I become, that I was amazed at the pain and outrage I felt if anyone else, even a less close relative, disparaged our mother in any way. I had not needed to consider my sense of loyalty, since my copious criticisms had been for my sister's ears only.

My presumption of the usefulness of a sibling is so strong, that it took me a while to hear different stories from the adolescents I studied. I waited for complaints about siblings to reveal themselves as superficial, yet many of them were not. Siblings clearly have the power to be confirming and supportive, but they also have the potential to be threatening—not only within the home, as rivals for parental attention, but also as a power to diminish a sense of personal worth, no matter how far one gets from home. Some people throughout their lives measure themselves against a sibling, seeing achievement and success, sexuality and beauty, and social relationships as having point and purpose only in so far as these out-distanced them from a sibling. At 21, Clare began describing her 23-year-old sister by describing her sister's view of her: "She's so good at putting me down—what a knack! We were both home last summer and we were there sitting in the garden, and my parents were so pleased because I had just got a part in a play. It was a small part, but it was a good company, and I don't get parts very often. So we were talking about that, and then [my sister] stands up and claps her hands together and says, 'Daddy, you're going to be 60 next month. I'm going to plan you a real big party.' So he goes all soppy. 'Oh, you're so sweet, you're too good. . . .' And I'm sitting thinking, 'Great. Next month I'll be in Sacramento. I'll be on stage every night. I won't be able to come. It will be her gift to him, and I won't be able to share it, because I have finally landed a very small job. What could I say? I couldn't complain that she was being mean by planning a party for my Dad. I sat in the garden chair and kept smiling. She wasn't looking at me, of course. She was all flushed and happy with her idea, and they kept talking about that.'' There is sometimes a wilful freezing of one's views of a sibling, a desire to diminish her, to devalue her, because the sense of competition is so great, that anything more than denigration would be threatening. "I give my sister a wide berth, that's the only way I manage to get on with her. Every time I hear about another prize she's won or another high mark she's got, I feel as though someone up there has decided once again to give me a big kick in the stomach. There's nothing to her. She has no more depth than a two-inch stream. It's not only me. My friends can't stand her, either. But of course my Dad thinks she's wonderful, and then what's wrong with me? What gets me is the way she prevents [my parents] from seeing what I'm really like, because all the time they're asking 'Why aren't you like her?' " When a girl remained angry at a sibling, she seemed to get some mileage from it, some belief that in thinking ill of a brother or sister, she has gotten further along in her own life. "All my life," Rebecca insisted, "my little brother's come first. With everyone. With my parents. With my grandparents. With my aunt. You name it, he got it. Now I'm going to college next year. You know where I'm going. All that to-do about my little brother and his brains and his talent and his beauty. Well, let's just see if he gets as far as I do. All that adulation has made him soft. I'll pull my own weight—you just wait and see."

Some adolescent siblings use their greater emotional control to pull away from one another. The reasons for withdrawal are almost always that of envy. A sibling is hated for being the family's "favourite," or for taking the role of "goody-goody" or the "successful one" or the "clever one," or the one who gets all the attention. Many parents, during their children's ad-

olescence, lose the show of fairness they have carefully culti-
vated in childhood. They may, in exasperation, set a good child
against an unruly one. As the adolescent becomes more highly
individualised, the parent herself may develop marked preferences for one child. The growth of the personality and of
techniques for having the personality recognised subjects the
parents to new biases. Seeming less vulnerable to the parent,
she is often less meticulous in suppressing her bias. She feels
less guilt at "not liking" an adolescent than a very young child.
Siblings can cause new, more subtle and profound pain to one
another at this time, through the parent's varying responses.
Two siblings within one household can actually feel as though
they had totally different histories, and describe very different
parents, since their parents treated them in different ways, valued them differently, and communicated and fought with them
differently.[8]

What is most sad is that these patterns of rejection outlast
their use. Some girls spoke of their intense jealousy towards
their siblings as arising quite suddenly in mid-adolescence,
driving them so far apart that they never made contact again.
Gelsey Kirkland speaks of this in her autobiography:[9] her sister
and she became such competitors in dance that they ignored
one another from 14 on, and then later, when the rivalry seemed
irrelevant and the desire for support emerged, the opportunities
were lost. Reparation is always possible, but it can also be so
difficult, and so filled with shattered vanities and shame that it
simply never gets done.

The relationship between siblings is regulated to a great
extent by the mother—certainly more directly than by the father. A father's favouritism does not tend to have the same day-
to-day impact as a mother's. "I get angry with my Dad when
he thinks [my brother] can do more than me. Even when he's
pleased with me I get annoyed, and wonder whether he's
pleased because he's surprised—because he didn't think I could
do it," said 18-year-old Jemma. "Mum's more even-handed.
She always says, 'Well [your brother] can do that, but you're
good at this,' and whenever anyone asks how [my brother's]
doing at university, she'll mention something good about me."

Even Clare, who felt badly upstaged by her sister's announcement that she would plan a party for their father, emphasised the impact her sister's tactics have on her mother. "It bugs me that my Mom doesn't see what she's up to. I mean my Dad—sure—someone's giving him a party, he's going to be all sentimental about it—but my Mom's a woman. I wish she'd see for once what my sister's up to. If only she saw. That's what gets me, the way [my sister] always gets away with things. She always charms them into not seeing what she's really up to. She's always been like that. I'm the actress—so they're always on the look out for me, but to them, [my sister] is all innocence. She's the real actress."

Siblings tend to be most helpful to one another if they have the same sort of problems with the parent, or many overlapping ones. I recognised my own previous position as a younger sister hopelessly in love with my older sister and all too easily at odds with my parents in 16-year-old Elizabeth's description of a domestic conundrum. She exhibits the mature superiority, the abiding protectiveness, and the mingling of amusement and empathy which, for me, is the crux of sibling support: "She gets the rougher treatment, mostly 'cause she's the baby, I guess. Sometimes, when I think Mom is being real unreasonable, I remind her what I was allowed to do at that age—or what I did anyway, even if I wasn't allowed. And [my little sister] isn't that tough, not really. She puts up a good fight, but when either Mom or Dad turn on her, she breaks down. I sometimes laugh at her, and she gets so sore—but I laugh because she's so cute. She just throws herself into it, and keeps shouting back even though they've made her cry so hard. Sometimes she's crying so much she turns blue. She can't get her breath to talk. She hits me when I go near her, because I've laughed at her. That makes her so mad. But I can usually get her out of it. She'll go away and cry and I'll come with her and just talk her through it. Then I tell her what she should say—you know, how to apologise, what to promise, that sort of thing. She does just what I tell her, and it usually works out okay."

SPECIAL FRIENDSHIP PROBLEMS IN LATE ADOLESCENCE

Siblings may be close, appreciative and supportive of one another, throughout mid-adolescence, and then, suddenly, in late adolescence, competitive and envious feelings may virtually wipe out the positive side of their attachment. Late adolescence seems particularly troubled by rivalry and envy. As a result, friendships do not tend to stabilise during that phase, in spite of the overall increase in maturity. Many girls find it necessary to make new friends. They may be moving into a new environment—to college, or to a job. Such conditions, at 17 or 18, often give rise to strong depressive feelings, to a sense that she is worth nothing, and that other people are worth far more. Self-uncertainty, even among those who had a fairly calm earlier adolescent history, is very common at this age. The stronger feelings of self-doubt and self-depletion in late adolescence may have gone unnoticed simply because a girl's greater maturity means that her problems become less troublesome to others—not to herself.

In late adolescence girls think of themselves as more conscientious, as more capable of being fair, of fulfilling responsibilities to a friend. They have better cognitive and moral strengths but often, in the new setting, away from home, where they are re-assessing their abilities, they regress to earlier stages of friendship, choosing as friends girls or boys whose association would give them the image they desired, or fill the absence of self-definition. Being lonely, they make friends simply to have a companion, someone to do things with, and frequently they choose as a companion someone who is available and non-threatening. As a result, in late adolescence they are more likely than in mid-adolescence to have "friends" of whom they are not particularly fond, whom they do not admire, and with whom they cannot establish a sense of trust.

"I thought I knew who I was. I thought I knew my capacities, I thought I had a pretty good opinion of myself," reported a sophomore at Johns Hopkins University in Washington, DC, "but one day here, and everything I thought about myself was just blown. Everyone seemed much more sure of herself than me. I smiled and tried to make friends. I was desperate to make friends, but the whole process took longer than I thought, and I was too depressed to go through with it. I'd talk to someone for a while and she might be real nice, and tell me lots of things—about herself, where she grew up—but she'd already have a boyfriend, and a major, and I'd feel an inch high next to her."

This depression, this depleted self-esteem can inhibit friendship. Feeling low, a girl may develop a pattern of initiating and then breaking off contact with others. A friendship is pursued because she is feeling lonely, and then, because her loneliness comes from a loss of self, she finds the connection threatening, and breaks it off. Feeling that she herself is inadequate, she will be threatened by rejection. "I know they're nice to me now," a college freshman admitted of the friends she was avoiding, "but they'll soon lose interest. They're chatting away, full of everything, and I have nothing to add. It makes me feel worse being with them, because all their liveliness just pounds against my emptiness." Many girls speak of their fear of being discovered to be "phony" or "fake."

Depression, in these young women, is linked to loneliness, and then to shame. A girl finds it difficult to form friendships because she is depressed, and she becomes depressed because she is lonely. She believes that her loneliness reflects some absence within her, some deep personal flaw. When depressed girls explain their predicament, they invariably cite themselves as being at fault, and the faults within themselves—they believe—cannot be corrected. This really is the crux of depression—the assumption of helplessness and changelessness, the assumption that improvement is not possible, the belief that no effort or determination can lead to improvement. When a girl is depressed because she is isolated she does not see her own behaviour as the cause of her isolation—not her on/off approach to friends, or her reluctance to join a group outing (because being in a group made her feel "left out"), or her sulky waiting to be approached. Instead, she cites an incorrigible character defect. She doesn't have "enough to offer," or she isn't sufficiently "interesting" or she is "ugly" or "clumsy" or "awkward." She sees her position as one that is uncorrectable: the problem is not with her circumstances, which might change, or the friend or group of friends she has chosen, or with her behaviour, which she would be able to improve. The problem, she believes, lies within herself. She sees it in terms of what she lacks and cannot get. Her view seems to lock her within her problem. In such circumstances, if a girl does gain a friend— either a boy or a girl—her expectation, and her dependence, will be sky-high. She thinks that without the friendship, she has nothing, and its loss will lead straight back to depression.

A common side-effect of loneliness, of being apart from the mother and being anxious about that separation, is weight gain. Feeling that she has no available source of human comfort, she can turn to food as that primitive comfort source. Many girls said they gained between ten and twenty-five pounds the first year they were away from home, "I would think, 'I miss my mother,' and then I would rush for the ice cream machine. It was a disaster." The girl who over-eats is trying literally to fill herself up with mother-love. Since most of the weight gain is within the first year of leaving home, it seems linked to the uncertainty that a connection with the mother can be sustained in spite of the physical separation.

Anger, too, inhibits friendship, and the anger of these girls, newly "independent," can take a very startling turn. "I walk around campus and I look at other people, and they all somehow look ugly. I see their mouths when they talk, look all twisted, and their shoes—I don't know, up-turned, with heavy soles—they seem ridiculous and hateful. When a boy talks to me, I keep looking at his chin, and I see all those muscles working, because he's self-conscious and self-important, and I just want to push him away." Anger such as this—a rejection of everyone else's claim to significance—is closely linked to depression, since it is a defence against self-doubt and self-despair.

During the first year, or even the first days, of college life, a girl may suffer from the impression that everyone around her is better defined, more distinctive, more significant than herself. Fearing the devastation of envy, her anger and fear twist admiration into disparagement. One girl, within three weeks of dormitory life, developed a nearly mad belief in her own superiority: "I stare at people, and I think 'I'm better than you' and I start hating them because they think so well of themselves. I see myself talking to them and laughing with them, but something inside me refuses to associate with them. I'm acting, but they're not. They really think they're great, and I want to shake them, kick them, because they don't see how much I'm worth."

Given the traditional model of adolescent development, these girls would have nearly completed separation from their parents. Yet, at 18, they miss their parents (particularly their mothers) dreadfully. Kim Chernin described how, when she left home, no bed was made smooth enough by anyone other than her mother, and how this small detail, the imperfectly made bed, seemed a sign that the fabric of her life could not hold together, as though the domestic care of her mother shaped her actual life.[10] Frequently, in the laundry room of the dorms, a girl would ruefully take out her laundry and say. "I can never get this as clean as my mother did." Or a tear in a blouse would be held up to the light, with the remark, "The only person I would trust this to is my mother." It is not that they pick up specific meaning from a pseudo-importance the mother gives household tasks. Many of these mothers worked, and did not consider themselves to be domestic creatures. But even working women do a great deal of housework, a great deal of domestic care, to which the daughter imparts great meaning, seeing in it a tangible sign of her love.

College girls do not miss their mothers every minute. They do not say that they would rather be at home. They had left home with great excitement, and they retain a sense of anticipation; but at the same time, they admit, they miss their mothers dreadfully, and much of their energy is spent in learning what it was like living without her. They want to learn this, they have a great sense of moving forward as they learn it, but the intimate, simple domestic care their mother had given them was to remain a standard, a point of emotive reference for them throughout their lives.

In late adolescence, the "growth of self" concept is often under great pressure, because it is not growing quite quickly enough, and it does not seem strong enough. The supportive friendships characteristic of mid-adolescence still occur, and are still valued but the sting of envy can get sharper, and many girls suffer terrible depressive feelings as they compare themselves to one another. "It's great how I'm now with people who take a much broader perspective of things," explained 19-year-old Ellen during her first year at university. "I can discuss all sorts of things I never would have dreamed of talking about with my friends in high school. I know I have something to contribute—when we talk about politics or women's issues. I know I have good ideas, like anyone else. But when I say something, the words often seem all flat and empty, and I can suddenly feel like a heel. How did these other girls grow up? How did they get to know so much? And they're so composed. I really admire their self-assurance. I watch them and think, 'Maybe I can learn to act like they do.' Maybe some day I'll even feel like they do." Girls seek friendships bravely, pursuing those they envy, trying to learn rather than trying to defend themselves against what they perceive as others' excellences, accomplishments and virtues. But the inner self that had seemed so sure when they were in their parents' homes now seems small. They had fought during early and mid-adolescence to gain their parents' acknowledgement of a new self, and that self had seemed strong and well worth fighting for even as it was threatened by their parents' outdated images of them. But in leaving home, in living among a new group of adolescents, these girls often regret the loss of the childhood comfort. They feel far more strongly at 19 than at 15 that they "don't know who they are." They are probably much closer to self-realisation—or at least self-definition—than they were five years before, but they do not feel that they are. Instead, they suffer a sharp self-doubt of which they tend to be ashamed. With their greater maturity they have more emotional control and greater capacity to conceal their doubts. These girls are very careful to present themselves well to adults. They value the image they present. They have learned that an appearance of maturity is rewarded with greater freedom and respect. To express their self-doubt would make them even more vulnerable, so they clothe it, disguise it with a well-groomed confidence.

DIARIES

It has been suggested that if Anne Frank had had a good friend, she would not have written her diary.[11] The urge to confide, to explain, to share secrets about the growing self, are usually exercised in adolescent friendships. The diary, which Anne Frank named "Kitty," and often referred to as a friend who might judge her or be slighted by her neglect, was a substitute for the friendship that was prohibited by Anne's isolation.

Yet diaries and young girls go hand-in-hand, however many friends are available. Along with poetry, it seems a way of slicing out some personal reality and making it more than merely personal, giving some special seriousness to feelings and moods and hopes which she knows she bestows with an irrational value. That special, romanticised valuing of the self, typical in adolescence, has some awareness that it is out of tune with others' assessments. For the audience of a friend is never perfectly admiring. The sympathy of a friend may not provide just the right intensity or quality of attention. A girl's friends take her seriously, but they may lack the super-seriousness with which she approaches her diary. The charm of the diary for an adolescent girl is not only that it is secret, but that it is a visible secret, an object in the world, between book covers, which proves she has a secret self. For as hard as a girl in middle or late adolescence works to make herself known to her mother and to her friends, as much as she needs confirmation and validation from them, she also needs to feel that there is something unknown within her. Muriel Spark has said that as a young girl she wrote love letters to herself and then hid them throughout the house, hoping her mother would find them and believe she had a secret lover. Many teenagers speak of the frustration of their parents being "too sure" of them, too confident about their knowledge of them, as though that knowledge in some way confines them. The diary is an object they can look at, and make sure others knew about, which proves there is a private, recorded life. The secrecy of the diary is sometimes a pawn, or a love trinket within a friendship. A girl may decide to show her diary as a sign of special trust to a friend, or she allows a friend access to certain marked pages of the diary. "This is how I really felt," she explains, handing the diary to a friend, as though the words written in that book carry a weight her spoken words lack. Any friendship involves self-presentation, and the adolescent, who may be learning to do this well, never believes she does it as well as she deserves, or as well as someone else does it.

Girls' special affinity to the diary as self-expression is actually linked to their greater communicativeness towards adults and friends. It corrects, not substitutes, for the imperfections of self-expression with people. The diary has most of its appeal in mid-adolescence, when girls are better than they were a few years before at setting out their thoughts. It tends to lose some appeal in late adolescence when, as an 18-year-old explained, "my problems are too big for those tiny lines. Just writing down my thoughts isn't going to solve anything. I have to make real decisions." A 15-year-old, however, finds the opportunity for self-reflection a luxury. "I have to sit down at my desk, and wait a while before the sound of my own voice fades. I can feel the privacy. It doesn't come straight away. But when it does it's like a vibration, a hum which drowns out other sounds. I pick up my pen and I can write more truthfully about how I feel. It isn't so much that I put in things I wouldn't tell anyone else. It's just that I can put everything down together, and more easily." Girls in mid-adolescence may talk freely about how they feel, but still find the weight of their feelings difficult to express. "There's always this fear of taking yourself too seriously when you talk to anyone else," explained a 14-year-old girl, her smile stiff with embarrassment. "I talk to my friends, but I often make a joke of everything, and then I make myself feel worse, laughing at myself like that. As though I've been disloyal to something inside me. I sort it out in my diary. I say 'This is how I really feel.' So I make it up to myself."

Girls in mid-adolescence learn how to present themselves

to friends, to express their ideas, thoughts and feelings, but no one does this perfectly, and the self-consciousness of adolescence makes her highly critical of her self-presentation. It is common for girls to express dissatisfaction with how they appeared to others. They believe that they appear superficial, or flighty, or silly, or "totally non-serious." "I can hear my own voice going 'Yak-yak-yak,' " 15-year-old Amy used her hand like a glove puppet to mimic her mouth movements, "and I know I sound stupid, and my smile is all wrong, but I keep chattering away. I don't really know what else to do. Sometimes I try to show how I really feel, and the more I show the emptier and sillier I feel. I can't wait to get away, and when I do I kind of shake myself all over to get rid of that awful feeling, like I'm so embarrassed I'm just full of the jitters. I have to calm down, and take a deep breath, and let this feeling pass, and then I'll sit down with my diary and try to say how I really feel. What's good is if I can get down the whole episode, so that I can say how silly I looked, then how I appeared isn't so much a part of me."

The diary can be a means of setting the record straight, of showing the appearance to be untrue, not the whole story. It can also be something to turn to under the pressure of depression, when there is a sadness or loneliness pushing the girl to write down her feelings, to give this apparently aimless pain some form, and perhaps some meaning. "I'll just be sitting at home, and everyone will be doing something ordinary. My sister will be drawing, and my mother will be sewing, and I'll just feel like a lump of ice right in the centre of me, and I'll have to move around, and I'll try to think 'Why do I feel this way?' and then I'll go upstairs and sit down with my diary, and try to describe this sensation, and it won't go away but somehow it will feel better, because I've written it down, and when I go back into the room where my sister and my mother are, I'll feel special, because I've been working out how I feel, and they don't know anything about it." Sometimes she wants to keep a record of her feelings because she does not see anyone around her who registers her pains and pleasures. Fearing the passing of this volatile self, she keeps it as a record for her

future self. "I want to be able to look back and see how I felt.
I don't want to be like the grown-ups I know, who never seem
to have been young themselves." The diary offers proof to the
girl that she knows herself in a way others do not, that she
knows things about herself no one else knows. It offers reprieve from the hard work she does with both her mother and
friends to realise and to communicate her maturing self. Hence
the diary often is loaded with sentimentality. It is the luxury
of a one-sided view, her private voice to a personal, imagined
audience.

NOTES

1. Coleman, 1961.
2. Erikson, 1956.
3. For a description of the bewildered disappointment that a revolution
   failed to take, see Davidson, 1976.
4. Blos, 1962.
5. The term "emotion management" is from Arlie Russel Hochschild
   The Managed Heart, 1985, where she discusses how commercial firms
   train employees in the art of being either always ready to please on
   the one hand (in airline stewardesses) or always threatening (among
   collection agencies) on the other. It was with the help of this concept
   that I noticed the work done among adolescent girls.
6. Goffman, 1969.
7. Goffman, 1969.
8. Dunn *et al*, 1985, p. 770.
9. Kirkland, 1985.
10. Chernin, 1983.
11. Dalsimer, 1986.

Chapter 6

RISK, DISCIPLINE
AND GROWTH

It is tempting to see the distinctive feature of adolescent and parent interactions as a power struggle.[1] The adolescent wants to live "her own life"; the parents see her as not yet ready. The adolescent wants freedom; the parent wants control. A struggle of wills between parent and child, however, does not suddenly emerge in adolescence. Throughout their lives together the parent and child have separate and frequently opposing wills. A balance between these wills is precariously effected through compromise, persuasion and love. Another common view is that adolescence is distinguished by the child's critical attitude towards the parent. But the child has been learning throughout her life to spot her parents' weaknesses and intractable prejudices or fears. Often she resists and despises them. Sometimes she fears them and seeks protection within them. Sometimes she wants to protect her parents from the fears that give rise to their prejudices and weaknesses. Yet there is no doubt that all these things—the battle of wills, the arguing, the criticism, take on a new seriousness—for some parents even a terror—in adolescence.

Aristotle saw the transition from youth to maturity as the emergence of a moral being, one capable of deliberation and responsible choice. Other, recent moral psychologists have described the way in which the child develops moral sophistication, moving from a pre-conventional morality, wherein she sees "good" and "bad" in terms of what brings on punishment or anger, displeasure or scolding, to a somewhat more sophisticated conventional morality, wherein the child accepts the rules laid down by society—in particular as society is represented and interpreted by the parents. Later, with the greater intellectual and critical skills of the adolescent, the child may develop a "post-conventional morality."[2] Having reached this phase the child no longer simply accepts her parents' principles. She needs reasons for believing in one principle rather than another. She sees principles as conclusions she herself must come to, rather than precepts which she adopts simply because her parents adhere to them. This development from viewing morality in terms of fear of punishment to viewing morality as principles derived from reasoned argument shows growth towards moral responsibility. Through taking charge of her own morality, the child becomes a responsible adult.

Any parent of an adolescent knows that this development is more idealised than real. The questioning skills of an adolescent are often more critical than positive and when they are positive they are impossibly idealistic. The adolescent's intellectual growth equips her with the ability to undermine others' arguments rather than with the wisdom necessary to construct her own. She feels the strength of her own righteousness through her criticisms of others. Other people are so blatantly wrong, in her view, that her own ideas have a luminous, necessary justification. But there is one crucial area in which she has not developed adequate skills, a weakness which she will not acknowledge because she lacks the skills to measure her weakness, a weakness which can terrify and terrorise the parent. In her transitional period from irresponsibility to responsibility she has not yet mastered one important aspect of taking responsibility, and that is assessing risk.

Teenagers are often stereotyped as impulsive and they often do act impulsively, with apparent thoughtlessness or recklessness. The problem with this stereotype is that it presents adolescents as acting without thinking, without caring about the consequences. This reinforces the accompanying assumption that teenagers do not care whether or not they hurt others, that indeed they have no concern for others. Many parents conclude that their adolescent children do not care about hurting themselves either, because they act with so much determination and with so litle regard for the outcome. During adolescence there is a pronounced split between the ability to reason and the ability to predict the outcome of an action. This leads to a split between the sophistication of thought and action. Adoles-

cents—and especially adolescent girls—tend to be highly conscientious in how they think about themselves and their
behaviour. Any crucial decision, for example, whether to have
an abortion, whether to get married, whether to go to college,
involves sensitive consideration of others' needs and wishes.
Under the pressure of making a crucial decision, adolescent
girls refer to what their father would think ("He would kill me
if I ever had an abortion," "He wants me to finish college before I get married, I'll break his heart if I don't.") to how their
mother would feel ("She'll feel as if she's the one who lost the
baby. I don't know whether I can do it to her." "She wants
me to be happy. She'll just smile, grit her teeth and hope for
the best." "She'd feel like she was a failure if I didn't go on, at
least to a 'poly.' ") and even to how her decision would affect
a brother or sister ("She's always looked up to me. I don't want
to disappoint her," "Her head's buzzing with all this. I've got
to show her how this all makes sense.")

An adolescent girl's responsiveness to and consideration of
other peoples' needs is so strong that Carol Gilligan has pow-
erfully concluded that girls' self-interest goes "underground"
during adolescence.[3] Whereas the adolescent boy uses his new
intellectual skills to argue for preservation and protection of his
own rights, the girl suppresses, even subverts her own needs
as she uses her reasoning and perspective-taking skills to consider how her actions will affect others. Whereas a boy sees a
duty to himself, a girl learns to see her responsibility in terms
of caring for others. Her moral priority is to avoid hurting
others. Though Gilligan values this perspective and emphasises
its legitimacy, she sees it as a possible threat to a girl's mature
development. The girl must learn to control her consideration
of others, and to view herself as a person with rights, as someone who has a right to act on her own behalf and to consider
her needs and wishes, first.

There is no doubt that Gilligan's view, which has become
enormously influential, is well supported by the way adolescent
girls speak and indeed think about their decisions and the consequences of their actions. Mothers, however, describe their
daughters in very different terms. Gilligan interviewed preg-

nant girls and young women who were considering whether
or not to have an abortion. She found that they were meticulous in considering the effect of their decisions upon others—
upon a mother, a father, or a boyfriend. I discovered, however,
that mothers take a very different view of their daughters. They
do not describe their daughters as thinking about others, and
considering others first. They describe them as "stupid,"
"thoughtless," "selfish," having "tunnel vision," refusing to
"consider the consequences of what she does." "You want to
know her trouble?" asked the mother of 20-year-old Gwen,
who waited until she was four months pregnant before telling
her parents. "Her trouble is that she's socially retarded. Don't
think she doesn't know what's what. She's had more lessons
than most about what contraceptives work and what don't.
We've discussed that openly, all through her childhood. I'm a
doctor, for Christ's sake! And she's a medical student—or was.
How do you like that? She must know something about reproduction. Even if she blocks out everything *I've* taught her, she
must have learned something in pre-med. But it's with only
one part of her mind. She doesn't think with the other part.
She thinks she must be different, some exception to all those
other girls. What goes through her mind? That's what I'd like
to know. She doesn't give a hoot about us—that's for sure. She
doesn't even have the good sense to come to us when she needs
help. What an insult! That's the real insult. It makes me so
angry when I think of it. She thinks we won't be able to help
her, that she knows it all. She can't see beyond her own reflection in the mirror."

The discrepancy between the mothers' views of their
daughters, and the daughters' views as recorded by Gilligan, is
not really a discrepancy between how we speak about our
decision-making process and what we actually do when we
decide,[4] but a discrepancy between what the adolescent girl
thinks she is doing, and what, because of her limited ability to
assess the consequences of her behaviour, she is actually doing.

Gilligan was looking at the way girls weighed various con-
siderations under stress. She found that the issues which they
emphasised, and the way these issues were balanced, revealed

a suppression of self-directed thoughts, and a proliferation of other-directed thoughts. The concerns were: how can I avoid causing others pain, and how can I meet others' needs? The girls' mothers, however, stress the behaviour which got them into the "mess" or the difficulty, and it is that behaviour, those previous, less documented decisions, which are the terror of parents of adolescents, who see the independence and maturity of their children as hollow. Freedom, in many parents' view, simply provides the daughter with the opportunity to bring disaster upon herself and others close to her.

The adolescent girl does think carefully about the consequences of her actions. She also acts "thoughtlessly," "selfishly," with "tunnel vision." There are two explanations of these apparent contradictions. First, though the adolescent does care about the consequences of her actions, she is unable to assess them. From her mother's point of view it looks as though she does not care. Secondly, it is well known to parents that the adolescent's capacity for concern and love is often mingled with anger, with a downright contrary independence. The mother fears this, and sees her daughter's divergence from parental rules as a destructive revolt. When the hard work of getting her mother to acknowledge her individuality seems to be going too slowly, or her mother is not sufficiently impressed, a daughter may prove this independence violently or crudely, caring more about making her point than acting in her self-interest. This strategy has been greatly over-rated because left out of account is the way the girl sees herself as acting. She believes she is acting responsibly, or responsibly enough. She believes she is taking care, or taking enough care. She does not intend to cause so much trouble because she cannot assess the risk of trouble. "I thought I was careful," Gwen told me. "I mean, I did use something, but I was drunk, and I guess I didn't put the foam in properly. My doctor, said, 'Yep, that's how it usually happens.' . . . Yes, I know foam isn't always considered the safest method, but the pill is a real bind, and most of my friends—real intelligent ones—say foam works for them. It's not any less safe than the condom which my mother's so keen on—is it? Anyway, I thought I could handle it myself. I tried to induce an abortion with some surgical tubing. My mother thinks this is outrageous. She thinks I could have killed myself, 'You'd rather kill yourself than come to me?' she says. Well, I didn't endanger my life, you know. And I did come to her eventually. The thing is, I didn't really believe I was pregnant, not until I got the results of the test. Then I just fell apart."

It has been thought that adolescents take risks under the influence of peer pressure. Fearing ridicule from their peers more than the consequences of the activity, an adolescent will experiment with cocaine, or will drive under the influence of alcohol or drugs, or will take some part in a robbery or in vandalism. This pressure from peers to act destructively or simply stupidly may also come from not wanting to be left out. Some girls admitted that they agreed to have sex because all their friends were doing it, and they felt their innocence made them a "freak" or "real peculiar" or "the odd one out." In addition, it has been supposed that there is some hormonal push towards impulsiveness, that the adolescent is "feeling her hormones," becomes jittery, has a need for action or excitement to match her inner unrest. Or, it is supposed that an adolescent's impulses and urges are simply stronger, and cannot be contained. Even the law courts accept this argument and create excuses from it. A judge may show lenience for a sexual crime, for example, because he sees it as a manifestation of the unruly impulses characteristic of the age rather than a moral failure of the person. Another explanation of the teenager's "foolhardiness" is that she simply cannot conceive of her death. The new self-consciousness of adolescence provides her with an "imaginary audience." She sees herself as always under scrutiny. Someone is watching, someone is judging, someone is assessing her every minute. This imaginary observer both plagues and protects her. She may suffer excruciating embarrassment, but she is also, as a result, unable to conceive the real possibility of death. Like Huckleberry Finn, when she imagines her death, she imagines her presence at her funeral.[5] Death is a fiction for her. She cannot evaluate risk, because she does not see her vulnerability.

All these explanations probably have some validity, but

they leave out of account the central, and most treatable, aspect of adolescent risk-taking—the teenager's inability to assess risks, her cognitive failure in dealing with the laws of probability. Early adolescents, in fact, have no ability whatsoever to cope with these laws.

There seems to be a dramatic break between the ease with which an adult can coerce a child through fear, and the raging frustration a parent feels as she tries to convince a teenager that what she is doing is simply not safe. Yet there is a carry over from the young child's very concrete sense of danger, which makes it (sometimes) easy to control her by making her afraid of the consequences of what she does, to the teenager's imperviousness to the risks she is taking. A 5-year-old will be terrified to touch a knife at any time, if an adult has told her that she could cut her arm off with it. Yet she will test it, and then conclude "See, I can do it. It's all right, I didn't get cut," or she may say "See, I can cross the road myself, and I didn't get hit by a car." The parent has to work hard to convince the child that something may be dangerous without being harmful every time. But because it might be very harmful, it should always be avoided, or done only with great care. The parent does this initially through control, by either making sure the child is watched the entire time, or by insisting that the child cannot cross the road by herself. Her motor ability becomes re-defined. She can walk, and is physically capable of walking across a road, but she is judged to be unable to do this in the sense that she is not able to eliminate unacceptable risk of doing so. The child's independence is thereby curtailed. She is told she cannot do what in some sense she actually can do.

Later, the child is allowed more independence, but only because the parent believes fear and rules have been reliably internalised. The child has more independence because she is deemed to be more controlled and predictable. The child will do what and only what she has been told to do. She has a set of rules at her finger tips ("Stop, look, and listen," "Know your green cross code") which she is relied upon to follow. It is other people's rules that have made the road safe for her.

Adolescents do not have, cannot have, and do not want to

have rules for every action; and the actions they are capable of, and the actions or decisions which are appropriate for them, do not have such clear guidelines. Hence they need common sense, and a sense of responsibility. When parents complain about their adolescent children this is what they complain about most: their absence of responsibility, their lack of common sense, their reluctance to plan ahead or even look ahead. These common flaws are often a genuine sign of immaturity, and not, as is often thought, a show of rebelliousness or anger or even bloody-mindedness. What seems a clear danger in the eyes of the adult may seem safe, or safe enough, to her teenage daughter. For the adolescent retains some of the 5-year-old's response to the parental fear, "See, Mum and Dad, it's all right, I can cross the road myself without getting hit by a car." Even in mid-adolescence a very narrow view of risk is taken. If a girl has done something a few times without detrimental consequences, then she believes it is safe. She genuinely believes she is not taking a risk. Or, if she has seen a friend do something—take drugs, drive under the influence of alcohol, have intercourse without using contraception, or while using an ineffective method of contraception, she will think that because others do it without coming to harm, then it is safe, or safe enough. Added to this narrow view of risk, is her biased assessment of how many other people do what she claims their doing proves safe. She tends to overestimate greatly how many of her friends are using cocaine without becoming addicted, or sleeping with a boyfriend without becoming pregnant, or smoking without it becoming a habit.

"All my friends are sleeping with their boyfriends," may well mean that about fifteen per cent of her girl friends are currently having sex regularly. In addition, it has been found that college students (and girls in late adolescence were more likely to use contraception than girls in mid-adolescence) over-estimated the effectiveness of their contraceptive methods by close to three times the accepted, or published, reliability. Most of these girls had access to reliability figures; many had these figures thrust upon them; some could quote the accepted reliability figures. When I pointed out the discrepancy between their personal assessment and the objective probabilities, they offered various, sometimes quite bizarre reasons for refusing to accept that the objective probability had anything to do with their use. "Well, I know my body very well, so I know when to be careful," or "Most people don't how to use these things, but we do," or even "We know a good position for lowering the chances of getting pregnant."

Only a very small minority of teenage girls have even a generally correct idea about fertility, and hardly any girls realise what the actual risks of pregnancy are. One-third of the adolescent girls who had intercourse before marriage, got pregnant before marriage.[6] One in three is terrible odds, yet no girls saw themselves as taking this risk. Half of premarital first pregnancies occur in the first six months of sexual activity, twenty per cent in the first month, and the younger the girl, the greater the risk. Ten per cent of those girls who are under 15 when they first have intercourse, get pregnant during the first month. This high rate of risk is directly due to the absence of contraceptives, or to the "use" of highly ineffective techniques. Young girls give all sorts of justifications for these failures. They do not want to consult a doctor: "My God, what would he think of me? I can't go to the doctor. He still thinks of me as a baby. He pats me on the head and calls me 'Poppet.'" Even more tangential objections are uttered quite sincerely. "I could see another doctor, I suppose, but someone my Mum knows might see me in the waiting room, and then she might say something to Mum—and then where would I be?" Some teenage girls think that using the contraceptive pill is a sign that they are easy game, or somehow non-serious sexual partners. They are even too embarrassed to face a salesperson at a chemist. They feel a kind of terror at admitting their sexuality to any adult. Ambivalent about it themselves, they panic at the thought of "what someone else will think of them." This panic leads to an awful clumsiness.

Given the ratio of sexuality to pregnancy in teenagers, it is tempting to conclude that an adolescent girl must know at some level what risk she is taking; that on some level she wants to become pregnant. However distressed she may be on learning that she is pregnant—and most are devastated—she must on some level believe that pregnancy and the birth of a child, will fulfil some need.

Adolescent sexuality and reproductive behaviour is highly complex. To say that pregnancy and child-bearing satisfies some need is certainly true, yet this is different from saying that this is what the teenage girl really wanted, or was really after, or even really thought would happen. Adolescent girls are trying harder than ever not to become pregnant, in that more and more are using some contraception. The trouble is that even the medical profession has shifts, even fads, in contraceptive use. When there was a move away from extensive use of the contraceptive pill, more teenagers used contraceptive methods, but with less success. Even those who consult doctors do not feel they have much help when they ask the risks of using the pill or the effectiveness of other methods. "I asked about the risk of thrombosis," 17-year-old Dee explained, "and wondered whether because my Mum had varicose veins, whether I was more likely to have trouble. But he just shrugged and said, 'I'd wait until you got them yourself.' I tried to feel reassured, but then I wondered whether I hadn't got them myself already, because I do have these broken blood vessels. I felt stupid about going back. But I was too frightened to keep using the pill." Another 17-year-old, Pamela, was confused by various accounts of the safety of the condom. "My doctor said it was perfectly all right if you used it properly. I kept those words 'Perfectly all right' clear in my mind when I was first worried about missing my period. I kept repeating them to myself. It was a long time before I admitted it wasn't 'Perfectly all right.' The language doctors and most of us use in speaking about contraceptive use, has a curious palliative effect on some girls, who see terms such as "precaution" or "protection" as optional, as though only if one is being extra-careful, even fussy, are such procedures required.

The majority of adolescent girls who become pregnant do not think of themselves as wanting to become pregnant. The girls I spoke to—many of whom ruled out abortion because it is "murder" or "the killing of an innocent baby" or because "my Dad would kill me if I ever did anything like that," or because they had tried, but failed and finally gave up on procuring an abortion—expressed a clear and comprehensive despondency. They spoke of feeling "locked in" or "helpless" or "cut off." "I feel like all the doors are being shut in my face, like I'm in a room, all walls, no doors, no windows. I can sit there and cry my eyes out, but nothing will change. Things are tearing apart inside me, and nothing on the outside gives a damn," explained a 14-year-old who kept staring out of the window as she spoke. "I feel like I'm stuck on this road, and I have to keep on walking, even though everything I wanted is behind me," said a college sophomore who had put off getting a pregnancy test until she was four months pregnant, when it seemed unlikely that she would be able to have an abortion within the legal time limit. "It's as though suddenly my life as I've always thought about it is over. There's been no war, no nuclear disaster, and nothing's happened to any of my friends, but for me everything has changed and I have to think of my life in completely different terms now." "Everything I thought I was, and everything I thought I would be is just gone now, and I have to make something different of everything," explained a 17-year-old who was six months pregnant, and who had once planned to be on her way to college at the moment she was speaking to me.

Most of these girls felt enormously unlucky. From an adult's point of view they had taken absurd risks, but from their point of view they had just done what everyone else had done, except they got caught. Indeed since many adults do not know precisely how risky teenage sexual activity is either, they tend to over-estimate a pregnant teenager's sexual activity, which in fact may be, and probably is, highly selective and seldom rampant. Teenage girls do not treat sexual activity lightly, nor do they tend to be obsessed by it. If a girl has sex with one boyfriend she will not necessarily have sex with a subsequent boyfriend. She weighs up her feelings, and her boyfriend's, anew, for each relationship. Losing her virginity does not make her easy game. If she is engaged in a sexual relationship she does not have sex every time she goes out with her boyfriend.

"Sometimes it happens. Sometimes it doesn't." Sexual activity to a young girl often seems less risky than it is because she knows it is less rampant than adults suppose. "My father thinks that if I screw once I'm going to have screwing on the brain forever. Talk to any adult—they think we're sex mad. My father thinks that as soon as a boy takes me out he's going to go for non-stop entry. So of course he's worried about me getting pregnant. How can you be careful if you're told not to go on the pill, but you're supposed to be having sex every time your parents blink? There are other things, too, that we think about besides sex, you know," Rebecca insisted.

A relationship that involves sex usually involves a great deal of other things too—yet usually not enough for the progenitor to offer paternal support. As one girl conceded, "I'd run away from this too, if I could. I hate him now, but I don't blame him."

Many girls came to hate the boys who had made them pregnant, though they cited "being in love" as a reason for having had sex. They felt they had been duped by temporary feelings of love, by foolish hopes for emotional support and attachment. They felt repelled by the boyfriend, and often extremely angry even towards those boys who offered support. "How could I marry him?" Gwen demanded after telling me that the man responsible for the pregnancy was willing to accept the child, and her as a wife. "Every time I think about him I just go wild. I imagine slicing him apart with a chop of my hand, or breaking his neck and stomping on him. I can't stand it when he touches me—even my hand—" and she shook both of her hands to dispel the sensation of his touch. There was nothing like the stress of pregnancy to make a girl wonder "What did I ever see in him?" Whatever unconscious desire the teenage girl has to become pregnant, then, it makes itself realised not because it is stronger than all other needs and wishes, but because it can so easily link itself to ignorance, high fertility and a poor ability to assess risks.

Some teenage girls are at special risk of early and "unwanted" pregnancy. Though accidental pregnancies happen to every kind of girl, of every class and every race, a girl with little self-confidence, low self-esteem and a diminished sense of direction or set of goals is considered to be more likely to get pregnant than someone with a strong opinion of herself and firm sense of direction and a commitment towards future goals. A girl with low self-esteem and low self-confidence will be more easily led by the pressures of a boy, and will have less sense of who is truly committed to her. She will be more afraid of losing a boyfriend by saying "no" (many girls explained this as a reason for having sex) and may be less willing to assert her concern about contraception. Also if she has little direction, or diffuse and unformulated goals, then she has less to lose in becoming pregnant. Having a baby, to her, may offer a substitute for a goal, because it provides her with a ready-made role which can easily occupy her full time. For girls suffering from this "identity diffusion," girls who have little sense of what they want to become, pregnancy provides an answer. They can have a limited but nonetheless clear directive. And, many of these girls, so close to childhood themselves, look upon infancy as an idyll of love. Taking part in that idyll will, they believe, make them feel cared for too. A girl may romanticise pregnancy as a state in which she will be cared for, coddled, indulged.

RISK CONFRONTATION

Pregnancy is certainly not the only risk that teenagers take, nor does it present to parents the greatest fear. The adolescent's tendency to take risks cuts across every aspect of her life. She often does not plan ahead, or think ahead, or accept the consequences of her actions. She seems to have an "I know best" attitude towards choices and decisions, and a "not me" attitude towards rueful consequences. The skills of independence and social coping which seemed overwhelming as a child are now itching to be exercised. She knows she has mastered these skills, yet her parents doubt her. She fights for freedom as a drowning person fights for air. She genuinely believes that her parents, who are trying to limit her freedom and cast doubt upon her decisions, are trying to harm her.

Parents, on the other hand, see an adolescent daughter as setting out deliberately to hurt herself, or even to hurt the parent by hurting herself. The parent's outraged cry "How can you do this to yourself?" will be dismissed with, "I know what I'm doing," or "Leave me alone," or "Get off my case." The teenager's job is to experiment, to see what suits her, to discover new things of which she is capable. It is extremely difficult for the parent, who cares so deeply about her and whose fears can be so easily activated, to distinguish risky activities as genuine, healthy "trying out" from risky activities as an expression of anger, despondency and a failure to care about the self.

Parents are sometimes more or less good at making such a distinction, because they are more or less good at distinguishing what they want for a child, what they hope her to be, and what she herself decides she wants and needs. Does the teenager know what risks she is taking? Does she take risks because she is not assessing how risky they are, or is she taking risks from a destructive urge? Or is she assessing risks differently? Does she feel that she is putting herself at greater risk if she faces the ridicule of her friends for refusing to join in their risky activities? Does she feel more threatened by exclusion or mockery than she does by drug addiction? Does the immediate risk of falling out with her friends seem more important than risk to her health or even her life?

Parents express enormous frustration with a risk-taking adolescent. Sometimes a mother is so terrified for her daughter, and feels so helpless in face of her resistance and determination, that she uses anything at all, no matter how distorted or ugly, to make her point to regain control, to coerce when she cannot persuade. Here is a mother trying to persuade her daughter not to go to a New Year's Eve party. Reason has failed, so she makes awful predictions and presents them as problems which the girl must be willing to solve. "Go ahead. Take that trip with your friends. The road is ice. Ice, I tell you. You'll have fun paying back all the money you'll owe me when you crash the car. And you'll probably kill someone into the bargain. How will that feel? I hope you think it's worth it."

Here is a mother who is reluctant to let her daughter go into London for the day. "Do I need to tell you what can happen to a girl on her own? Don't you listen to the news? If you go, I won't be expecting you back. I'll be waiting to find you dredged up from some river." Many mothers who use these techniques explain that they do not believe their daughter "hears a word I say." Their "nastiness" expresses a sense of impotence. They exaggerate because more subtle and rational arguments have no effect. The daughters do, however, hear a mother. Her words have far more effect that she guesses, though they are not effective in the way she hopes. "When my mother goes on like that," Donna said, "telling me how sorry I'm going to be for doing what I want to do, I just go rigid inside. It's like a nightmare—you know you're standing in a tunnel and there's this piercing sound of a train that keeps coming at you. That's how her voice is—this sort of siren which is drilling through my head. She's just hysterical. How can I take her seriously? I don't even feel like answering her properly. There's no point in telling her I'll be careful, or I won't go if the roads are really bad. She's not going to listen to me when she's in that state. I feel just like making monkey faces at her—" and she puffed out her lower lip by tucking her tongue inside it and began scratching herself, monkey-fashion. What she responded to was her mother's panic, and her mother's frantic desire to control her. The daughter was sufficiently rational to measure the exaggeration of the mother's predictions, and thus she withdrew further from her mother's influence. She saw that the mother was trying to manipulate her. Her mother's arguments were correctly seen to be extreme. Therefore her mother was wrong. Therefore she was right.

All children, all adolescents, need discipline, need parental control, but they tend to respond to different types of control with well identified patterns. It has been fairly well established that certain types of discipline are more conducive to maturity, in terms of self-control, social control, self-responsibility, and even the ability to see things from another point of view.[7] Coercion, or any attempt at domestic dictatorship, impedes maturity, and gives rise to girls who lack self-confidence and self-direction. The permissive parent, the parent who believes that her home should be run like a democracy, and that the children should decide what is best for them, or have a large say in every decision regarding them, gives rise to an under-controlled child, a child who does not take responsibility for the consequences of her actions, does not consider the impact of her behaviour upon others. The egalitarian parent seems to join hands with the tyrannical parent, both of whom raise under-directed and under-motivated children. The parent who controls too little, and the parent who controls too much, each deprives her child of the ability to control herself, to learn how her decisions lead to specific consequences, to develop the confidence in her ability to make decisions and control the outcome of her actions.

The authoritarian parent, who bases her power on her position in the family, who says "You must do this because I say so," and "You must obey me because I am a parent," gives the daughter no training in the logic of acting upon principles which go beyond parental dictation. The adolescent of an authoritarian parent will be as ill-equipped as the daughter of a permissive parent in controlling her self and her actions, and in assessing her effect on others.

The type of parental discipline which does seem to allow for both control and growth is labelled "authoritative," and is characterised by a parent's use of control and argument. The parent presents rules as principles based upon reasons, "You must never do that," or "You must do that. You have no choice," are placed within a framework that makes sense to the child, since these directives are accompanied, frequently enough, by explanations. Reasons behind rules are not "because I say so," but "because you might get hurt," or "because you will annoy everyone else," or "because it wouldn't be fair to your sister," or "because you'll get too tired." This type of discipline promotes mature control because the child does not feel cut off from the sources of discipline. The demands made upon her develop rather than thwart her intellect. Yet because there is a match between personal development and discipline, authoritative parents face a most exhausting task. Once a child learns that reasons lie behind rules and that reasons are constructed through a verbal logic of emphasis and balance, she will learn that rules and directions can be challenged through argument.

"I try to reason with her, but it's no good." "I explain to her until I'm blue in the face that if she goes about things her way, she'll come to grief," "I've tried to be fair. For seventeen years I've tried to be fair. I've treated each of the children the same, given them each a present when any one got one. And all I get is protests about how I'm not fair, it isn't fair, I listen to one more than the other, I'm nicer to one more than to the other. So now I say, 'Look. Don't argue. I say you're to do this. Do this. I'm worn out arguing now.'" "I'll ask my daughter to help carry in the shopping, and she'll start explaining a hundred and one things to me about why it's really her sister's turn to do it, and I never ask anyone else, and if I let her go on, the ice-cream will be melting in the car, so I just give up and do it myself."

No parent needs to be reminded how exhausting a child's arguments can be. As a child learns the rules of argument, which she does with a great leap in adolescence, she can spin the parent's sense of reason and fairness into a web that trips the parent up. Trying to explain, the parent decides it is easier and more efficient to become either permissive or tyrannical. Fortunately most parents weather this stage, battered, fatigued, but with the energy of their love intact.

Even through discipline the child must feel acknowledged. Authoritarian parents offer no flexibility, and no respect for her point of view—which, for an adolescent, is deeply humiliating and therefore enraging. Yet when the parent is truly seen to be fighting for the well-being of the child, this triptych of discipline types and effects may not hold. A startling finding is that authoritarian parents in black families do not raise under-controlled or less self-confident or less self-responsible children, or passive and dependent girls; instead they raise self-assertive, independent and generally competent girls.[8] The differences in effect are due in part to the different context, and partly to the different interpretation of behaviour. "Our mother fights tooth and nail to keep us straight and make sure we do well at school. She's peeling carrots and talking to the little ones: 'What's two plus two?' She can't do that to me anymore—my math isn't that simple! But she checks my homework and looks at it after it's been marked, and no way can I go out or even talk on the phone until it's done." Sixteen-year-old Nell saw her controlling mother as working against a trend—a trend not to finish high school, not to do well, not to succeed. The children recognise that the mother's greater bid for authority is based upon a lack of support elsewhere. The degree of authority must be measured not only with regard to behaviour within the domestic arena but also with reference to possible, or usual influences outside the home.

The main and very difficult task of the parent is to discipline an adolescent without humiliating her—too much—without alienating her, without making it impossible, in the child's view, to live with her parents and to love them and trust them. Somehow the mother must show her daughter that she has great faith in her, even while she protects her, and hence constrains her, from her own ignorance. This fine line is seldom trod gracefully, for mother and daughter each sees a wilful malice in the other's behaviour. Suspicion and rage surrounding discipline can be overcome only in the context of good, sound personal validation, which the mother gives her daughter in other, more peaceful times. The tasks which have traditionally been seen as those of the parent dealing with an adolescent—"letting go" and "setting limits"—are so ineffective because the "setting limits" will only be accepted by the adolescent when she views them in the context of the parent's continuing confirmation, trust and love. The parent can set limits only when she refuses to let go, only when individuation is aided and separation denied.

DIVORCE

The entire process of adolescent development is set askew when the family itself is disrupted. The adolescent's sense of things being disjointed within herself is mimicked and enlarged by her parents' betrayal, for from her point of view the family in which she was born is a God-made unit, and any change of form is a transgression. People are not fair to family members. They make a series of demands upon them, demands stemming from needs. Fairness is irrelevant, especially the child's fairness to a parent. Many adults feel that an adolescent understands divorce better than a younger child—and perhaps that is so, but the understanding does not create ease or acceptance.

It is impossible to consider any aspect of parent and child today without considering the effects of divorce. In Canada 100,000 children a year experience the divorce of their parents. In the United States the parents of one million children become divorced each year. In England, though the total number is much smaller, nearly thirty percent of children under 16 experience the divorce of their parents. Divorce, though common, is not an epidemic, for now the percentage, which has been on a steady rise since the beginning of the century (with an uncharacteristic period of stability in the 1950s) is levelling off. Nonetheless divorce as a common experience of children is here to stay.

Many parents try to stay together until the children are old enough, though children of all ages find divorce difficult to accept. One surprising recent finding is that the poor effects of divorce on children actually seem to increase as the child gets older—at least up the age of 18.[9] But waiting until the children are old enough to understand may mean waiting until they are ready to feel outrage at the betrayal of one parent to another, or when their own sexuality, especially a girl's, is so tentative and confused, that sexual vacillation, or betrayal, or the sexual visibility that comes with changing partners, is "disgusting," "revolting," giving rise to the adolescent's belief that her age group has a monopoly on sex. A mother who expects her adolescent daughter to accept her sexuality and her sexual needs, will be disappointed. The fact that the daughter herself is experiencing the emergence of sexual needs does not make her more tolerant of her mother's. Understanding them more fully, she is less tolerant. A daughter may seem to accept it, but only because she is "getting used to it" or "doesn't have to think about it anymore." The secret of acceptance of the parents' sex life is that it is not brought to her attention, that it is part of the normal and hidden domestic framework.

Adolescents, more than younger children, are aware, frightened and resentful of the drastic cut in domestic income that often follows a divorce. Younger children, with their greater innocence about financial matters, take each limitation as it comes, whereas the adolescent will be oppressed by the overall picture, and pressured into either finding ways to help or finding ways to compensate for these new limitations. Adolescents are better at assessing the situation, and knowing what they fear, at naming dreadful things. They may not feel the primitive fear of a child that as her parents separate from one another they will abandon her. The adolescent may not suffer from the guilt common to a younger child that she is the cause for the divorce, or that the divorce occurred because she was bad, that in some nebulous but moral way it was her fault. But even in late adolescence, the adolescent's best strategy is to withdraw, to turn to her own concerns, and keep clear of her parents' difficulties. She needs her mother, yet her mother is often under too much stress to heed her needs. The considerable needs of an adolescent are often less loudly proclaimed, and hence seem less overwhelming and urgent than the needs of a young child. Moreover, the adolescent's needs are more difficult to meet, involving as they do the sympathy of the mother, the acknowledgement of her daughter's maturity and change.

However intrusive, however upsetting, girls fare better than boys, even though they tend to face greater pressure from divorce. The daughter is more likely than the son to be chosen as a confidant of the mother, and that kind of symmetrical support isn't the best kind of support. The mother's need to confide in the daughter is a loaded, or mixed, blessing: it is good in so far as the daughter gets more attention, but it is bad in that this type of support forces her into an alliance with the mother and against the father. Normally she wants to remain loyal to each parent. If the mother uses her as a confidant, asking her to sympathise with her complaints against the husband, then the daughter is drawn away from her father and cannot feel loyal to him, without thereby disappointing her mother. Moreover, if the mother is under stress, and seeks support from her daughter, then it is difficult for her daughter to seek support from her. "I can't bother her with that now," or "I keep my problems to myself now," adolescent girls repeatedly said when their parents were undergoing a separation or divorce. There was a subtle but significant difference between the way in which a girl seeks to protect her mother from the daughter's problems and the way in which a boy seeks to protect himself: "I keep myself to myself, now." "I come home and go straight to my room, and I do my work and then go out to see my friends. I take care of myself, and let others take care of themselves."

The young men who describe themselves so clearly as avoiding contact are protecting themselves from the confidences or complaints of a parent. They are looking out for themselves, not from hard-heartedness so much as, in the context of divorcing parents, from a good, healthy strategy. Girls do not like being drawn into the battle between parents, and though some girls are proud to be a help to their mother, proud that "she turns to me, because I'm the oldest, and I'm really the only one who can help her," the mother's dependency on them curtails their freedom. This restraint, however, is usually gladly accepted. While girls railed against their mothers for being intrusive, querulous, restrictive, they never complained about them being dependent. Adolescent girls do not like their mothers seeing them as children. They do not like being reminded of their dependence upon their mothers, but they never complain when a mother is dependent upon them. Though this dependence cannot be good for them, they may be too frightened of the mother's needs to fail the mother. They tend to be proud, too, of their ability to fulfil her needs.

The boys seemed to avoid being used as a confidant not because they were unsympathetic, but because they considered themselves unable to help. "When my Mum starts crying, I run out of the house. I can't do anything for her, and I know it's crude—getting up and going out like that. But there's like this lightning inside me, and I just go," explained a 17-year-old boy whose father had suddenly decided to try "living on his own." Yet his 15-year-old sister explained what she did when her mother cried, "Well—" she put her fingers to her lips as though trying to remember, "I just sit with her, tell her it'll be all right, and that sort of thing, I don't do anything really." Whereas the boy didn't know what to do, the girl knew what to do, but said she "didn't do anything, really." She did not think of her comfort in terms of doing anything. She was simply there, she simply sat beside her mother. The boy ran away because he felt the burden of having to do something, and thought he was incapable of doing anything. The girl offered comfort, and "did something" because she saw there was nothing to do, except be there. She knew that her presence was enough, or at least was all she could be expected to give. She was more effective because she felt that there were fewer demands made upon her.

The most recent evidence about children and divorce, shows that girls are better off if they are allowed to maintain the bond with their mother—they show less emotional disturbance, less signs of stress, exhibit fewer behavioural problems if they remain in the sole custody of their mother.[10] The first important studies about the effect of father-absence on adolescent girls revealed significant differences in dating patterns, which at first were thought to be highly significant, but subsequently were seen as an isolated immaturity, or compensation, a feature which was less disturbing when seen in the context of their overall development. The only detriment to their well-being, if deprived of their father, is that in regard to boys they seem less mature, that they tend, more often, to be sexually precocious, in that they are more receptive to and interested in boys. This aspect of their development tends to endure past adolescence—they tend to marry earlier, have sex earlier, and have their first pregnancy earlier. These girls are either hungry for male companionship and love, or they want to take determined steps away from their mother's single status.[11]

While the girls turn to men to make up for their fatherless adolescence, or to avoid following their mother's pattern, they have no other immaturity. They do not suffer from lower self-esteem or self-confidence or independence. They do tend to be very close to their mothers, but closeness is not at odds with independence. Many of these girls living with a single mother are also careful to prepare for a career or profession, and to avoid the financial trap of being a single woman with no job skills. What I found interesting was to see how a girl might shift, from a view at 13, that she was going to marry someone rich, because she had seen her mother work so hard, for so little, to a much more considered and positive view at 17 or 18, that she was going to have a profession, because in this way she would overcome the financial stress her mother had faced, along with loneliness and low self-esteem.

PARENTAL HUMILIATION

All good and trusted parents suffer blame from their children. Mothers bear the brunt of the child's anger, in particular the daughter's whose deep identification and need for the mother makes her ready to blame her whenever anything is not right. As a child the daughter blames the mother when circumstances are less than perfect. Expecting her mother to represent her world, and to present it well, the mother is implicated in every disappointment. In adolescence—and beyond—the daughter blames the mother for the faults she finds within herself. She may suffer a raging hatred which eats into her. Seeing herself as half her mother, she may want to rip out the mother within her in order to save herself.

Thus it is that the feminist movement became so easily linked to an anger against the mother. The realisation that many of her constraints are inside her did not mitigate her resentment of the "male conspiracy" in which her mother played a crucial part. The daughter experiences the social order through the mother. Hence the mother is held responsible for all those limitations from which the daughter now sees herself to be suffering. The mother's failure to draw from her daughter the best self possible, is a crime. The daughter knows she cannot correct this without her mother's help, or without a huge push against the patterns "imposed" upon her by the mother. The enduring bond to her mother seems like a defeat, an attachment which clings to her like a preying tiger. When women became highly critical of their social and psychological position, they tried to begin anew, but were held back by their own priorities. Something must be wrong with her and her mother, the feminist concluded. The problem seemed to lie in her continued identification with her mother. She continued to bear the burden of her childhood influences; she continued to be influenced by her. The blame for that continuing attachment was placed at the mother's door. It was the mother who would not let go, the mother who needed the daughter. The daughter felt she was responding to the mother's need, but in fact she was so keenly sensitive to this need because it was within herself, too.

The anger, even revulsion, many feminists felt towards their mothers, did not arise suddenly, or uniquely, nor was its first expression in feminist writings. It began at home, and in all probability the mother was the first to hear of it, the first who was asked to validate it. "I've always tried to be available to [my daughter] and to listen to whatever it was she had to say. Okay, sometimes I couldn't talk the minute she wanted me to, but I'd make an effort to sit down with her later in the day," insisted the mother of 18-year-old Lauren. "But now, when I do that, when I sit down and prepare myself to hear what she has to say, I'm completely at a loss, because what she's telling me is that everything I do—everything I did—is wrong. Sometimes she seems to be saying I loved her too much, and sometimes she seems to be saying I didn't love her enough. I never left her alone, she'll say one minute, and the next she's complaining that I never supported her enough. I sit down thinking we're about to have an open discussion, and I discover that I'm consenting to hear her judgement against me." With the daughter's new reflective and consolidating capacity, she can look back on her childhood, and how her mother was when she was a child, and see new depths of insults and wounds in previous behaviour, often coloured by misbalancing or misperceptions, often involving the gross unfairness that is common to descriptions of behaviour of family members—whether it is parents describing a child's behaviour or a child describing a parent's behaviour. Most parents know the injustice and outrage of a child protesting, "You always play with my little sister, but you never played with me when I was that age," or "You never let me do anything I want to do." What they are less aware of is how grossly they themselves misrepresent a child's behaviour. The mother tends to over-estimate—by a factor of 600%!—the amount of whining, coaxing and nagging her child engages in.[12] The irritating behaviour of her child becomes clustered into an image which, under pressure, she may insist is what the child is. "Why do you always have to nag?" "Why can't you ever listen to what I have to say?" show a parent who—at the moment she says this—is taking only what she dislikes in the child and presenting it as the child's complete self. In effect, she is stereotyping the child through her anger and frustration. She stereotypes the child because she is frustrated. The mother has no opportunity to present her own case. She is humiliated by the child's unfairness, by the child's narrow perspective and distorted memory. She passes the narrowness and meanness back to the daughter. She sulks as her daughter dismisses, disregards, or denies the love within her anger.

As mother and daughter face one another with the bonds of loving hatred, they seek to find blame for this impasse outside themselves. Each believes that her feelings are fundamentally good, that her object is to maintain the attachment, or to change so that it can be maintained. The daughter, when angry, feels that her mother is being unfair to her. The adolescent's use of "fairness" or "unfair," when applied to her family's behaviour, is not much better than the child's. She may have a better grasp of the logic of general principles, she may be better than she was as a child at balancing or spotting the significant differences in different circumstances, but her domestic use of these terms will be as self-interested, beyond rational argument, and ignorantly self-righteous as that of a 9-year-old. Her need to argue her anger is part of her need for self-validation. She needs her mother to see her point, and to accept it. She begs her mother, it seems, to turn against herself. Never would it occur to her to keep her criticisms of her mother's behaviour or lifestyle to herself. For her criticisms lack punch unless the mother confirms them—at the very least, by being hurt or made angry by them.

The mother is much better at this sucker's job than the father. Her greater capacity to take the daughter's point of view, and her sympathy with the daughter's need to persuade her mother to share a view of her self, makes her willing to listen to criticisms—up to a point, and the point up to which she is willing to listen tends to be the point of explosion. Whereas the father will break off a blaming session before it gets rolling, the mother will wait and listen, watching for some possible compromise or correction, some clue to understanding the problems behind the complaints. The mother will never be totally sure that she is right and the daughter wrong. While the daughter will feel herself to be magnificently self-justified, doubt will linger. Depending so greatly upon her mother for her sense of her self, she will expect confirmation from her mother even for her criticisms of her mother.

"I can't make her see what she's doing to me. Little things— she thinks they're little—will make me so angry, and she just looks at me, as if to say 'What's up?' She says I should be wearing something different, or tells me how to do something, and she puts me in such an awful mood. I get this sinking feeling, like she's talking inside of me. She doesn't see how bad those little things are, how they ruin my day." As this 17-year-old girl spoke, she made fists with her hands, which she then rhythmically beat against her thighs. She was angry with her mother for having such a huge effect upon her, angry with herself for being so sensitive, and frustrated because she could not hold up her view of her mother, and convince her mother to face this view as a looking glass. In her anger, the adolescent girl seeks her mother's aid in the anger towards her.

People are not generally good at observing their own behaviour. Since many quarrels between daughter and mother involve irritable and angry suppositions about what each is doing to the other, the arguments are characterised by hypercriticism, and by brooding upon mutual injustices. A mother feels that the daughter started the quarrel, by picking on her, showing disrespect for her, trying to upset her, disobeying her, or, as I heard repeatedly, refusing to "listen to her"—which meant a number of things, from simply ignoring what she said to not accepting the truth of what she said. The daughter is sure that she did nothing, that the mother started the quarrel, or took offence at some insignificant remark, or misinterpreted her, or did not believe her, or in turn didn't listen to her. In her anger, and her wish to justify this anger, each makes statements such as "You always suspect the worst of me," "You're always criticising me," "You never listen to a word I say," "You always back-talk," "Why do you have to complain about everything?" "Why do you always have to whine?" The atmosphere can become rich with accusation and counter-accusation. The mother feels her love is being rejected; the daughter feels that her new personality is being devalued: "I'm not discarding her," Gwen insisted, "that's what she says, isn't it? [about her waiting so long before coming to her with her problematic pregnancy]. Anyway—what is *she* doing to *me*? It's like she's looking at my whole life through this one mistake, as though she's taking every move I've made on my own and screwing it up into a ball and throwing it away. She's using this mess to prove to me that everything I've done on my own is wrong."

The daughter's anger is so vehement because she believes it is ineffective. She sees her mother as unchanging. Yet from the mother's point of view, the daughter's anger is controlling. She feels blackmailed by these accusations. She is enraged that the love and fairness she has tried to give, is rejected. Mother and daughter inflict pain on one another through shouting, through sulking, through ignoring one another, trying to invalidate one another even as the presence and reality of the other is all too real, all too deeply felt by each.

Yet, in the strange configurations of domestic logic, daughters only blame mothers in a context of trust and gratitude. She blames her, having high expectations of her. It is these expectations, and this blame which are thought to be resolved through "separation," which is the psychological term

for the process of "growing up" and coming to terms with the
fact that one's mother is a separate and imperfect individual
who is not always available and who cannot satisfy all one's
needs and expectations. It is the remarkably persistent "difficulty" with these aims that persuaded me to form a new model
which would make sense of a girl's abiding psychological dependency on her mother, and to help the mother see the positive and loving force behind the passionately rough time her
daughter gives her. I felt supported in this task by the fact that
the girls who seemed most "separate" from their mothers—in
that they were most likely to accept the mother as being a
separate and imperfect person—were girls who had become autonomous through sheer disappointment. In extremely troubled families, or among extremely troubled adolescent girls,
blame was more sparse than in productive and reasonably normal homes. Having more cause to reject or blame her mother,
the delinquent girl seems to have an increased need to hold on
to a childhood attachment to her. Having more cause to blame
her, the delinquent girl offers excuses for her: "It was my stepfather who really turned her against me," "Those drugs just
tore up her mind," "She's ill. She's hooked on those drinks and
she tries, but it keeps on at her," "She's done what she could,
but there was never any money and with all the worrying about
that, she couldn't see to all of us too."

Aggressive and destructive behaviour in adolescent girls
rests primarily on the absence of a closeness with a mother who
cares about her, and who does her job in responding to her
maturing personality.[13] The aggressive failure to care about
herself is a way of expressing her anger and disappointment in
failing to find someone who will care about her, and validate
her, and thus ensure her self-value. Also, the failure to care
about what is happening to her may be a defence against the
awful things that are happening or have happened to her. When
she has been abused or neglected by the people she was born
to love, and whose job is to love her, she is taught that she has
no value, and accepting that lesson is the best way to keep her
love intact, to keep the rage at bay, and to neglect the consequences of her actions which express the threads of anger that
remain.

Though mourning for the loss of childhood (and the depression this engenders) has been considered a normal part of adolescent development,[14] I found it only among delinquent girls. These were the girls who mused, "If only I could do it all over again," or "If only I knew then what I know now," or "I wish I could go back, and just be a baby again." Yet these girls were looking back not to a stage of real joy, but to a fanciful idyll. Most of them had committed some delinquent act before the age of 10, and one girl had tried to cash her first forged cheque when she was 5. Finding angry and anxious feelings particularly difficult to cope with, girls turn to drugs and to alcohol not so much as a stimulus, but for escape. When girls said that alcohol heightened their experience, when it made them more rather than less sensitive, they avoided it. Girls like alcohol when it soothes them, calms them, suppresses memory and anxiety.[15]

THE LOSS OF A MOTHER

The adolescent's relationship with her mother provides enormous opportunity for growth, and she will make use of it, if she can. However, some girls do survive without mothers. They find other people to give them what a mother cannot, or will not give her. They develop a self-mothering capacity, which both defines and cushions their loss. "I call it up as I fall asleep," 15-year-old Nina explained. "It's a hand that I reach up to, just floating above my head. I love sleep. Even during the day, when I don't feel it, I know it's there, and it's something I look forward to. No one would guess this about me. Everyone says how well I cope, how grown-up I am. But I have that comfort at night."

Measuring the effect of actual loss of a mother on the child—the final loss, through death—remains an elusive quest. The consensus position is that very young children, because of their psychological immaturity, are unable to mourn the death of a parent—until adolescence. Any reactions to the death of a parent before adolescence, it is thought, are generally defensive. That is, they guard against the realisation of the death, they prevent the child from facing the loss, so that even bereaved children who are functioning well and developing normally are considered "precarious" and appear fragile and tentative in their maturational steps.[16] But in adolescence a normal process of mourning becomes possible; by this time a girl has developed a sufficient memory capacity to form a concept of another person and sustain that conception during her absence. She can therefore (it is supposed) confront the loss, work through it, accept it, and move forward.

There is very little clinical or statistical information about the effect on an adolescent of a mother's death. This was clearly different from maternal neglect or abuse. I sought out a small handful of adolescent girls whose mothers had died. Though each girl "confronted" her mother's death—that is, she thought about it, spoke about it, felt it—there was little sign that it was being worked through. One woman of 30, whose mother had died when she was 15, said, "I still feel as close to that day [of her mother's death] now as I did then. In some way nothing has happened since then. I don't cry about it anymore, but somehow it's always the same, like it's still happening, or just happened." A 14-year-old girl, Laurie, whose mother had died from cancer six months before I spoke to her, described her first day back at school, after the relatives who had come to town for the funeral, left her home. "I walked into school and suddenly all the girls were surrounding me. 'How are you?' they wanted to know. 'Are you all right?' 'Is there anything we can do?' You know, it was such a shock to discover they knew all about it. I hadn't thought about that. It had never occurred to me that they had been told, and I was furious. 'I'm fine,' I told them. 'Why shouldn't I be fine?' and I went straight to my locker and took off my coat and got my books and went into the classroom, snubbing every last one of them. It took me a long time to deal with that anger, that sense that someone had betrayed me, that they'd all whispered behind my back about my mother's death. I never said anything to any of them about it, because I just didn't see how any words I used could explain what I felt, and it seemed an awful cheek for them to try to get something out of me."

The language of friendship, for all its intimacy, is not the language of mourning, and not the language of maternal love. "Friends can help," explained a 16-year-old whose mother had gone into hospital for an apparently routine operation on her back, and had suddenly died under anaesthetic, "just by being around, you don't feel so lonely. But I don't want to talk to them about it. I keep them at arm's length when they try to find out how I really feel about it."

From my small sample of bereaved girls, it seemed that the older they were, the worse they suffered. Whereas the 14-year-old felt that friends helped, and that her relatives, especially her mother's sister, were being very nice, a 17-year-old, whose mother had died seventeen days after being in an automobile accident, said, "Nothing helps. There's nothing I can do to get away from it," and the strangest thing for this older adolescent was that she felt she had not been close to her mother, that they had drifted apart, and quarrelled terribly, and "hadn't quite sorted things out yet." "I spend half my time still arguing with her, in my head, and then suddenly I realise she's not there to fight back. That really makes me angry!" She laughed ruefully.

The mourning seemed to be "resolved" as they found their mother's attributes and their mother's roles in other people. Some girls—the lucky ones—developed a sudden closeness to the father. One girl said her relationship with her father changed "overnight," that she no longer thought of him as an unworthy confidant. "I used to get the jitters whenever he tried to talk to me. You know, I would get so irritated, and start tapping my foot or my finger, showing him how I couldn't wait for him to go away, because whatever he said seemed so stupid and so wide of the mark that there was no point to discussion. And now suddenly he seems to understand me, and care for me, and he's not asking too much of me. I dreaded seeing him again, after my mother died because I thought he'd be sulking and wanting me to comfort him. But he just seems to be there for me now. He's much more real—well, he loves me more effectively than I ever thought he could." The 30-year-old woman, who felt her mother's death was as close to her now as the day she died fifteen years before, said that she thought her husband had many of her mother's qualities, "and sometimes I catch myself saying things to him in the same tone of voice I might have used with my mother."

THE LIFE-LONG DIALOGUE

The adolescent daughter needs her mother. She needs to fight with her, to come to self-awareness by forcing her mother to see the new person within her. The mother often finds this exhausting work. She may also find it disheartening, for she may not like the person her daughter is becoming. She knows that she is playing a large part in this development. Her daughter's demands upon her make this very clear. Yet she does not always believe she has control upon her influence. She tries to influence her daughter in one direction, but her wishes push her daughter in another direction. It is maddening, having this powerful influence yet being unable to direct it, to feel that what she does has enormous impact on her daughter without being able to predict its effect. Her daughter's responses seem, given the twists of psychological logic, bizarre and irrational. Though her daughter continues to use her as a mirror or a sounding board, the mother herself has lost her daughter as a simple and direct reflector of the mother's love.

If people close to us change, and change rapidly, we may be thrilled, but we may also be threatened. We may not like what they are. In some ways mothers are more "objective" about a teenage daughter than about a much younger daughter. As she changes, they see her more clearly. They see her from a greater distance. If they do not like what they see, they feel that bitter anger which only a disappointed parent feels. But not liking them, they continue to love them, and try to change them.

As a very young adult, a woman often has, towards her mother, a cooling off or brushing off phase. Disappointed by her "failure" to separate during adolescence, she tries to draw boundaries between them. She is a woman, too, now, and an equal of her mother. Her self-boundaries should be well-defined, should they not? If she is fortunate, if she has some success, some direction, and forms some good attachments outside her family, then these "boundaries" will take good shape within new contexts, and her demands upon her mother will diminish. Yet many young women, as they receive the first thrills of adult confirmation in their work, stack up these successes like a pile of grudges, reserved ammunition against the mother, who did not believe in her enough, or failed to recognise that skill, that capacity. "My mother thought I couldn't be a lawyer. She thought I wanted to go to law school just to stay in school a few years longer. She didn't think I was career-minded. And now she sees my salary cheque—well, that impresses her. I never could convince her, but this pay-in slip sure does." "My mother was always sure I wouldn't make it through college. She thought I had the brains, but somehow not the stamina. I want her to come to my graduation—she'd better come—because I want her to sit there and see that I've done it. Without a slip. Without a tremor. I've done it, and she was wrong to be afraid." "When I walk on to the stage," said a young opera singer, "the most nervous person in the hall is my mother. She told me she had dreams, just before I first performed at the Wigmore Hall, that I forgot the music, that I just broke off, and there was nothing she could do to help me. I always feel particularly sassy [smug, impudent] when she's watching me. I want to prove I have all the confidence I need." "Here I am, living on my own—and living pretty well—miles away from her," explained an apparently highly independent woman of 23, "but each time—a hundred times a day!—I'll find myself talking to her, as though she's here, arguing with me. It could be any little thing. She might be asking me why I'm buying this or that at the supermarket, and I'll find myself trying to come up with an explanation that will suit her. Or it might be a conversation with a much larger framework. I'll be telling her how satisfying I find this job, what good work I can hope to do as a lawyer, and how right she was to back me. Anything in my life that wouldn't appeal to her tends to crop up. Sometimes I'm annoyed and sometimes I feel as though I'm getting somewhere, that she's really able to understand and accept all of me. It's not a huge issue—it doesn't take up my whole consciousness. I'll just catch myself doing it. It can be peripheral—but then of course I can also brood long and hard over it."

The desire to make the mother proud is twisted into anger, anger that it is still necessary to fight for recognition. The mother's protectiveness is so ingrained that it takes some time to get used to her daughter's ability to plough through life without her. The daughter offers her independence like a gift, and then finds that it is received with suspicion. Or, when she has proved that her life as an adult is pretty much in order, a less dependent sister may seem to absorb the greater part of passion and attachment that parents retain for their adult children. The good work done between them during adolescence creates high expectation, and hence offers many grounds for disappointment and complaint.

Mothers and daughters continue to quarrel because neither gives up on the other. Underlying the continuing quarrels is the hope that needs will be met. Each quarrel is an attempt to get, this time, the right response, the correct effect. A mother continues to haunt her daughter, for better or for worse, throughout her life. This intimacy is due not only, and perhaps not primarily, to the emotional bonding of infancy, but to the type of personal growth she battles through during adolescence, a growth which is like a persuasion. It is impossible ever to forget the role she has played in this development, and it is impossible ever to forgive those bad patches which reside within us all. Well into adulthood, long past adolescence, daughters ponder over the meaning their mothers had for them. A woman may fear becoming a mother herself as she acknowledges the terrible burden of her personality, as something which is bound to affect her daughter as much as her mother's affected her. This intimate exchange of identity is a secret dread of many women, which can be heightened as they themselves become mothers of daughters. The daughter's need for her mother's confirmation cannot be conceived as a weakness, but as a fact of female psychology. Letters between mothers and daughters document this continued need for the daughter to explain herself, to justify herself through explanation, through making her mother see, understand, accept, verify, confirm.[17] This form of written communication is particularly revealing. Sometimes it urges forward the more positive feelings, which may be buried under daily, minor irritations.[18] Sometimes the negative feelings surface, which are normally buried under the fear of causing pain, or of retaliation. In letters the daughter takes on a more adult and circumspect persona. The daughter feels she has the chance to have her full say, without interruption. She can qualify her remarks at her own pace. The hectic ping-pong effect of the adolescent smashing with a spin each remark her mother hands to her, turns into a more refined dialogue, wherein the mother is able to explain herself and her love anew, to someone who had known it all along, but who can now understand it. This dialogue continues in some form as long as the mother and daughter can look at one another, and acknowledge what they see.

The greatest change in adulthood is not the final breaking of the bond between mother and daughter, but the daughter's acceptance of the fact that it is not the mother who forces the bond upon her. Whereas the daughter may continue to pick fights, or to seek confirmation, or to expect praise, the mother herself loosens her hold, and wonders at the tenacity of her daughter's complaints, her continued fantasy that the mother is "governing" her life. "In a voice remarkably free of emotion— a voice, detached, curious, only wanting information—she says to me, 'Why don't you go already? Why don't you walk away from my life? I'm not stopping you,'" demands an elderly mother of her middle-aged daughter, finding her demands and complaints exhausting and confusing. Standing "half in, half out" of the mother's room, the adult daughter acknowledges, "I know you're not Ma."[19] The daughter grows into womanhood, still puzzled by that tricky equation between her identity and her mother's, still prepared to fight one more battle to make their different positions clear, and for her mother to offer the banner of acceptance and admiration. In moments of enlightenment, she sees that the argument is no longer between her mother and herself, but between her self and the history which formed that self.

NOTES

1. Lillian Rublin, "Generations in Conflict," talk presented at Oakland Children's Hospital, 26 March 1988 (book under same title forthcoming).
2. Kohlberg, 1976.
3. Gilligan, 1982.
4. Haan, et al., 1985, suggests that if you want to discover someone's moral priorities the researcher should not listen to what the person says but look at what she does.
5. Elkind, 1981.
6. *Family Planning Perspectives*, 1980, 1977 (updated reprint, 1980).
7. Maccoby, 1980.
8. Baumrind, 1978.
9. Jan Johnston, recent research and data analysis in the Family Dynamics Seminar.
10. Jan Johnston, also reporting recent update of work with Wallerstein.
11. Hetherington, 1972, and follow-up study.
12. Patterson and Forgatch, 1987.
13. One exception to this link between aggressive behaviour and absence of a strong bond to the mother involves adolescent suicides. Recent data from San Francisco Children's Hospital indicates that only adolescents within a family setting commit suicide or attempt suicide. Children who have run away from home do not commit suicide. Only adolescents who remain at home commit or attempt suicide. The data at the moment is merely suggestive. However, it is possible that suicide involves extreme anger towards others, anger which makes the victim feel that she is already destroyed. This particular combination of defeat and anger may well occur, for the adolescent, only if she remains linked to her parents.
14. Blos, 1962.
15. Konopka, 1972.
16. Garber, 1983.
17. Payne, 1983.
18. Plath, 3 March 1956.
19. Gornick, 1987.

BIBLIOGRAPHY

Adelson, Joseph (ed.), *Handbook of Adolescent Psychology*, New York: John Wiley, 1980.

Anthony, E. James, "The reactions of adults to adolescents and their behaviour," in Gerald Caplan and Serge Lebovici (eds.), *Adolescence*, New York: Basic Books, 1969.

Apter, Terri, *Why Women Don't Have Wives*, London: Macmillan Press; New York: Schocken, 1985.

Aries, Peter, *Centuries of Childhood*, New York: Vintage, 1962; Harmondsworth: Penguin, 1981.

Baldwin, W., "Adolescent pregnancy and childrearing—growing concerns for Americans," *Population Bulletin*, vol. 31, no. 2, 1977 (updated reprint, 1980).

Banks, Stephen and Michael Kahn, *The Sibling Bond*, New York: Basic Books, 1982.

Bardwick, Judith M. and E. Douvan, "Ambivalence: the socialization of women," in V. Gornick and B.K. Moran (eds.), *Women in a Sexist Society: Studies in power and powerlessness*, New York: Basic Books, 1971.

Bardwick, Judith M., Elizabeth Douvan, Matina Horner and David Gutman, *Feminine Personality and Conflict*, Belmont, California: Brooks/Cole Publishing, 1970; London: Greenwoods Press, 1981.

Baumrind, D., "Parental disciplinary patterns and social competence in children," *Youth and Society*, vol. 9, no. 3, pp. 249–76, 1978.

Bell, David C. and Linda G. Bell, "Parental validation and support in the development of adolescent daughters," in H.D. Grotevant and C. R. Cooper (eds.), *Adolescent Development in the Family*, San Francisco: Jossey-Bass, 1983.

Bernard, Jessie Shirley, *The Future of Marriage*, New York: World Publications, 1972; London: Souvenir, 1973.

Bernard, Jessie Shirley, *The Female World*, New York: Free Press; London: Collier Macmillan, 1981.

Block, Joan H., *Lives Through Time*, Berkeley: Bancroft, 1973.

Block, Joan H., "Another look at sex differentiation in the socialization behaviors of mothers and fathers," in J. Sherman and F. Denmark (eds.), *Psychology of Women: Future directions of research*, New York: Psychological Dimensions, 1978.

Block, Joan H., *Personality Development in Males and Females: The influence of differential socialization*, unpublished manuscript, University of California, 1981.

Blos, Peter, *On Adolescence: A psychoanalytic interpretation*, New York: Free Press, 1962.

Blos, Peter, "The second individuation process in adolescence," *Psychoanalytic Study of the Child*, vol. 22, pp.162–86, 1967.

Blos, Peter, *The Adolescent Passage*, New York: International Universities Press, 1979.

Blos, Peter, "Modifications in the traditional psychoanalytic theory of female adolescent development," *Adolescent Psychiatry*, vol. 8, pp. 8–24, 1980.

Bowlby, John, "Process of mourning," *International Journal of Psychoanalysis*, vol. 442, pp. 317–40, 1961.

Bowlby, John, "Pathological mourning and childhood mourning," *Journal of the American Psychoanalytic Association*, vol. 11, pp. 500–41, 1963.

Brooks-Gunn, Jeanne and Anne C. Petersen (eds.), *Girls at Puberty: Biological and psychosocial perspectives*, New York: Plenum Press, 1983.

Chernin, Kim, *In My Mother's House*, New York: Ticknor and Fields, 1983; London: Virago, 1985.

Chodorow, Nancy, *The Reproduction of Mothering: Psychoanalysis and the sociology of gender*, Berkeley: University of California Press, 1978.

Chodorow, Nancy and Susan Contratto, "The fantasy of the perfect mother" in Barrie Thorne with Marilyn Yalom (eds.), *Rethinking the Family: Some feminist questions*, New York and London: Longman, 1982.

Clausen, John A., "The social meaning of differential physical and sexual maturation," in S. E. Dragastin and G. H. Elder (eds.), *Adolesence in the Life Cycle: Psychosocial change and social context*, Washington, DC: Hemisphere, 1975.

Cohen, Betsy, *The Snow White Syndrome: All about envy*, New York: Macmillan, 1986.

Coleman, John S., *The Adolescent Society*, New York: Free Press, 1961.

Cooper, Catherine R. and Harold D. Grotevant, "Gender issues in the interface of family experience and adolescents' friendship and dating identity," *Journal of Youth and Adolescence*, vol. 16, pp. 247–264, 1987.

Dalsimer, Katherine, *Female Adolescence: Psychoanalytic reflections on works of literature*, New Haven and London: Yale University Press, 1986.

Darling, Carol A. and Mary W. Hicks, "Parental influence on adolescent sexuality: implications for parents as educators," *Journal of Youth and Adolescence*, vol. 12, no. 6, 1983.

Davidson, Sara, *Loose Change: Three women of the sixties*, London: Collins, 1977.

Degler, Carl N., *At odds: Women and the family in America from the revolution to the present*, New York: Oxford University Press, 1980.

Demos, J. and V. Demos, "Adolescence in historical perspective," *Journal of Marriage and the Family*, vol. 31, pp. 632–8, 1969.

Deutsch, Helen, *The Psychology of Women*, 2 vols, New York: Grune and Stratton, 1944.

Deutsch, Helen, *Selected Problems of Adolescence: With emphasis on group formation*, New York: International Universities Press, 1967.

Dinnerstein, Dorothy, *The Mermaid and the Minotaur: Sexual arrangements and human malaise*, New York: Harper & Row, 1976.

Dinnerstein, Dorothy, *The Rocking of the Cradle and the Ruling of the World*, London: Souvenir Press, 1978.

Douvan, Elizabeth, and Joseph Adelson, *The Adolescent Experience*, New York: John Wiley, 1966.

Dunn, Judy, Denise Daniels, Frank F. Furstenburg, and Robert Plomin, "Environmental differences within the family," *Child Development*, vol. 56, pp.764–74, 1985.

Ehrensaft, Diane, *Parenting Together: Men and women sharing the care of their children*, New York: Free Press; London: Collier Macmillan, 1987.

Elkind, David, *The Hurried Child: Growing up too fast too soon*, Reading, Massachusetts: Addison-Wesley, 1981.

Elliot, Gregroy C., "Self-esteem and Self-presentation among the young as a function of age and gender," *Journal of Youth and Adolescence*, Vol. 12, no. 3, pp. 135–53, 1983.

Erikson, Erik, "The concept of ego identity," *The Journal of the American Pschoanalytic Association*, vol. 4, pp. 56–121, 1956.

Erikson, Erik, *Identity and the Life Cycle: Psychological issues*, vol. 1, no. 1, 1959.

Erikson, Erik, *Childhood and Society*, New York: Norton, 1963; Harmondsworth: Penguin, 1965.

Erikson, Erik, *Identity: Youth and Crisis*, New York: Norton, 1968; London: Faber, 1971.

Erikson, Erik, "Once more the inner space," in J. Strouse (ed.), *Women and Analysis*, New York: Grossman, pp. 320–40, 1974.

Erkut, Sumru, "Daughters talking about their mothers," revised version of a talk given at the Wellesley College Center for Research on Women's Daughters and Mothers Colloquium, 11 February

1984, Working Paper 127. Wellesley, Massachusetts: Wellesley College, Center for Research on Women.

Esman, Aaron H. (ed.), *The Psychology of Adolescence*, New York: International Universities Press, 1975.

Esman, Aaron H. "Adolescence and the 'new sexuality,' " in *On Sexuality: Psychoanalytic observations*, International Universities Press, 19–28, 1979.

Esman, Aaron H., (ed.), *International Annals of Adolescent Psychiatry*, vol. 1, Chicago and London: University of Chicago Press, 1988.

Family Planning Perspectives, "Sexual activity, contraceptive use and pregnancy among metropolitan-area teenagers: 1971–9," *FPP*, vol. 12, no. 5, 1980.

Fine, Stuart, "Children in divorce, custody and access situations: an update," *Journal of Child Psychiatry*, pp. 361–64, 1987.

Frank, Anne, *The Diary of a Young Girl*, 1947, trans. R. Mannheim and M. Mok, New York: Pocket Books, 1953; Harmondsworth: Penguin, 1986.

Freeman, Derek, *Margaret Mead and Samoa*, Cambridge, Massachusetts: Harvard University Press, 1982.

Freud, Anna, "Adolescence," *The Psychoanalytic Study of the Child*, vol. 13, pp. 255–78, 1958.

Freud, Sigmund, *Three Essays on the Theory of Sexuality*, in James Strachy (ed.), Standard Edition, vol. 7, pp.125–78, London: Hogarth Press, 1953.

Freud, Sigmund, "The dissolution of the Oedipus complex," Standard Edition, vol. 19, pp.171–9, London: Hogarth Press, 1961.

Freud, Sigmund, "Female sexuality," Standard Edition, vol. 21, p. 225–43, London: Hogarth Press, 1961.

Freud, Sigmund, *New Introductory Lectures on Psychoanalysis*, Standard Edition, vol. 22, pp. 7–182, London: Hogarth Press, 1964.

Freud, Sigmund, "An outline of psychoanalysis," Standard Edition, vol. 23, pp.139–207, London: Hogarth Press, 1964.

Friday, Nancy, *My Mother, My Self: The daughter's search for identity*, New York: Delacorte Press, 1977; London: Sheldon Press, 1979.

Friday, Nancy, *Jealousy*, New York: Morrow, 1985; London: Collins, 1986.

Friedan, Betty, *The Feminine Mystique*, London: Gollancz, 1963.

Friedan, Betty, *The Second Stage*, New York: Summit Books, 1981.

Gagnon, John and W. Simon, *Sexual Conduct: The social sources of human sexuality*, Chicago: Adeline, 1973.

Garber, Benjamin, "Some thoughts on normal adolescents who lost a parent by death," *Journal of Youth and Adolescence*, vol. 12, pp.175–85, 1983.

Gilligan, Carol, *In a Different Voice: Psychological theories and women's development*, Cambridge, Massachusetts and London: Harvard University Press, 1982.

Goffman, Erving, *The Presentation of Self in Everyday Life*, New York: Doubleday, 1959; Harmondsworth: Penguin, 1971.

Goffman, Erving, *Strategic Interactions*, University of Pennsylvania Press, 1969, Oxford: Oxford University Press, 1970.

Gornick, Vivian, *Fierce Attachments*, New York: Strauss, Farrar, Giroux, 1987.

Greenacre, P., "Special problems in early female sexual development," *Psychoanalytic Study of the Child*, vol. 5, pp.112–38, 1950.

Greenberg, Mark, T., Judith M. Siegel and Cynthia J. Leitch, "The nature and importance of attachment relationships to parents and peers during adolescence," *Journal of Youth and Adolescence*, vol. 12, p. 373, 1983.

Grotevant, Harold D., and Catherine Cooper (eds.), *Adolescent Development in the Family*, San Francisco: Jossey-Bass, 1983.

Gutman, David, "New sources of conflict in females at adolescence and early adulthood," in J. Bardwick (ed.), *Feminine Personality and Conflict*, Belmont: Brooks/Cole Publishing Co., 1970; London: Greenwood Press, 1981.

Haan, Norma, M.B. Smith, and J. Block, "Moral reasoning in young adults: political–social behaviour, family background, and personality correlates," *Journal of Personality and Social Psychology*, vol. 10, pp.183–201, 1968.

Haan, Norma, Elaine Aerts and Bruce A. B. Cooper, *On Moral Grounds: The search for practical morality*, New York and London: New York University Press, 1985.

Hall, Stanley, *Adolescence*, New York: Appleton, 1904.

Hamburg, B., "Early adolescence: a specific and stressful stage of the life cycle," in G. Coelo, D. Hamburg, and J. Adams (eds.), *Coping and Adaptation*, New York: Basic Books, pp.101–124.

Henning, Margaret and Anne Jardim, *The Managerial Woman*, New York: Pocket Books, 1977; London: Boyars, 1978.

Hetherington, E.M., "Effects of father-absence on personality development in adolescent daughters," *Developmental Psychology*, vol. 7, pp. 313–26, 1972.

Hochschild, Arlie Russel, *The Managed Heart: The commercialization of human feeling*, Berkeley: University of California Press, 1983.

Hock, Robert A. and John F. Curry, "Sex role identification of normal adolescent males and females as related to school achievement," *Journal of Youth and Adolescence*, vol. 12, pp. 461–70, 1983.

Hoffman, M.L., "Parental discipline and the child's consideration for others," *Child Development*, vol. 34, pp. 573–88, 1963.

Hoffman, M.L., "Father-absence and conscience development," *Developmental Psychology*, vol. 4. pp. 400–6, 1971.

Hoffman, M.L., "Moral internalization, parental power, and the nature of parent-child interaction," *Developmental Psychology*, vol. 11, pp. 228–39, 1975.

Hoffman, M.L. and H.D. Saltzstein, "Parental discipline and the child's moral development," *Journal of Personality and Social Psychology*, vol. 5, pp. 45–57, 1967.

Horner, Matina, "Fail Bright Women," *Psychology Today*, vol. 3, no. 6, p. 36, 1969.

Horner, Matina, "Towards an understanding of achievement-related conflicts in women," *Journal of Social Issues*, vol. 28, pp.157–76, 1972.

Horney, Karen, "The dread of women. Observations on a specific difference in the dread felt by men and women respectively for the opposite sex," *International Journal of Psychoanalysis*, vol. 13, pp. 348–60, 1932.

Ivy, M.E. and J.M. Bardwick, "Patterns of affective fluctuation in menstrual cycle," *Psychosomatic Medicine*, vol. 30, pp. 336–45, 1968.

Jacob, T, "Patterns of family conflict and dominance as a function of child age and social class," *Developmental Psychology*, vol. 10, pp. 1–12, 1974.

Jones, Ernest, "The early development of female sexuality," *International Journal of Psychoanalysis*, vol. 8, pp. 459–72, 1927.

Jones, Ernest, "Early female sexuality," *International Journal of Psychoanalysis*, vol. 14, pp.1–33, 1932.

Kaplan, E. B., "Manifestations of aggression in latency and preadolescent girls," *Psychoanalytic Study of the Child*, vol. 31, pp. 63–78, 1976.

Kaplan, Louise J., *Adolescence: The farewell to childhood*, New York: Simon and Schuster, 1984.

Kett, Joseph F., *Rites of Passage: Adolescence in America, 1790 to the present*, New York: Basic Books, 1977.

Keyes, Susan and John Coleman, "Sex role conflicts and personal adjustment: a study of British adolescents," *Journal of Youth and Adolescence*, vol. 12, pp. 443–59, 1983.

Kirkland, Gelsey, *Dancing on my Grave: An autobiography with Greg Lawrence*, London: Hamilton, 1987.

Kleeman, J., "The establishment of core identity in normal girls," *Archives of Sexual Behavior*, vol. 1, pp.103–29, 1971.

Kohlberg, Laurence, "Development of moral character and moral ideology," in M.L. Hoffman and L.W. Hoffman (eds.), *Review of*

Child Development Research, vol. 1, New York: Russell Sage Foundation, 1964.

Kohlberg, Laurence, "Moral stages and moralization: the cognitive-developmental approach," in T. Likona (ed.), *Moral Development and Behaviour*, New York: Holt, Reinhart and Winston, 1976.

Kohlberg, Laurence and Carol Gilligan, "The adolescent as a philosopher: the discovery of the self in a postconventional world," *Daedalus*, vol. 100, pp. 1051–86, 1971.

Kohlberg, Laurence and R. Kramer, "Continuities and discontinuities in childhood and adult moral development," *Human Development*, vol. 12, pp. 93–120, 1969.

Kohut, Heinz, *The Analysis of the Self*, New York: International Universities Press, 1971.

Konopka, Gisela, *The Adolescent Girl in Conflict*, Englewood Cliffs, New Jersey: Prentice Hall, 1972.

Konopka, Gisela, *Young Girls: A portrait of adolescence*, Englewood Cliffs, New Jersey: Prentice Hall, 1976.

Lamb, Michael and Brian Sutton-Smith, *Sibling Relationships: Their nature and significance across the life span*, Hillsdale, New Jersey: L. Erlbaum Associates, 1982.

Lawrence, D.H., *Sons and Lovers*, Harmondsworth: Penguin, 1948.

Loevinger, Jane, with the assistance of Augusto Blasi, *Ego Development: Conceptions and theories*, San Francisco: Jossey-Bass Publishers, 1976.

Maccoby, Eleanor E., *Social Development: Psychological growth and the parent-child relationship*, New York and London: Harcourt Brace Jovanovich, 1980.

McCullers, Carson, *The Member of the Wedding*, Boston: Houghton Mifflin, 1946; Harmondsworth: Penguin, 1962.

Mahler, Margaret S., "Thoughts about development and individuation," *The Psychoanalytic Study of the Child*, vol. 18, pp. 307–24, 1963.

Mahler, Margaret S., F. Pine, and A. Bergman, *The Psychological Birth of the Human Infant*, New York: Basic Books, 1975.

Masterson, J. F., "The psychiatric significance of adolescent turmoil," *The American Journal of Psychiatry*, vol. 124, pp.1549–54, 1968.

Mead, Margaret, "Adolescence in primitive and modern society," in V.F. Calverton and S. Schmalhausen (eds.), *The New Generation*, New York: Macaulay, 1930.

Montemayor, Robert, "Picking up the pieces: the effects of parental divorce on adolescents with some suggestions for school based intervention programs, *Journal of Early Adolescence*, vol. 4, pp. 289–314, 1984.

Nagera, H, "Children's reactions to the death of important objects," *Psychoanalytic Study of the Child*, vol. 25, pp. 360–400, 1970.

Offer, Daniel, *The Psychological World of the Teenager: A study of normal adolescent boys*, New York: Basic Books, 1969.

Offer, Daniel and M. Shashin (eds.), *Normality and the Life Cycle*, New York: Basic Books, 1984.

Openshaw, Kim D., Darwin L. Thomas, and Boyd C. Rollins, "Parental influences on adolescent self-esteem," *Journal of Early Adolescence*, vol. 4, pp. 259–74, 1984.

Patterson, George, *Mothers: The unacknowledged victims*, Eugene, Oregon: Castalia Publishing, 1980.

Patterson, George and Marion Forgatch, *Parents and Adolescents: Living Together*, part 1: *The Basics*, Eugene, Oregon: Castalia Publishing, 1987.

Payne, Karen (ed.), *Between Ourselves: Letters between mothers and daughters, 1750–1982*, Boston: Houghton Mifflin, 1983.

Person, E., "Women working: fears of failure, deviance and success," *Journal of the American Academy of PSA*, vol. 10, pp. 67–84, 1982.

Peterson, A. C., *The Self Image Questionnaire for Young Adolescents*, Chicago: Laboratory for the Study of Adolescence, Michael Reese Hospital and Medical Center, 1980.

Piaget, Jean, *The Moral Judgement of the Child*, New York: Harcourt, 1932.

Plath, Sylvia, *Letters Home: Correspondence 1950–63*, Aurelia Plath (ed.), New York: Harper and Row, 1975.

Powell, M., "Age and sex differences in degree of conflict within certain areas of psychological adjustment," *Psychological Monographs*, vol. 69, no. 378, 1955.

Powers, Sally and Stuart Hauser, "Adolescent ego development and family interaction," in H. Grotevant and C. Cooper (eds.), *Adolescent Development in the Family*, San Francisco: Jossey Bass, 1983.

Prien, N. and M. Vincent, "Parents et enfants dans un monde en-changement," *Revue de Neuropsychiatrie Infantil*, 26, pp. 706–17, 1978.

Rich, Adrienne, *Of Woman Born: Motherhood as experience and institution*, New York: W.W. Norton and Co., 1976; London: Virago, 1977.

Rierdan, Jill, Elissa Koff, and Margaret L. Stubbs, "Depression and body image in adolescent girls," Working Paper 165, Wellesley, Massachusetts: Wellesley College, Center for Research on Women, 1986.

Ritvo, S., "Adolescent to woman," *Journal of the American Psychiatric Association*, vol. 24, pp.127–37, 1976.

Rosenberg, Morris, *Conceiving the Self*, New York: Basic Books, 1976.

Rosenthal, I., "Reliability of retrospective reports of adolescence," *Journal of Consulting Psychology*, vol. 27, pp.189–98, 1963.

Roth, Philip, *Portnoy's Complaint*, New York: Random House; London: Cape, 1969.

Roth, Philip, *The Breast*, New York: Holt, Rinehart and Winston, 1972; Harmondsworth: Penguin, 1980.

Rubin, Lillian, *Just Friends: The role of friendship in our lives*, New York: Harper and Row, 1985.

Sassen, Georgia, "Success anxiety in women: A constructivist interpretation of its source and significance," *Harvard Educational Review*, vol. 50, no. 1, pp.13–24, February 1980.

Shafer, R., "Concepts of self and identity and the experience of separation-individuation in adolescence," *Psychoanalytic Quarterly*, vol. 42, pp. 42–9, 1973.

Silverberg, Susan B. and Laurence Steinberg, "Adolescent autonomy, parent–adolescent conflict, and parental well-being," *Journal of Youth and Adolescence*, vol. 16, pp.293–313, 1987.

Simmons, R.G. and F. Rosenberg, "Disturbance in the self image at adolescence," *American Sociological Review*, vol. 38, pp. 553–68, 1973.

Smollar, Jacqueline and James Youniss, "Parent–adolescent relations in adolescents whose parents are divorced," *Journal of Early Adolescence*, vol. 5, pp. 129–44, 1985.

Solnit, A.J., "Adolescence and the changing reality," in I.M. Marcus (ed.), *Currents in Psychoanalysis*, New York: International Universities Press, 1972.

Spacks, P.M., *The Adolescent Idea: Myths of Youth and the Adult Imagination*, New York: Basic Books, 1981; London: Faber, 1982.

Steinberg, Lawrence D., "Transformations in family relationships at puberty," *Developmental Psychology*, vol. 24, pp. 189–98, 1963.

Stern, Daniel, *The Interpersonal World of the Infant: A view from psychoanalysis and development psychology*, New York: Basic Books, 1985.

Stoller, Robert, "The sense of femaleness," *Psychoanalytic Quarterly*, vol. 37, pp. 42–55, 1968.

Stoller, Robert, "Primary femininity," *Journal of the American Psychoanalytic Association*, vol. 24, pp. 59–78, 1976.

Stone, Lawrence, *The Family, Sex and Marriage in England, 1500–1800*, New York: Harper and Row, 1977.

Sugar, Max, *Female Adolescent Development*, New York: Bruner/Mazel, 1979.

Sullivan, Henry Stack, *The Interpersonal Theory of Psychiatry*, New York: Norton, 1953.

Ticho, G.R., "Female autonomy and young adult women," *Journal of the American Psychoanalytic Association*, vol. 24, pp.139–55, 1976.

Tobin-Richards, H. Maryse, Andrew M. Boxer, and Anne C. Petersen, "The Psychological Significance of Pubertal Change: Sex Differences in Perceptions of Self during Early Adolescence," in Jeanne Brooks-Gunn and Anne C. Petersen (eds.), *Girls at Puberty: Biological and psychological pespectives*, New York: Plenum Press, 1983, pp.127–254.

Viorst, Judith, *Necessary Losses*, New York: Ballantine Books, 1987.

Wallerstein, Judith and Joan Berlin Kelly, *Surviving the Breakup: How children and parents cope with divorce*, New York: Basic Books; London: Grant McIntyre, 1980.

Weissman, S. and P. Barglow, "Recent contributions to the theory of female psychological development," *Adolescent Psychiatry*, vol. 8, pp. 214–30, 1980.

White, Robert, *Lives in Progress: Study of the natural growth of personality*, New York: Holt, Reinhart and Winston, 1975.

Winnicott, Donald W., *Playing and Reality*, London: Tavistock Publications, 1971.

Youniss, James and Jacqueline Smollar, *Adolescent Relations with Mothers, Fathers and Friends*, Chicago: University of Chicago Press, 1985.

About the Author

Terri Apter is a Research Fellow at Clare Hall, Cambridge. She is the author of *Why Women Don't Have Wives: Professional Success and Motherhood*. She lives with her husband and two teenage daughters, in Cambridge, England